NEW MEDIA JOURNALISM

EMERGING MEDIA AND NEW PRACTICES IN JOURNALISM

NEW MEDIA JOURNALISM

EMERGING MEDIA AND NEW PRACTICES IN JOURNALISM

Edited by

Prof. (Dr) Anubhuti Yadav

STERLING

STERLING PUBLISHERS (P) LTD.
Regd. Office: A1/256, Safdarjung Enclave, New Delhi-110029.
Cin: U22110DL1964PTC211907
Phone: +91 82877 98380/ +91 120-6251823
E-mail: mail@sterlingpublishers.in
www.sterlingpublishers.in

New Media Journalism: Emerging Media and New Practices in Journalism

ISBN 978 93 93853 07 3

Printed and Published in India

Sterling Publishers Pvt. Ltd.,
Plot No. 13, Ecotech-III, Greater Noida -201306, U.P. India

Contents

Foreword

The global pandemic has certainly transformed how we communicate with each other, and how we understand our world. Within this context, *New Media Journalism* is an important text that provides considerable insight into the role and impact of the media on Indian journalism during the pandemic era – and beyond.

New Media Journalism features an impressive collection of perspectives by media scholars that examines:

- The development and dissemination of media content
- The impact of media on audience attitudes, beliefs, and behaviors
- Strategies for interpretation of media content
- The relationship between media producers and their audience
- Innovations in media technology
- Ways in which producers of media content communicate with their audiences effectively

India has emerged as a global leader in the field of media literacy and scholarship. Thus, while *New Media Journalism* focuses on the role of the media in India, it is also a valuable resource for international media literacy scholarship, as we consider the evolving nature of media communications throughout the globe.

Art Silverblatt, PhD

Emeritus Professor, Webster University (US)

Co-founder, DIMLE (Digital International Media Literacy Education)

Acknowledgements

This book is possible because of the support and assistance of many. I owe a special debt to the contributors of the chapters, who shared their vast experiences and knowledge for this volume. I am grateful to Mr Surinder Ghai, Director, Sterling Publishers (P) Ltd & Chairman, Institute of Book Publishing to recognize the value of the book for the students of journalism and mass communication. I am also grateful to Mr. Sanjiv Sarin for going through the manuscript meticulously and offering suggestions. My heartfelt thanks to Ms. Nisa Askari, Ms. Sarima Thakur, Ms. Riya Gupta, Ms. Shivangi Garg, and Ms. Aditi Sharma for going through the chapters and helping me with the edits and graphics. Finally, thanks to my students who have been asking for a book on New Media. I am sure you'll like it and I would appreciate your feedback at newmediabookay@gmail.com.

Preface

This book is written at a time when a lot is happening in the field of New Media in India and across the world. The Covid-19 pandemic brought many changes to the media and entertainment industry. The most affected was New Media, but in a positive manner. Before the pandemic New Media was growing very fast as compared to any other medium but in 2020, when people were restricted to their homes because of the lockdown, the growth was unprecedented. Overnight, people switched from print to e-newspapers.

In India a complete lockdown was announced by Prime Minister Narendra Modi on 25 March 2020 to contain the spread of Covid-19. The next day, many people did not receive newspapers. People took to social media to share their anguish. Many resident welfare associations (RWAs) across the country banned the entry of newspaper vendors as that could lead to the spread of virus. The vendors too had a fear of contracting the virus. They refused to deliver newspapers. Many newspapers could not be printed. Many newspapers and magazines suspended print editions and the focus moved to digital. In the absence of print newspapers, people started reading online editions.

The government maintained that an uninterrupted supply of newspapers was vital. In a letter to the chief secretaries of all states and union territories, the Ministry of Information and Broadcasting noted that proper functioning of news networks was required not only to create awareness among people and to give important messages, but also to keep the nation updated on the latest events and prevent the spread of false and fake news. The letter mentioned that printing presses and distribution infrastructure of newspapers and magazines were critical infrastructures for the uninterrupted operation of information networks.

Despite government directives, advisories by health professionals and campaigns run by media organisations, the newspaper industry saw an unprecedented slump. The *Times of India*, to recoup some of the damage done due to Covid-19, launched a campaign #NewspaperMornings which captured the relationship between readers of newspapers and the emotion one experiences when an integral part of their daily life is missing. '*Bina akhbar ke, chai subah ki adhoori lagti hain . . . na din chadhta hain poora, na poori aankh khulti hain* (without the newspaper the morning tea appear incomplete, the day does not start, the eyes do not open completely) and #WantMyPaper campaign that asked readers to reclaim their right to information by supporting the daily newspaper.

The financial year 2020, despite all efforts, remained an unfavourable year for Print (printed newspaper and magazines) with a decline of 8 per cent, mainly due to advertisement spending slowing down. This particularly impacted the English segment which also had a decline in circulation due to stagnation in key metro markets. Hindi and regional segments had a lower decline due to diversified local and national customers and greater reach in Tier II and smaller towns.[1]

While Print witnessed a downward trend with growth in financial year 2020 registered at minus 8 per cent, Digital and OTT witnessed a growth of 26 per cent, which was the second highest after gaming, where the growth was 45 per cent. Technology-led innovations were the key to this growth. Many new technologies gained traction. According to the KPMG report, technologies like AR/VR, Virtual Production, Artificial Intelligence and Blockchain have the potential to disrupt the status quo. Also, with the huge amount of data generated around Covid-19, the number of data-based stories increased.

Journalists started experimenting with the new tools to create interactive content around Covid-19. Institutions like IITs, IISC, and IIIT developed apps and came up with innovative ideas to provide solutions for fight against Covid-19. There were apps that worked as a complete Infodemic Management System like the Wash Karo app. The app delivered government advisories from official pages and contained symptom trackers. The app was presented at a conference organised by the World Health Organisation (WHO). The app also had Covid-19 tracking, worked on a peer-to-peer network and used Bluetooth technology to tell if someone in proximity was Covid-19 positive. The government came out with apps – the Arogya Setu app to keep a track of the cases and concentration of infections and the COWIN app which was projected as the go-to app for vaccine monitoring and distribution. Media houses too launched apps on Covid-19 case counts to debunk rumours. The Director-General of WHO, Dr Tedros Adhanom Gnebreyesus, said at the Munich Security Conference, 'We are not just fighting an epidemic; we are fighting an infodemic.' This became the opening line for all the training and workshops on fact-checking and verification. WHO introduced a section on their website called 'Myth Busters' in which they debunked all misinformation and disinformation related to Covid-19. Media houses and fact-checking organisations became vigilant and clarified many rumours. New digital tools were explored and used for countering misinformation. Amidst all this, the Government of India announced social media rules to curb its misuse. The social media platforms were required to provide information, including information related to verification and identity, to lawfully authorised agencies within seventy-two hours. In a press conference, Electronics and Information Technology Minister Ravi Shankar Prasad said that the basic essence of the Information Technology (Intermediary Guidelines and Digital Media Ethics Codes) Rules, 2021,[2] was 'soft-touch oversight' mechanism to deal with issues such as the persistent spread of fake news.

Covid-19 has been very hard on journalism. When people were limited to their homes because of lockdown, journalists did not have any choice but to go out and cover stories. Since the need for information on Covid-19 was more, journalists had to constantly provide it. This meant more visits to hospitals, more interaction with the healthcare workers and patients and hence more exposure. Journalists paid a heavy price while covering Covid-19 in India. According to a report by the Delhi-based Institute of Perception Studies, 238 journalists died due to Covid-19 infection from 20 April 2020 to 16 May 2021. However, if we go by the reports of news media, the figure was around three hundred.

The Editor Guild of India and the Press Club of India asked the Central Government to declare journalists as frontline workers and ensure they were vaccinated on priority. Many states like Bihar, Orissa and Madhya Pradesh did that and also extended financial help to them. The Press Council of India also recommended to the Central and state governments to include journalists in the category of Covid-19 warriors and provide immediate financial assistance to the families of those who lost their lives due to this disease. It also called for framing and implementing a group insurance scheme for journalists.

The pandemic has taught us that the journalist fraternity has to prepare itself for such catastrophes in the future. This time the pandemic caught all of us unprepared. The result was a loss of life, shutting down of businesses and so on. Everyone, irrespective of the field they were in, started exploring and experimenting with new ways of working, interacting and engaging with their intended audience. Many lessons were learned and solutions found in terms of technology-driven innovation for many businesses. They are here to stay. According to the report, 'New powers, New Responsibilities: A Global Survey of Journalism and Artificial Intelligence'[3] based on a survey conducted by the London School of Economics and Political Science and Google News Initiative, artificial intelligence (AI) can free up the time of journalists so that they can work on creating better journalism. This is very useful at a time when the news industry is fighting for economic sustainability, public trust and relevance. AI can also help the public cope with news overload and misinformation and connect them in a convenient way to credible content that is relevant, useful and stimulating for them.

Journalists need to embrace new technologies and constantly innovate to connect with their audience in a meaningful way. While those who are currently working will be expected to up-skill themselves, new entrants will face a lot of expectations in the area of technology-driven journalism. Unfortunately, institutes at present are not providing such skilled professionals to the industry. While newsrooms in different parts of the world are talking about artificial intelligence, blockchain technology and immersive media, most educational institutes are still following the age-old curriculum barring a few which have the autonomy to revise their curriculum to make it relevant for today's time,

In India, the model curriculum in Mass Communication drafted by the Curriculum Development Committee in April 2012 does mention New Media but much more is required. In the last twenty years, there have been substantial changes in the industry. The way journalists are working has changed, and the way newsrooms are functioning has undergone a massive transformation. These changes that ideally should define the curriculum have not been taken into consideration by the Unfortunately, University Grant Commission (UGC). Though there are universities, institutes and some faculty members who are proactive and have introduced the much-required changes this is happening only at the institutional level. There is a need for national-level consultation on Journalism and Mass Communication education curriculum.

There cannot be a better time than this to discuss and deliberate on these important issues in Journalism and Mass Communication. The National Education Policy (NEP) has just been approved and media education in India has completed a hundred years This is the time to look back and appreciate what has been achieved and reflect upon what should be the vision for the next hundred years.

Because of the NEP, some of the key areas that require discussion are – a multidisciplinary approach in media education, the curriculum framework, promoting research and innovation, and industry-academia linkage for knowledge sharing.

According to the report 'Framework of Industry–University Linkage in Research' prepared by the Department of Scientific and Industrial Research, Ministry of Science and Technology, Government of India,[4] India is at a very nascent stage of developing strong industry-university linkages. While there are successful partnerships and collaborations between universities and industries in the sectors like textiles, automobiles, engineering, biotechnology and so on, there are not many such tie-ups and collaborations in the media and communications sector. What little we witness involves media professionals in curriculum development and teaching. There is much more that can be achieved through such tie-ups. In this book, an attempt has been made to bring in industry experts to share their knowledge and experience. Most of them are pioneers in their field. The idea is to document all the innovative practices adopted in the newsrooms and share them with media educators and students.

This book, *New Media Journalism*, aims to bring journalistic experiences and academic understanding of New Media together. It introduces readers to the new technologies that are used in newsrooms and what opportunities a knowledge of such new technologies offers. It also talks about the challenges faced by the journalists while embracing these new technologies.

The topics explored in this book are extremely relevant and useful for working journalists as well as teachers and students of journalism. My students in Journalism, Advertising and Public Relations courses at the Indian Institute of Mass Communication continue to be the early adopters of these technologies. It is their eagerness to learn more that has motivated me to produce this book. The interest shown by my Twitter, Facebook and LinkedIn friends has always driven me to explore new digital tools that can be of use to teachers, students and media practitioners.

I hope this book will contribute to the ongoing discussions and debates we all are having in the field of digital media and help media faculty, students and practitioners to learn and explore more in this fast-changing digital world.

Notes

1. KPMG, *A Year Off Script: A Time for Resilience*, September 2020, https://assets.kpmg/content/dam/kpmg/in/pdf/2020/09/synopsis-kpmg-india-media-and-entertainment-2020.pdf.
2. Ministry of Electronics and Information Technology Notification, New Delhi, 25 February 2021, https://mib.gov.in/sites/default/files/IT%28Intermediary%20Guidelines%20and%20Digital%20Media%20Ethics%20Code%29%20Rules%2C%202021%20English.pdf.
3. Charlie Beckett, *New Powers, New Responsibilities: A Global Survey of Journalism and Artificial Intelligence*, November 2019, https://drive.google.com/file/d/1utmAMCmd4rfJHrUfLLfSJ-clpFTjyef1/view.
4. *Framework of Industry–University Linkage in Research*, October 2019, https://www.phdcci.in/wp-content/uploads/2019/10/Framework-of-University-Industry-Linkages-in-Research-DSIR-16-Oct_-Forweb.pdf.

Chapter 1

New Media Journalism

Dr Anubhuti Yadav

Around 73 per cent of our respondents from India access news through smartphones. Social media access is high with 53 per cent using WhatsApp and YouTube for news.

–Reuters 2021 Digital News Report[1]

Introduction

News consumption pattern has changed tremendously in the past few years. Reading newspapers watching the news and listening to radio bulletins – every media consumption experience has witnessed a paradigm shift. All this happened because of the emergence of new technologies. Most people have stopped consuming media the way they used to earlier. The habit of reading newspapers with a cup of tea or coffee in the morning is replaced by reading them on laptops, tablets and smartphones. Even while reading the printed text, there is always an urge to go online to watch a video using the QR code placed next to the story. While reading text online, there is always an option to listen to the story than read it. These new ways of consuming content are the result of integrating new technology in the newsrooms which makes it possible for the news producers to produce content in a variety of ways. These new technologies not only help in packaging the content in a variety of ways but also in publishing it in different formats and disseminating it via different platforms.

New Media, as it is termed by the experts in the industry and academia, is posing tough competition to Print and TV. People are consuming media messages not only from the television channel but by also from YouTube. Radio sets in households often lie unused as people tune into their favourite channels using smartphones. This medium has not only affected the consumption pattern but also the way media messages are produced. New technologies have impacted every function in the media house. Old ways of working on many products have been replaced by new ways of packaging information, which are influenced by new technologies.

In this chapter, we shall discuss the concept of New Media, its emergence, its characteristics New Media landscape, its impact on traditional media along with the opportunities and challenges that come with it. In media industry and academia there are various terms that are being used interchangeably for New Media like online media, digital media, Information and Communication Technology (ICT), Convergent Media and so on. All these terms will be discussed for better conceptual understanding.

New Media[2]

The new technologies have not only made various tasks of journalists, advertising and public relations professionals easier but have enabled them to reach out to niche audiences with the use of right medium. Personalised messaging by the communication professionals delivers specific message at the right time to its target audience. Such messages are more relevant to the users' needs rather than those sent out as generalised messages to all. This requires development of a variety of messages for the audiences that are diverse, and pushing them through the right medium. Keeping in view the varied usage of new technologies, new departments are being created and new job profiles, which were unheard of earlier, have come into being. Some of the job opportunities posted by the *New York Times* (as on 1 September 2022) elucidate the need for new job roles in the digital age:

Product Manager, Search and Personalisation

Analyst, Data and Insights (Games)

Data Scientist

Social Editor

Manager, Advertising Analytics

Audience Insights Analysts

Insight Product manager

Instagram Staff Editors

NDTV, in its job section, has also advertised for Software Developers to work on its digital platforms and the *New Indian Express* is looking for Content Writer (Social Media with SEO knowledge), Data Entry Analyst, Manager Digital Advertisement Sales, UI/UX Designer, (retrieved on 1 September 2022).

All these job profiles require knowledge of new technologies. There are very few Media institutes which are preparing their students for these emerging careers. Therefore Media organisations have to look for young talent in engineering colleges. Students in engineering college might be proficient in technology but they are not trained in communication. Hence it has become extremely important to update curriculum of Journalism schools so that they are able to provide skilled workforce to the Media Industry.

Newsrooms are also organising training programmes to upskill their employees so that they are relevant in the Digital age.

There are a number of terms used to explain this emerging trend of using new technologies in the newsrooms. While in this book we will be using term 'New Media', it is equally important to understand other terms associated with these technologies.

Before discussing other terms, it is important to understand two terms – digital and internet – which are the foundation of New Media. The term 'digital' refers to a technology that stores data as a binary code. The data can be information stored as text, photographs, graphics, audio and video. The term 'internet' refers to a distribution system for information.[3] All the terms which we are going to discuss now emerge from these two terms whose technology has opened up huge number of new possibilities.

Understanding New Media and Other Terms

In the context of New Media, several terms are used interchangeably, like New Media, ICT, Digital Media, Online Media, Multimedia, Convergence Media and so on. There are some overlaps, and the meaning often varies with the context. Let us explore the meaning of these terms:

Information and Communication Technology: Information and Communication Technology (ICT) consists of hardware, software, networks and media for the collection, storage, processing, transmission and presentation of information (voice, data, text, images, videos) (The World Bank).

Digital Media: The digital process converts all information (data, text graphics, audio, pictures, or videos) into a sequence of numbers (digits), transports it by wire or wirelessly to a destination, and then re-constructs it back into its original form. Digital media refers to audio, video and picture content that has been encoded (digitally converted). Encoding content involves converting audio and video input into a digital media file such as a Windows Media file. A digital file can be easily manipulated, distributed and rendered (played) by computers and mobile phones, and is easily transmitted over internet and computer networks. Examples of digital media types include Windows Media Audio (WMA), Windows Media Video (WMV), MP3, JPEG and AVI.

New Media: New Media refers to those digital Media that are interactive, incorporate two-way communication and involve some form of computing as opposed to 'old media' such as telephone, radio and TV.[4]

Lev Manovich says thinking of New Media as digital is only half the story.[5] The digital elements may be present in older media forms as well. The new elements that point to a significant change in the media are that they are the result of the convergence between the computational logic characteristics of the computer and the communicative logic characteristics of the media.

Online Media: This is a generic term often used loosely to describe digital information access, retrieval or dissemination. This means accessing the information on the internet via a modem or a telephone line.[6]

Multimedia: As name suggests, it is the use of more than one technique (text, audio, still images, moving images) to tell a story. A multimedia news story is any piece that uses two or more media to narrate it.

The terms mentioned are deeply linked and thus are difficult to distinguish separately. The significance of limiting the definitions is largely contextual. While ICT encompasses everything from hardware to software and also includes the dissemination of information, the focus in the definition of Digital Media is on what makes any information digital. In New Media, the stress is on how the digital media is being used with interactive and two-way communication as its important feature. Multimedia, however, is the combination of two or more techniques which is easily possible only when the information is available in digital format. While there is an overlapping basis for these, however, each of these terms has some distinct feature.[7]

As Eugenia Siapera puts it, different names bring to the fore different attributes and by prioritising different elements, they focus attention on some aspects and overlook others.[8]

For this book, the term New Media will include online platforms, social media, new digital tools, and the new ways of packaging and disseminating information, all in the context of the News Media Industry.

Characteristics of New Media

New Media has opened up thousands of possibilities for not only content creators but also for the consumers. Before the advent of internet all media formats existed in silos. Print was just print, radio was just radio and television was just TV. They had their own distribution systems which were exclusive to one another. Now everything is riding on internet technology. When you are reading content on any news portal, you are not only reading text you can also listen to the story, you can also watch the story. Each media format is residing next to the other providing a satisfying experience to the consumer. The consumer not only consumes the content but also has the opportunity to provide feedback there and then. Consuming content on New Media is gratifying because of its following characteristics:

New Media Is Interactive

Interactivity in New Media happens at three levels. At the first level, users can interact with the content. Users prepare their own pattern of consuming any story. Instead of a linear form of the story which starts with a headline, followed by the lead and then the body, in New Media stories are presented in non-linear manner. The story starts with the headline, then there could be lead, audio, video or infographic accompanying the story. At this time the reader chooses what he or she wants to consume, unlike the traditional format of a story where the readers have to read or watch the story from the beginning to the end to make sense of it.

Another interaction takes place with the content, leading to a personalised experience. For example, in 2019 BBC India on launched an experimental interactive election chatbot in Hindi and English on Facebook's Messenger platform as part of a series on content related to the Indian general elections. The chatbot allowed users to interact with the BBC and ask specific questions and get updates on elections. In this innovative way of storytelling, people could use Google Assistant and say, 'OK Google, Talk to BBC Elections' to receive latest updates. This feature was available in Hindi language too.

In yet another interactive initiative, the *Times of India* put together the data of all the Indian elections from 1980 to 2019. Instead of reading the entire story, in this case the readers could decide what they wanted to read and by using filters like candidates, constituencies, alliances and regions, they could access the content that was relevant to them. This data hub can be accessed at https://timesofindia.indiatimes.com/elections/constituency-map.

The second level of interaction is in the form of rating, liking, commenting and sharing of the content. Earlier, the interactivity was limited. For newspapers, it was limited to a letter to editor and for TV and Radio, some feedback programme. Thus, very few customer voices were heard. In New Media, anyone who is interested in providing feedback can give that in the comments section of the story.

The third level of interaction takes place between the media organisation/journalist and the readers. Many journalists use New Media as a platform to crowd source ideas for their story. The suggestions are taken on what kind of stories people would like to read or watch.

Interactivity is extremely important for audience engagement which can help in building loyal audience base.

Most news portals offer opportunities to users to interact with the content (in case of interactive stories), interact with the producers of the content and are also providing space for user-generated content.

The 'iReport for CNN' is an example of how mainstream media encourages its audience to interact with the platform. Here, the interaction is not just by writing comments or rating stories done by CNN. The 'iReport for CNN' is an interactive, international, monthly half-hour TV programme showcasing the most newsworthy and informative iReport contributions and reports of citizen journalists on the internet. Besides sending their content to the platform, citizens journalists can post it on Facebook, Instagram or Twitter with the hashtag #CNNiReport.[9]

'Your Turn' section of the *Print* also encourages its subscribers to write stories.[10]

This dimension of interactivity can be unsettling for traditional journalists. It challenges the whole premise of the journalist as a gatekeeper and information provider.

It also raises all sorts of issues about accuracy, veracity and perspectives of that information and reportage.[11]

However, journalists and media houses today look at interactivity as an opportunity as it helps them to:

1. Receive feedback on their stories
2. Connect with the sources
3. Crowdsource story ideas

New Media Is Immediate

Nowadays, often when we pick up a newspaper in the morning or watch news on TV in the evening, we have a feeling of 'already read' or 'already watched'. Yes, we might have come across that content on our smartphone. In New Media, news is updated as it is happening by the reporters or chance witnesses. When the Supertech Twin Towers in Noida were demolished on 28 August 2022 on the orders of the Supreme Court, people did not wait for the newspapers for the story. They watched live the 32-storey and 29-storey buildings brought down to ground controlled explosions. This live coverage was not only done by the media houses but a lot of it was by people witnessing the event and sharing the footage on social media. Even after the demolition, people were glued to their TV sets or small screens to get the latest updates. The power of New Media is that stories can be updated in real time.

During the Russia–Ukraine war of 2022, Twitch was used to livestream the war. Some Twitch streamers attempt to counter or question the narratives presented by mainstream news. Others sought to train their audiences so they were not so easy to mislead. Most just hoped to cut through the clutter and gain a firm grasp on what was happening during a time of unprecedented chaos – and in front of a massive live viewership. Streamers see their ability to do so while in direct conversation with their audiences as a unique strength.[13]

Convergence

New Media has brought all the media formats together. It has made the merging of different mass communication formats like print, television and radio possible. On the internet, every medium resides next to another. A person can listen to an audio interview, watch the event and read the story at the same time. Journalists use one media format to tell one aspect of the story and another to tell another aspect. For example, a story on Covid-19 might use an explainer video to explain the immunisation process, photographs to tell how it is being implemented, text to analyse the initiative and audio for interviews with people. All these elements could be combined to tell the story on immunisation.

This is also called 'multimedia journalism'. In this case, each media element is an important part of the story. Multimedia reporting is often confused with parallel reporting. In parallel reporting, two or three journalists cover a story for print, video or audio. In these cases, these stories are independent of one another as they are separate stories told by different journalists. Even if they are uploaded on a website, the only thing they have in common is the subject; otherwise stories are different.[13]

In multimedia journalism, many media elements are weaved into the story according to the requirement. Several digital tools can help journalists to write multimedia stories. Some examples of multimedia stories can be seen at https://infogr.am/examples and https://storymaps-classic.arcgis.com/en/gallery/#s=.

Longer Shelf Life

Digital Permanence makes content creation on New Media different from the one that is created for the legacy media. Once anything is uploaded on the internet, it remains there for a long time. This has its own advantages and disadvantages. The advantage is that efforts that are made for a story do not become irrelevant. The stories do not vanish as in the case of newspaper or television. The shelf life of news stories thus increases. These stories can be referred any time and can become background material for newer stories. Readers can refer to them any time and journalists can easily access them and build upon them.

While it is a good idea to archive content for future use, it is important that it is stored in such a way that it is searchable. Tags and keywords are important to search archived content. Hence it is important to add relevant keywords and tags to the articles. The archived content also adds depth to the story. While writing about a one particular issue or an event, one can always provide a link to an archived story which has some commonality. For example, an article on National Education Policy can be accessed by typing a search query in the search box. If the article is given a tags like Education, NEP and so on, it will be easy to retrieve the article from the repository which may contain millions of articles. Internet Archive's[14] Wayback Machine[15] has made it very easy to archive as well as access archived material (Figure 1.1).

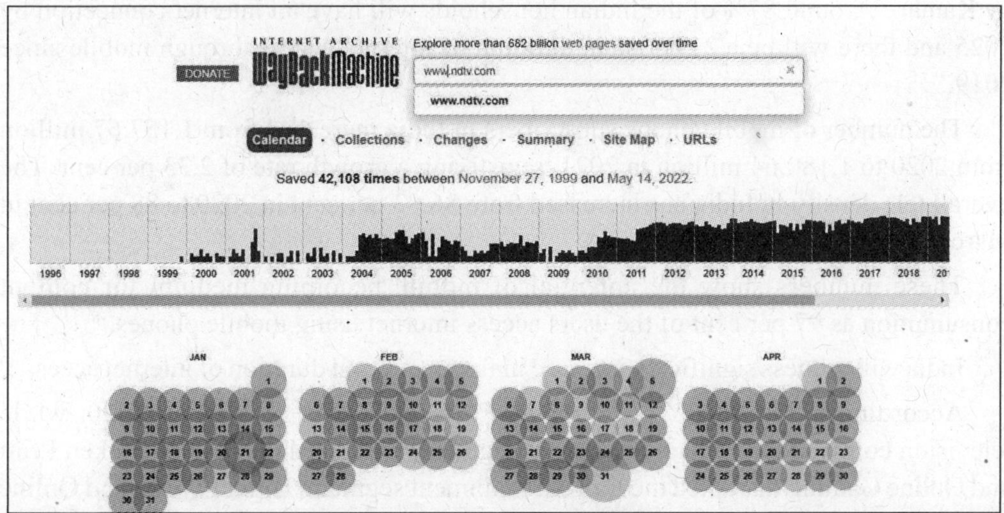

Figure 1.1: Wayback Machine

Source: Wayback Machine

Connecting Threads

Archiving of the web makes linkages possible. It is easy to link an article to something which was written earlier or with an article on the same subject written by someone else (or even another article by the same author). Linkages provide depth to a story.

In New Media, for any story the amount of space is limited, and so is the case in print, TV and radio. In legacy media the challenge is to tell the entire story in the limited time and space allocated. However, New Media overcomes this challenge by providing links to other material which is relevant to the story. This linkage could be for an article on the same website or it could be some report lying outside the website.

While linkage broadens the scope of the story and multiple angles can be explored at a time, it also poses the risk of losing the reader to the linked website or content. It becomes very difficult to bring readers back to the site once they are navigated out to read alternate content. Therefore, in any story it is important to use linkages strategically.[16]

New Media in India

India is leading the world in the digital revolution. The government's commitment to the use of digital technology in welfare programmes and services delivery is changing the lives of the people of the country, said Prime Minister Narendra Modi while launching multiple digital portals at the Digital India Week 2022.

The total number of internet users in the country has increased from 795.18 million in 2020 to 825.30 million in March 2021 according to a report from the Telecom Regulatory Authority of India (TRAI). The growth India has seen in terms of internet penetration is unprecedented. India has become the second-largest country in the world (after China) in terms of internet users with 825 million people connected to the internet. The penetration is 60.73 according to TRAI. According to the study 'Digital @2025' by Kantar. 'Around 87% of the Indian households will have an internet connection by 2025 and there will be a 21% rise in duration of internet access through mobile since 2019.'[17]

The number of mobile phone subscribers in India increased from 1,157.67 million from 2020 to 1,180.64 million in 2021, registering a growth rate of 2.33 per cent. The overall tele density in India has increased from 86.83 per cent in 2020 to 88 per cent in March 2021.

These numbers show the potential of mobile becoming medium for content consumption as 97 per cent of the users access internet using mobile phones.[18]

India will witness significant increase in frequency and duration of internet access.[19]

According to FICCI-EY 2021 report *Playing by New Rules*,[20] in 2020, while television continued to remain the largest segment, Digital Media had overtaken Print and Online Gaming disrupted the film entertainment segment. Digital Media and Online Gaming were the only segments that grew in 2020. As far as the news consumption is concerned, according to 2021 Reuters Digital News Report, India is a strongly mobile-focused market, with 72 per cent people accessing news through smartphones and just 35 per cent via computers. News aggregator platforms and apps such as Google News (53 per cent), Daily Hunt (25 per cent), InShorts (19 per cent), and NewsPoint (17 per cent) have become an important source to access news and are valued for convenience. The digital platforms like Newslaundry, News Minute, Quint and Wire have emerged as platforms giving tough competition to the legacy media. While these platforms are popular among the English-speaking audience, their reach is limited.

As a document on languages uploaded on the Ministry of Education website says, India writes in many languages and speaks in many more tongues. Hence it is important to create content in different languages. The Indian Constitution recognises twenty-two languages of India as 'official languages' in what is known as the '8th Schedule' of the Constitution. Besides the scheduled languages, the Indian census recorded 1,576 rationalised languages as well as 1,796 other mother tongues.[21] Unfortunately, we do not see much content in vernacular languages despite the fact there is a demand for that. According to 'Year in Search 2020' conducted by Google, India's internet users may have multiplied, but each individual continues to have a unique set of needs. In their pursuit for new information, fresh ideas and engaging entertainment – much of it in languages and formats of their preference – the growth of 3Vs (Voice, Video and Vernacular language) has accelerated at an unprecedented rate. People across the country have used Google Translate features over 17 billion times in the 2019 to translate web pages into Indic languages.[22] Hindi and other local-language digital journalism start-ups are few and far between, especially when it comes to original, on-the-ground reporting. New Media start-ups in India primarily started with English speaking audience but the New Media start-ups in other languages are also coming up to cater to the niche audience.

From digital versions of the legacy media to the New Media start-ups catering to niche audience, New Media in India has come a long way but as compared to New Media practices at international level, there is lot needs to be done and a lot needs to explored.

Emerging Trends

Artificial Intelligence (AI) is the new electricity. 'I can hardly imagine an industry which is not going to be transformed by AI,' says Andrew Ng, CEO, Landing AI and deeplearning.ai.[23]

AI, as in other fields, has become important in journalism too. While AI is criticised for taking over jobs of journalists, it has become the norm in the newsrooms. In many countries, robots are used to present stories. China's State-run Xinhua News Agency launched an AI news anchor in 2018 (Figure 1.2). Claimed as the first AI anchor, it debuted at the World Internet Conference 2018. According to the video posted on Xinhua News Twitter handle, the English AI anchor introduced himself to the world and promised to work tirelessly.[24] In 2019, Xinhua launched the first female AI news anchor Xin Xaomeng. According to Xinhua, robotic news employees have taken their roles with enthusiasm and since their launch they have published some 3,400 reports totalling over 10,000 minutes in length.[25]

Figure 1.2: AI News Anchor

The concern the world over is whether AI will replace journalists. Stressing upon human-centric journalism, Unnati Sharma wrote in her article titled, 'AI is already putting journalists out of job but there will never be AI Arnab or Ravish' about how compassion and humanity are essential parts of being a reporter. She quoted a tweet by Barkha Dutt with the picture of 70-year-old woman stranded in Mumbai waiting outside the railway station. Robots can never have such connect so there are number of jobs that robots cannot do.[26]

There have been occasions when an algorithm goes wrong. For example, Microsoft's Twitter bot Tay, tweeted racist content. The company released an official apology after the AI program went on an embarrassing tirade, likening feminism to cancer and suggesting the Holocaust did not happen.[27] Similarly, in 2018, Amazon 'scrapped' its AI-based recruiting engine after realising that the system had taught itself to favour male candidates and it downgraded resumes that included the word 'women'.[28]

This means there has to be human intervention to monitor algorithms when they malfunction.

Still, AI can be of great help in journalism in discovering, developing, editing, promoting and distributing stories. This does not mean journalists will lose their jobs. This means they need to up-skill themselves to develop and use these technologies to do their jobs more effectively and efficiently.

AR and VR in Journalism

Because of the advent of new technologies, audiences have moved from being passive consumers of content to active consumers of the content. Now, they can interact with the stories like never before. They can like, comment and share. They can also choose how they would like to consume the story by deciding whether to read just the headline or the entire text or see the infographics or listen to the story or to watch the story. Here the focus is on how the consumers would like to consume the content and interact with the content. For engagement and immersive experience AR and VR can play an important role as these technologies can engage and build connection with the audience. Such experiences many stories require huge investment not only by the content creators but also those who are consuming. That is the reason that despite having so many advantages, this has not taken off in the newsrooms the way it should have.

Audio and Video Stories

The three Vs – Voice, Video and Vernacular – define how Indians are consuming content on internet. This means a lot of content has to be produced in audio and video format and in the language that people understand.

Use of digital formats continues to gain momentum as Indian consumers immerse themselves online. Streaming on a connected TV has taken off, and short videos are becoming popular quickly. When people take a break from the screen, they're opting for content like podcasts and audiobooks, which they can enjoy on-the-go. Hence it is important to develop more and more video and audio content. This also makes it possible to take news to those who cannot read and write.

According to an analysis done by Judith Argila for Reuters Institute for the Study of Journalism, of how eight British and Spanish newsrooms tackle video production for Facebook, Twitter, Instagram and YouTube – and what kind of videos have made them successful, 'The most common video type, accounting for more than 40% of the successful cases, is what we defined as "short-texted videos": a video less than 4 minutes long where graphics and/or text narration is used over a sequence of images, without a voice narration.' This format, with subtle differences, is shared by all the news organizations. Newsrooms in India have come up with any such short videos and podcasts.

Podcasts

In focus: The Hindu

On the Record: The Hindustan Times

News Wrap: The Times of India

Reporters without Borders: News Laundry

We the People: NDTV

The Big Story: Quint

Three Things: Indian Express

More than 200 million Indians watched short-form videos at least once in 2020, with active users spending up to 45 minutes a day on these platforms. By 2025, three in four internet users, or 600 million to 650 million Indians, will consume short-form videos, with active users spending up to 55 to 60 minutes per day.[29]

Presently this format is very popular among those who would like to produce and consume entertainment content and also amongst advertisers as it gives them a huge scope to reach out to those people who spend lot of time on platforms like Moj, Josh, MX TakaTak, Roposo, Zili, Instagram Reels, Facebook Reels, YouTube Shorts.

NFTs in Journalism

NFT stands for non-fungible tokens. They are digital certificates of ownership of any assigned digital asset that cannot be duplicated. NFTs in journalism came in to prominence with the article 'Buy This Column in Blockchain' by the *New York Times*. This article was originally sold for 350 Ether, which is around $1.5 Million dollars.[30]

In January 2022, the Associated Press (AP) announced it was starting its own NFT marketplace for photojournalism. It would offer non-fungible tokens – digital certificates for digital images, traded using cryptocurrency – to buyers looking for 'exclusive, historic, and stunning visual content'. Collectors would be able to buy virtual tokens of the news agency's 'award-winning contemporary and historic photojournalism'.[31]

Any digital assets like pictures, videos, gifs, courses, articles can become an NFT which can be sold and bought. NFTs can be a financial investment, a sentimental purchase, a collectible item or a way for the buyer to feel more connected to the NFT's creator, like an artist or a brand.[32] While very few international media organisations are leveraging this because of the lack of knowledge and also scepticism about its legitimacy. In the times to come more and more media organisation will explore NFTs as this can be alternate business model. But the big question is – Who is going to buy them and why? Do watch the interview of Kevin Roose, whose column was sold for 350 Ether at https://www.youtube.com/watch?v=2vaGdd2MtqE.

Data Driven Journalism

Data journalism, big data, data analytics – these are all buzzwords nowadays. Data is used by media houses to tell stories. The open data movement has made it easier for communicators and journalists to access and use data. Many countries are releasing their data as 'open' data so that it can be used freely why the public. In India, the website www.data.gov.in hosts data from all the ministries and departments.

The website data.gov.in is the result of the National Data Sharing and Accessibility Policy (NDSAP) which was notified by the Government of India in March 2012 to promote a culture of data sharing and using data for larger socioeconomic goals. Adhering to the norms laid out by this policy, the National Informatics Centre (NIC) has set up Open Government Data (OGD) platform which is a state-of-the-art dynamic data sharing platform.[33] The portal has many rich features to support the open data policy such as:

Search and Discovery mechanism for instant access to numerous datasets of great importance.

Community engagements around published datasets for innovative applications of open data with an ability to provide customised citizen services. Tools, apps and visualisations developed by using this platform have played a pivotal role in increasing the level of transparency and citizens' participation in the governance process.

DataPortals.org is the most comprehensive list of open data portals in the world. It is curated by a group of leading Open Data experts from around the world, including representatives from local, regional and national governments, international organisations such as the World Bank and numerous NGOs. The data available on these platforms is freely available for the researchers. We will discuss this topic in detail in the chapter 'Data Journalism'.

Digital Tools

As more and more people want to consume content in different formats and on different platforms, it becomes increasingly necessary for the journalists to upskill themselves so that they are in a position to create content in a variety of ways. From researching for the stories to developing one, from its distribution to its marketing, each and every function requires the knowledge of digital tools. There are hundreds of tools that can be used by the journalists while working on their stories. Some of the tools are as follows:

Online Research: Google Alerts, Google Trends, RSS Readers, Netvibes.com, Feedly.com, Flipboard.com, Twitterlist, Tweetdeck, Follower.wonk, Wefollow, Twellow, Bluenod, Twitter advanced search, Hashtagify.me, Sonar solo, Buzz sumo.

Video: Videopad, Videoeditor, Filmors, Movavi, Videosnap, Inshot, Invideo, Director, Spice, Filmicpro, Wirewax, Director.

Audio: Anchor, Cogi, Opinion, Soundcite, Transcribe.

Mapping and Timelines: Google Maps, Storymap JS, TikiToki, Timescape, Mapbox, Infogram, Flourish, Canca, Vengage.

Social Media: Everypost, Twxplorer, Hootsuite, Landscape.

Factchecking and Verification: Google Reverse Image Search, Invid, Tineye, Reveye.

Summary

New Media in India is growing at a very fast pace. Keeping in view the various initiatives under 'Digital India' programme to strengthen the digital infrastructure, this trend will continue. The Indian media industry has embraced new technologies and all the platforms including print, magazines, TV, and radio are adapting themselves to remain relevant in the digital era. This chapter deconstructed New Media and what advantages it has over traditional media. The chapter also discussed the emerging trends like AI, AR and VR in Journalism, Short Videos, Podcasts and NFTs in journalism.

Tools and Tricks

- Boolean Basics: How to write a search query for newsgathering that works: https://firstdraftnews.org/articles/boolean-basics-how-to-write-a-search-query-for-newsgathering-that-works/.
- Open-source investigations and media literacy resources: https://www.osintessentials.com/.
- Introduction to New Media: https://www.youtube.com/watch?v=8HcMGrlF738&t=1168s.

Questions

1. Discuss four characteristics of New Media.
2. With Digital Media there is a shift from limited interactivity to unlimited interactivity. Discuss.
3. Discuss the impact of New Media on Legacy Media.
4. Discuss the impact of the Covid-19 pandemic on New Media.

Notes

1. Reuters Institute for the Study of Journalism, *Digital News Report 2021*, https://reutersinstitute.politics.ox.ac.uk/digital-news-report/2021.
2. Anubhuti Yadav, 'Unit-10: Emergence of Digital Media', *Indira Gandhi National Open University*, New Delhi, 2020, http://egyankosh.ac.in//handle/123456789/57026.
3. Lucy Kung, Robert G. Picard and Ruth Towse, *The Internet and the Mass Media* (London: Sage, 2008).
4. Robert K. Logan, *Understanding New Media: Extending Marshall McLuhan* (New York: Peter Lang, 2010).
5. Lev Manovich, *The Language of New Media*, series editor Roger F. Malina (Cambridge, London: MIT Press, 2002).
6. Mike Ward, *Journalism Online* (New York: Routledge, 2002).
7. Anubhuti Yadav, 'Unit-10: Emergence of Digital Media', *Indira Gandhi National Open University*, New Delhi, 2020, http://egyankosh.ac.in//handle/123456789/57026.
8. Eugiena Siapera, *Understanding New Media* (London: Sage, 2012).
9. 'iReport for CNN', *CNN International Edition*, accessed 14 February 2022, http://edition.cnn.com/CNNI/Programs/ireport/.
10. 'YourTurn Archives', *The Print*, accessed 14 February 2022, https://theprint.in/category/yourturn/.
11. Mike Ward, *Journalism Online* (New York: Routledge, 2002).
12. Nathan Grayson, 'Twitch in Wartime', *Washington Post*, 10 March 2012, https://www.washingtonpost.com/video-games/2022/03/10/twitch-streamers-russia-ukraine-hasan-cnn/.
13. Anubhuti Yadav, 'Unit-10 Emergence of Digital Media' *Indira Gandhi National Open University*, New Delhi, 2020, http://egyankosh.ac.in//handle/123456789/57026.
14. https://archive.org/.
15. https://web.archive.org/.
16. Anubhuti Yadav, 'Unit-10: Emergence of Digital Media', *Indira Gandhi National Open University*, New Delhi, 2020, http://egyankosh.ac.in//handle/123456789/57026.
17. Bhavya Dilipkumar, 'India Will Witness Significant Increase in Frequency and Duration of Internet Access: Study', *The Economic Times*, 26 April 2022, https://economictimes.indiatimes.com/tech/

technology/india-will-witness-significant-increase-in-frequency-and-duration-of-internet-access-study/articleshow/91012991.cms.

18. '97% of Users Access Internet through Mobiles: Study', *The Hindu BusinessLine*, 6 March 2019, https://www.thehindubusinessline.com/info-tech/97-per-cent-of-users-access-internet-through-mobiles-study/article26449028.ece.
19. B. Dilipkumar, 'India Will Witness Significant Increase in Frequency and Duration of Internet Access: Study', *The Economic Times*, 26 April 2022, https://economictimes.indiatimes.com/tech/technology/india-will-witness-significant-increase-in-frequency-and-duration-of-internet-access-study/articleshow/91012991.cms.
20. FICI and EY, *Playing by New Rules*, 2021, https://assets.ey.com/content/dam/ey-sites/ey-com/en_in/topics/media-and-entertainment/2021/ey-india-media-and-entertainment-sector-reboots.pdf.
21. https://www.education.gov.in/hi/sites/upload_files/mhrd/files/upload_document/languagebr.pdf.
22. Google, *Year Search 2020*, https://www.thinkwithgoogle.com/_qs/documents/11063/Year_in_Search_2020_-_India.pdf.
23. World Intellectual Property Organization, *WIPO Technology Trends 2019: Artificial Intelligence*, 2019, https://www.wipo.int/edocs/pubdocs/en/wipo_pub_1055.pdf.
24. China Xinhua News @XHNews, 'Xinhua's first English #AI anchor makes debut at the World Internet Conference that opens in Wuzhen, China Wednesday', *Twitter*, 7 November 2018, 6:57 pm, 'https://twitter.com/XHNews/status/1060161714123984901?s=20&t=CF5H7oGU44Gk9q98_FVn6w.
25. Isabella Steger, 'Chinese State Media's Latest Innovation Is an AI Female News Anchor', *Quartz*, 20 February 2019, https://qz.com/1554471/chinas-xinhua-launches-worlds-first-ai-female-news-anchor/.
26. Unnati Sharma, 'AI is already putting journalists out of job. But there will never be AI Arnab or Ravish', *The Print*, 1 June 2020, https://theprint.in/opinion/pov/ai-is-already-putting-journalists-out-of-job-but-there-will-never-be-ai-arnab-or-ravish/433250/.
27. 'Microsoft "Deeply Sorry" for Racist and Sexist Tweets by AI Chatbot', *The Guardian*, 26 March 2016, https://www.theguardian.com/technology/2016/mar/26/microsoft-deeply-sorry-for-offensive-tweets-by-ai-chatbot.
28. Chaitra Vedullapalli, 'Reviewing the Top AI Ethics Issues That Could Affect the Future of Women in Tech and How to Combat Them', *Forbes*, 1 April 2021, https://www.forbes.com/sites/forbestechcouncil/2021/04/01/reviewing-the-top-ai-ethics-issues-that-could-affect-the-future-of-women-in-tech-and-how-to-combat-them/.
29. 'Short-Form Video Is Poised to Grow to 600 to 650 Million Users in India by 2025', *Bain*, 6 October 2021, https://www.bain.com/about/media-center/press-releases/2022/short-form-video-india/.
30. Zach Wise, 'NFT FTW: Exploring NFTs for Journalism', *KnightLab*, https://studio.knightlab.com/projects/crypto-nft/.
31. Cristin Leach, 'NFTs Are Not about Art or Journalism; They Are about Money', *The Times*, 12 March 2022, https://www.thetimes.co.uk/article/nfts-are-not-about-art-or-journalism-they-are-about-money-2fzkqt3fn.
32. Kayleigh Barber, 'WTF Is an NFT', *Digiday*, 11 March 2021, https://digiday.com/media/wtf-is-an-nft/.
33. 'Open Government Data (OGD) Platform India', https://data.gov.in/.

Chapter 2

Cybersecurity in Journalism

Dr Abhay Chawla

Any digital database will inevitably be hacked. There is nothing called foolproof security.

Digital media, like any other technology, besides enabling daily life has its downsides. For journalists tasked with informing society, understanding the downsides and indulging in best practices enables them to perform their job efficiently as well as keeping them safe from personal and professional harm.

Introduction

The 2007 Hollywood movie the *Bourne Ultimatum* has a scene where they show a British journalist Simon Ross of the *Guardian* newspaper doing an investigating story on the protagonist Jason Bourne. The scene shows him meeting a source and subsequently how his mobile communication with his editor is intercepted by a government agency by locking on to the keywords of interest which the journalist utters in his conversation. This then leads him getting targeted by the dodgy individuals in the federal agency under the guise of national security. He is put under physical and virtual surveillance and the scene ends with the journalist being assassinated by a hired shooter.

The movie is obviously a hyperbole on the dangers faced by a journalist in a digital world. But due to the role played by journalists in showing a mirror to the society and the powers that be, the digital world has made their lives both easy and difficult, especially in terms of securing their communications, ideas, sources, story and so on.

New technologies have brought about a proliferation of different kinds of media. What are the consequences of this? The main outcome has been the discovery that news is a commodity whose sale and distribution can generate large profits.[1] So while some news can help people choose a particular outcome, another can devastate established outcomes. Profit has been one of the biggest and oldest motives for all crime in the world.

When looking at cybersecurity in journalism, it is important to first understand what the terms mean before proceeding on why and how. The phrase comprises three words – cyber, security and journalism. Getting to understand what they mean will help us understand how they are connected and the importance of this chapter.

The word 'cyber' as per the *Oxford English Dictionary* (*OED*) is a shortened form of the word 'cybernetics'. The field of cybernetics was pioneered in the late 1940s by an interdisciplinary group of specialists and was concerned with the study of communication and control systems in living beings and machines. 'Cybernetic' itself comes from the Greek word 'kubernētēs' (κυβερνᾶν) meaning 'steersman' and the current usage of the term involves things associated with computers. The term 'cyberspace' only appeared in 1982, apparently coined by William Gibson in his science fiction novella *Burning Chrome*. According to its *OED* entry, cyberspace is 'the space of Virtual Reality; the notional environment within which electronic communication (especially via the internet) occurs'.

As per the *Online Etymology Dictionary*, the word 'secure' entered the English language in the 16th century, derived from Latin 'securus', meaning 'freedom from anxiety'.

Finally, *Cambridge Dictionary* defines the word 'journalism' as the work of collecting, writing, and publishing news stories and articles in newspapers and magazines or broadcasting them on the radio and television.

Why should security be a matter of concern to a journalist? Do the security issues surrounding a journalist in a digital landscape be any different from the earlier media landscape of analogue?

The answers to these questions will set the background to our understanding of the subject, cybersecurity in journalism.

Maturity of Media

As the world of media matured it started becoming an entity in itself. With multiple media and umpteen channels, it was a dog-eat-dog world with each journalist keeping a close eye on what the others were doing. It was important to get your news before the person next to you did. Getting a scoop became a matter of life and death. This explains why, even when several major events are occurring simultaneously in the world, the media tends to cover only one – the one that has attracted the pack.[2]

However, the basic tenets of journalism were in the notion of the 'Fourth Estate', a term coined by Edmund Burke to describe how journalism acted as a fourth branch of governance, holding public officials accountable and informing citizens of prominent issues.[3]

But with the commoditisation of news, the product which the journalist produces is of value and needs to be secured before it is sold. The product not only needs to be secured before it is sold, the whole production process for the news product needs to be secured lest it is scuttled before seeing the light of the day. This would also include the external sources which, if compromised, result in the loss of the news product and hence a loss to the journalist.

Joshua Oliver writing in *Columbia Journalism Review* narrates the following story:

> Towards the end of a long workday, one last email dropped into Jawar Mohammed's inbox. It looked like a news tip, forwarded from an Ethiopian radio station. Mohammed, head of an independent broadcaster based in Minnesota and a leading figure in the Ethiopian opposition movement, wasn't fooled. He didn't click the link [inside the email].
>
> Instead, Mohammed forwarded the message to researchers at the Citizen Lab, a research group at the University of Toronto, who confirmed his suspicions. Clicking the link would have turned his phone or computer into the ultimate spying tool: recording sound, video, calls, texts, and passwords—possibly putting Mohammed's contacts in serious danger. Luckily, Mohammed didn't need an army of paid hackers to defend against this threat. His own sense for digital security was enough.
>
> Others have not been so fortunate. The *New York Times* said that operators based in China probably used the same type of email deception to break into their systems in 2012. In Mexico, journalists have been systematically targeted with sophisticated commercial spyware purchased by the Mexican government in an ongoing spying scandal. And these instances of probable state-sponsored spying represent only one type of digital threat against journalists today.[4]

The major change which has happened with the coming of digital is that it not only become easy to copy content from a computer but also with the subsequent networking of individuals and organizations, this copying could be done anonymously from a remote location.

As Joshua Oliver explains:

> One misguided click or weak password could let intruders into a whole news organization's system. These days, bad security habits could betray your sources, or the sources of the reporter sitting next to you.[5]

Why Security in the Digital World Is So Little Understood

First and foremost, this has to do with the way humans understand the world around them. Humans are material beings, that is, they tend to believe things they can see, touch and feel. Traditionally, security, as we understood it, was to hide or put things away under a lock-and-key. Computer systems have been designed to mimic the traditional human processes. Usernames and passwords are like lock-and-key and that's the reason why many websites show a symbol of lock next to the space where a password needs to be entered. However, humans cannot visualise digital data in the way they can visualise material things like a notebook, telephone diary and slips of paper. When I want to keep my diary secure, I look at hiding it or keeping it under a lock-and-key at home or office or in a bank. I am assured of the security as I can physically verify that the item is hidden or the lock has not been picked or tampered. If an intruder was to break in or find the hiding place, he would need to physically carry away the item and on verification I would find the item missing.

With digital data, the whole concept of security takes a different meaning right from the creation of a digital asset to its processing and finally its storage. The ease of digital copying not only makes the task of security difficult, the fact that copying doesn't lead to carrying away or destroying of a digital asset makes the intrusion difficult to detect or prove until it is very late or the damage is done.

For a journalist, data was always valuable but now, besides being valuable, it is portable and vulnerable. The threat landscape has changed, reducing effectiveness of spatial isolation, network firewalls, vulnerability scanners and other point solutions. To mitigate risk, individuals and media organisations now need to secure entire ecosystems of connected devices and systems while being mindful that there is no such thing as a totally invulnerable security solution.

Keng Lim, chairman and CEO at NextLabs, a security company, says security solutions have to encompass the entire data lifecycle. This means protecting data as it is shared, transformed, uploaded and downloaded. Security must continue over time and even as multiple individuals access the data for different, authorised purposes. Most important, the data owner must be able to retrieve or restrict the data access and usage as needed.

This scenario is a common occurrence in most organisations including media organisations especially where groups of journalists work on explosive stories. For example, the story done on extrajudicial killings in UP in February 2018 would have involved multiple sources and multiple journalists following those sources and procuring information from government records. While the story was being built and evidence collected using sources, the data that was collected and being interpreted as well as the story headline, idea and shape had to be protected from the various state powers lest the story was killed or the journalists came in harm's way.

Similarly, on an international scale, a story on the huge leak of documents from a Panama law firm called Mossack Fonseca lifted the lid on the financial skulduggery of the wealthy across the world. The records were obtained from an anonymous source by the German newspaper *Süddeutsche Zeitung*, which shared them with the International Consortium of Investigative Journalists (ICIJ).

The ICIJ then shared them with a large network of international partners, including the *Guardian* and the BBC. As the documents involved information on how the rich and the powerful of the world used uses tax havens to hide their wealth, the investigation by the journalists had to be done discretely and securely lest the story got out. This involved around four hundred journalists from more than a hundred media organisations in over eighty countries, who took part in researching the documents. This required a security protocol for communication between the journalists as well as for processing and sharing documents.

That this process of investigative journalism is fraught with security risks is borne by the story of Daphne Caruana Galizia. Writing in the *Guardian*, Garside said:

> The journalist who led the Panama Papers investigation into corruption in Malta was killed on Monday in a car bomb near her home. Daphne Caruana Galizia died on Monday afternoon when her car, a Peugeot 108, was destroyed by a powerful explosive device which blew the vehicle into several pieces and threw the debris into a nearby field.
>
> A blogger whose posts often attracted more readers than the combined circulation of the country's newspapers, Caruana Galizia was recently described by the Politico website as a 'one-woman WikiLeaks'. Her blogs were a thorn in the side of both the establishment and underworld figures that hold sway in Europe's smallest member state. Her most recent revelations pointed the finger at Malta's prime minister, Joseph Muscat, and two of his closest aides, connecting offshore companies linked to the three men with the sale of Maltese passports and payments from the government of Azerbaijan.[6]

Publishing a story is obviously fraught with risks as it is natural that the affluent and influential state and non-state actors would be extremely sensitive to exposes about them and their business and other interests. They would have some sort of espionage mechanisms on reputed journalist to prevent any sensitive information about them seeing the light of the day. The digital ecosystem has made such surveillance mechanisms simple to execute behind the cloak of anonymity and hence the important subject of cybersecurity for journalists.

Digital Security for Journalists

Digital security in journalism includes many aspects. A few of them are:

1. In basic reporting, the need to store notes and contacts securely in case the journalist's devices are searched.
2. In photojournalism, how metadata of photos can reveal the location of the journalist or where the photo was taken, putting sources at risk.
3. How journalists need to lock their social media accounts and how to cope with online threats.
4. Investigative journalists should be aware of ways to store sensitive information. Such documents should not be uploaded on cloud. In case it is required, then it is important to review privacy policies of the cloud.

Security is a constant worry when it comes to information technology. Data theft, hacking, malware and a host of other threats are a nightmare for any Information Technology (IT) professional. For a journalist who is not an expert in technology, it could be a tremendous setback in case of loss of highly important information.

Media and journalism courses still do not prepare prospective journalists for good cybersecurity practices. Considering that though computers and other connected devices are the frequently used tools of a journalist for data gathering, analysis and reporting, it would be hard to find cybersecurity best practices policy document circulated in any media college or school.

Security needs to be made a habit early into media training. Questions that any media professional needs to address include:

- How does digital technology change the working landscape?
- What information do I need to protect?
- Who might be trying to attack me?
- When am I at greater risk?
- How can I protect myself?

The kinds of security tools available are changing so fast that practical training in a specific tool becomes redundant unless the basic reason for using that tool is first understood. At the end of this chapter some digital tools and tips will be shared to make things easier for journalists.

Oliver, in his article on cybersecurity in the *Columbia Journalism Review* writes about Steve Doig, a Pulitzer Prize-winning reporter and professor at the Walter Cronkite School of Journalism and his digital security class. Doig looked at cybersecurity not as a 'how to' session. He wanted his students to be able to assess risks. He was conscious that security tools change so quickly that practical training swiftly goes out of date.[7]

Journalists can seek out technical knowledge and expert support in cybersecurity to protect their professional practice and don't need to become an expert in IT. Dailey, in an article 'A Guide to Easy Cybersecurity for Journalists', says, 'For most reporters, cybersecurity should probably be the digital equivalent of locking windows, doors and file cabinets before leaving home.'[8]

Ironically, the efficiencies of online and mobile devices may be putting the reporters and their sources at risk. A reporter who loses an unprotected phone or USB drive could inadvertently disclose volumes information about themselves and their sources – and cause irreparable harm.

New Age Tools for Security

There is always a risk of data theft whenever a journalist is using a computing device like a computer, smart phone, pen drive and so on. This risk increases multifold on wireless connections as the data can be captured by people or organisations without the knowledge of the journalist, for example, while using an unprotected public Wi-Fi.

Wi-Fi Protected Access (WPA) and Wi-Fi Protected Access II (WPA2) are two security protocols and security certification programs developed by the Wi-Fi Alliance to secure wireless computer networks. These were defined in response to the serious weaknesses researchers had found in the previous system, Wired Equivalent Privacy (WEP).

Then there is the VPN or virtual private networks. VPN services are provided by many companies. VPN creates a secure internet connection from almost anywhere. VPN operates by creating an encrypted tunnel in a public network like the internet. Encryption is the process of encoding a message or information in such a way that it will appear garbage to anyone illegally accessing the message or information. Encrypted message or information needs to be decrypted and can only be done by an authorised recipient with the key provided by the originator to recipients. This key will not be available to unauthorised users.

Marshall, writing in Techradar.pro about the best VPN services says:

> Ideally, a good VPN provider should offer quality customer support round-the-clock to address any issues swiftly and accordingly. Everything else is a bonus, although it's always good to have straightforward and user-friendly native clients (and preferably strong mobile app support).

His recommendations include services like ExpressVPN, Surfshark, NordVPN, ProtonVPN, CyberGhost based on the two primary concerns in this matter – privacy and security.[9]

Portable storage devices like hard drives and USB drives can transport large amounts of data. Cloud storage is a boon for journalists, allowing them to access documents from almost anywhere. However, these technologies are a security risk in themselves. For example, dozens of personal and intimate photos of celebrities like Anne Hathaway, Miley Cyrus, Kristen Stewart, Katharine McPhee, golfer Tiger Woods and his ex-partner Lindsey Vonn have been leaked on the internet and widely shared on social media. This was apparently done when an unidentified hacker or a group of hackers gained access to the celebs' Apple accounts.

It is important for journalists to use software that can lock drives and prevent unauthorised access. Simple things like Microsoft Word and Excel's password protection help unauthorised editing or opening of your documents.

USB or pen drives can be password-protected using encryption. Madhuparna writes about the need to password-protect a USB:

> While the USB flash drives are the most popular portable storage mediums based on the convenience and reliability, they are also prone to get lost, stolen or damaged. And, if you had any sensitive or private data in the USB it can be a great matter of concern. Hence, encryption of your USB drive becomes extremely imperative.[10]

Some of the software utilities to protect USBs include freeware like Rohos Disk Encryption, USB Flash Security, USB Safeguard, DiskCryptor, VeraCrypt and so on. Paid software includes Gilisoft USB Stick Encryption and Kakasoft USB Security.

One very important note of caution for journalists is never to write passwords on sticky notes and place them under keyboards or stick them on notice boards. There are password management softwares that help remember and use secure passwords. Kim Key writing in *PCMag* about the best free password managers for 2022 writes:

> A hacker can easily guess or brute-force a simple password. A data breach can expose whatever complex password you create, too, thus potentially compromising each account using it. The only solution is to use a different password for every account and make them long and random.[11]

She suggests adding password managers to our security arsenal to replace weak and duplicate passwords with strong, unguessable passwords. Some of the password managers she recommends are Bitwarden, Robofom and Dashlane.

Communication is the bread-and-butter of a journalist. Conversations on a mobile phone are not always confidential. Even though improvements in phone encryption standards are being done regularly to protect networks from unauthorised access, there is no guarantee of absolute security from espionage and hackers. Hence mobile phone call encryption and encrypted messages are crucial to a journalist. There are mobile encryption apps like the German T-systems for call encryption. The app generates an individual key each time the app is used, encoding the conversation or message and this key expires immediately after the call ends. This makes electronic eavesdropping (also called 'man-in-the-middle' attacks) impossible. The app also encrypts and stores contact information, messages and texts, assigning them a password as well.

Apps like Signal, an encrypted instant messaging and voice calling application for Android and iOS, has been developed by Open Whisper Systems. It was developed using free and open-source software. The advantage of open-source software is that it allows the cyber community to detect shortcomings and allows the community itself to remove them. Additionally, as the app is not owned by a large commercial conglomerate, the user-data governance is more transparent and subject to defined rules. As was disclosed by whistle-blower Edward Snowden in his leaked documents, American intelligence agencies routinely use American private technical businesses to do illegal surveillance for the US. The same would be the practice of many other state agencies around the world. In contrast, a journalist's job is to write fearlessly against state excesses. Hence there is a conflict of interest.

A Quick Overview of Message Apps

Today, many journalists use social media tools like WhatsApp, Facebook Messenger, Snapchat and so on for communication. All these have encryption facilities. Popular media uses the term 'end-to-end encryption', which means that only the sender and the recipient of the particular message can see each other's messages, that is, the messages cannot be decoded and unravelled by outsiders or even the maker of the application.

WhatsApp is perhaps the most popular messaging app because it enables easy communication across global networks. It has an encryption based on the Signal protocol – the same tech also used by open source messenger Signal referred earlier.

Facebook Messenger rolled out encryption in 2016 but users have to activate the encryption for every new message. It does not appear to allow encryption of old message chains, either. Facebook does not list the feature in its update notes, but on downloading version 381.0.0.29.105 or a later version, a user can mark a message as secret.

Snapchat allows messages to be encrypted in transit. However, Snapchat messages are encrypted while at-rest on Snapchat's servers and Snaps are deleted from the servers as soon as they're opened by the intended recipient. Unopened Snaps are kept on the servers for thirty days before being deleted and could be an area of concern.

Lastly, there are softwares like Tor (free software) available for anonymous communication. The name is derived from an acronym of the name of the original software project 'The Onion Router'.[12] Tor directs internet traffic through a free, worldwide, volunteer overlay network consisting of more than seven thousand relays to conceal a user's location and usage from anyone conducting network surveillance or traffic analysis.

Using Tor makes it more difficult to trace internet activity of the user including 'visits to Web sites, online posts, instant messages, and other communication forms'.[13] Tor essentially protects the personal privacy of its users allowing them the freedom to conduct confidential communication without being monitored.

This aspect can be understood by looking at the level of monitoring done by sites like Google, Facebook, YouTube, Amazon and so on.

A sample on the kind of data Google stores can be seen from the tweets of a Irish user Dylan Curran tweeting under the handle @iamdylancurran on 24 March 2018. He writes:

> Google stores your location (if you have it turned on) every time you turn on your phone, and you can see a timeline from the first day you started using Google on your phone.[14]
>
> Google stores search history across all your devices on a separate database, so even if you delete your search history and phone history, Google still stores everything until you go in and delete everything, and you have to do this on all devices.[15]
>
> Google creates an advertisement profile based on your information, including your location, gender, age, hobbies, career, interests, relationship status, possible weight (need to lose 10 lbs in one day?) and income.[16]
>
> Google stores information on every app and extension you use, how often you use them, where you use them, and who you use them to interact with (who do you talk

to on Facebook, what countries are you speaking with, what time you go to sleep at).[17]

Google stores all of your YouTube history, so they know whether you're going to be a parent soon, if you're a conservative, if you're a progressive, if you're Jewish, Christian, or Muslim, if you're feeling depressed or suicidal, if you're anorexic . . .[18]

This link includes your bookmarks, emails, contacts, your Google Drive files, all of the above information, your YouTube videos, the photos you've taken on your phone, the businesses you've bought from, the products you've bought through Google . . .[19]

Your calendar, your Google hangout sessions, your location history, the music you listen to, the Google books you've purchased, the Google groups you're in, the websites you've created, the phones you've owned, the pages you've shared, how many steps you walk in a day . . .[20]

Google offers an option to download all of the data it stores about you. Curran requested to download it and the file he received was 5.5 GB, which is roughly 3 million Word documents.

Among the search history document, which had 90,000 different entries, even showing the images he downloaded and the websites he accessed, was the 'ThePirateBay' section, a Torrent downloading site which shows him viewing copyright content against a federal law.

If you have the Windows 10 operating system installed (Windows 11 is likely to have similar features), the privacy option has sixteen different sub-menus. In the default option on installation, all options are enabled and you have to disable some of them before using the software.

The options include tracking where you are, what applications you have installed, when you use them, what you use them for, access to your webcam and microphone at any time, your contacts, your emails, your calendar, your call history, the messages you send and receive, the files you download, the games you play, your photos and videos, your music, your search history, your browsing history, even what radio stations you listen to. In an enabled state all the sub-menus can lead to a serious encroachment on your privacy and hence make you unsecure.

Some Practices for Cybersecurity

For a journalist, the goal of cybersecurity should follow two overarching principles:

1. Confidentiality of information and sources
2. Integrity of information where any breach or unauthorised use is preventable or at least detected

There are many best practices for cybersecurity. Some are generic while others are specific. Let us look at some generic practices.[21]

Password-based authentication systems have shortcomings. It is assumed that journalists will access computers and networks with secure passwords and will unfailingly comply with good password discipline. A weak password is one that is easy to figure out like dictionary passwords and names. In a survey done by the erstwhile computer company Compaq in the city of London[22] (Wilding, 2017), it was found some of the commonly used passwords include:

Sexual or abusive swearword or term (30 per cent)

Partner's name or nickname (16 per cent)

Favourite holiday destination (15 per cent)

Favourite sports team or sports personality (13 per cent)

Object on a person's desk (8 per cent)

Some of the ways in which passwords are compromised include guessing, verbal disclosure, written disclosure, duress, deception and phishing, trash search and spyware. Discarding of old devices like computers and mobile phones has also become a matter of concern considering that the stored data does not get deleted unless a proper electronic formatting has been done of the storage devices – merely deleting and emptying the trash folder is not enough.

All media professionals must have a good antivirus application package on their devices. The package must not be a free one as those are usually stripped-down versions and unable to detect and remove latest threats. The antivirus application should be updated regularly and its subscription should be regularly renewed so that the antivirus application is updated with the newly detected virus threats. The antivirus package should also include protection from Trojans specially spywares which can record computer keystrokes and switch on the mike or the camera of your device to gather data about the journalist and his or her workplace.

In the current digital ecosystem, a journalist's mobile device has become extremely vulnerable, especially with mobile apps increasingly coming with spyware having the ability to switch on the camera and microphone without the user's knowledge. It's always a good practice in desktops and laptops to stick a masking tape over the camera and in the case of mobiles, to switch off the mobile during secret meetings with sources. One has always to make sure location information in photographs is turned off lest it can be determined from the photograph's metadata where a sensitive photo was taken, leading to problems later.

All individuals working with a journalist should be assigned only the minimum privileges needed to carry out their responsibilities. Assigning minimum privileges reduces the chance that the assisting personnel walks out of the door with all the story or source data.

Journalists must use independent defences including decentralised data processing and storage for protection from data attackers. A single defence and a centralized data may be convenient but can spell doom. This doesn't prevent attack but reduces chances of being completely overrun. When senior NDTV journalist Barkha Dutt's email account was hacked, the hackers dumped the complete email records of over 1.2 GB in public domain. The public was informed by a tweet on the Twitter timeline of another senior journalist, Ravish Kumar, whose Twitter account was also hacked.[23]

Journalists must plan for failure and to minimise the consequences of a breach. This not only limits damage caused by a breach but also prevents one. Backup of all data in an offline, encrypted or physical mode is one way to plan for failure.[24]

Summary

Password-only based authentication systems have shortcomings.

Any digital database will be inevitably be hacked. There is nothing called fool proof security.

Journalists must use independent defences including decentralised data processing and storage as a precaution against data attackers.

All individuals working with a journalist should be assigned the minimum privileges needed to carry out their responsibilities

All media professionals must have a good antivirus application package on the devices being used.

Questions

1. Why should a journalist be concerned about cybersecurity?
2. Why is it important for journalist to make friends in the digital community whose help can be taken to secure digital assets?
3. Why is data storage a big concern with regards to cybersecurity?
4. How has mobile phone become the weakest link in a journalist's information gathering activity?
5. How and why should a journalist plan for failure to minimise the consequences of a breach?

Cyberlinks Compiled by Stephen Cobb

RSF.org: Reporters Sans Frontières (RSF), or Reporters Without Borders (RWB), is an international non-profit, non-governmental organisation that 'promotes and defends freedom of information and freedom of the press'. The RSF Online Survival Kit offers 'practical tools, advice and techniques that teach you how to circumvent censorship and to secure your communications and data'.

CPJ.org: The non-profit Committee to Protect Journalists (CPJ) offers a comprehensive 'Journalist Security Guide' which offers potentially life-saving advice on all aspects of security, from crime to natural disasters.

AccessNow.org: While not purely focused on journalism, Access Now is a good org to know about because its mission is to 'defend and extend the digital rights of users at risk around the world'. They have a good section on digital security and offer a Digital Security Helpline.

EFF.org: Electronic Frontier Foundation (EFF) offers a wealth of information on protecting yourself online, plus tools to help you educate (EFF) your colleagues.

CitizenLab.ca: Citizen Lab, a Canada-based interdisciplinary laboratory, focuses on 'research, development, and high-level strategic policy and legal engagement at the intersection of information and communication technologies, human rights, and global security'. The website has good advice on topics like secure messaging, plus reports on the hacking of journalists and political abuses of technology.

Reading List

1. Brian Krebs, *Spam Nation: The Inside Story of Organized Cybercrime—from Global Epidemic to Your Front Door,* audiobook, narrator Christopher Lane (Brilliance Audio, 2014).
2. Kevin Mitnick and William L. Simon, *The Art of Deception* (John Wiley & Sons, 2001).
3. Lawrence C. Miller, *Cybersecurity for Dummies* (John Wiley & Son, 2014).
4. Marc Goodman, *Future Crimes: Inside the Digital Underground and the Battle for Our Connected World* (Knopf Doubleday Publishing Group, 2016).
5. Raef Meeuwisse, *Cybersecurity for Beginners* (Cyber Simplicity Limited, 2017).
6. Ted Claypoole and Theresa Payton, *Protecting Your Internet Identity: Are You Naked Online?* (Rowman & Littlefield Publishers, 2016).

Notes

1. Ryszard Kapuscinski, 'Media as Mirror to the World', *Le Monde diplomatique*, August 1999, https://mondediplo.com/1999/08/05media.
2. Ryszard Kapuscinski, 'Media as Mirror to the World'.
3. Julianne Schultz, *Reviving the Fourth Estate* (Cambridge, England: Cambridge University Press, 1998).
4. Joshua Oliver, 'Journalism Schools Still Behind on Cybersecurity Training, New Survey Finds', *Columbia Journalism Review*, 8 January 2018, https://www.cjr.org/innovations/journalism-schools-behind-cybersecurity.php.
5. Joshua Oliver, 'Journalism Schools Still Behind on Cybersecurity Training, New Survey Finds'.
6. Juliette Garside, 'Malta Car Bomb Kills Panama Papers Journalist, *The Guardian*, 16 October 2017, https://www.theguardian.com/world/2017/oct/16/malta-car-bomb-kills-panama-papers-journalist.
7. Joshua Oliver, 'Journalism Schools Still Behind on Cybersecurity Training, New Survey Finds'.

8. Larry Dailey, 'A Guide to Easy Cybersecurity for Journalists', *Mediashift*, 4 March 2015, https://mediashift.org/2015/03/a-guide-to-cybersecurity-for-journalists/.
9. Adam Marshall, 'The Best VPN 2022', *TechRadar*, 26 April 2020, https://www.techradar.com/vpn/best-india-vpn.
10. Madhuparna, '15 Best Free USB Encryption Tools to Password Protect Your USB', *The Geek Page*, 4 March 2022, https://thegeekpage.com/free-usb-encryption-tools-to-password-protect/.
11. Kim Key, 'The Best Free Password Managers for 2022', *PC Mag*, 3 August 2022, https://www.pcmag.com/picks/the-best-free-password-managers.
12. Bingdong Li, Esra Erdin, Mehmet Hadi Gunes, George Bebis and Todd Shipley, 'An Analysis of Anonymizer Technology Usage', paper presented at 'Conference on 'Traffic Monitoring and Analysis: Third International Workshop', Vienna, Austria, 27 April 2011, DOI 10.1007/978-3-642-20305-3_10.
13. Jonathan D. Glater, 'Privacy for People Who Don't Show Their Navels', *The New York Times*, 25 January 2006, https://www.nytimes.com/2006/01/25/technology/techspecial2/privacy-for-people-who-dont-show-their-navels.html.
14. Dylan Curran @iamdylancurran, *Twitter*, https://twitter.com/iamdylancurran/status/977560174117474304.
15. Dylan Curran @iamdylancurran, *Twitter*, https://twitter.com/iamdylancurran/status/977561196571381762.
16. Dylan Curran @iamdylancurran, *Twitter*, https://twitter.com/iamdylancurran/status/977561752849338370.
17. Dylan Curran @iamdylancurran, *Twitter*, https://twitter.com/iamdylancurran/status/977562253594648578.
18. Dylan Curran @iamdylancurran, *Twitter*, https://twitter.com/iamdylancurran/status/977562812233977857.
19. Dylan Curran @iamdylancurran, *Twitter*, https://twitter.com/iamdylancurran/status/977563903919099906.
20. Dylan Curran @iamdylancurran, *Twitter*, https://twitter.com/iamdylancurran/status/977564384779227137.
21. Claudio Buttice, 'The 7 Basic Principles of IT Security', *techopedia*, 28 October 2020, https://www.techopedia.com/2/27825/security/the-basic-principles-of-it-security
22. Edward Wilding, *Information Risk and Security: Preventing and Investigating Workplace Computer Crime* (New York: Routledge, 2017).
23. 'Journalists Barkha Dutt, Ravish Kumar's Twitter Accounts Hacked by Legion', *Firstpost*, 11 December 2016, http://www.firstpost.com/india/journalists-barkha-dutt-ravish-kumars-twitter-accounts-hacked-by-legion-3150546.html.
24. Stephen Cobb, 'Cybersecurity for journalists and the news media', *welivesecurity*, 21 November 2017, https://www.welivesecurity.com/2017/11/21/cybersecurity-journalists-news-medi/.

Chapter 3

Immersive Journalism

Clyde D'Souza

Don't just watch the news. Come with me to ground zero, and experience it.

Introduction

To paraphrase a line from a well-known movie; 'If you fall in virtual reality, do you fall in real life?'

Anyone who's had the chance to try on a Virtual Reality (VR) headset and has 'walked-the-plank' – a popular VR game with many variations, will nod in the affirmative. Our brain knows we're on solid ground, yet with the VR headset on, the immersion is so complete (we are hundreds of feet from the ground and on the ledge of a skyscraper), that taking even a few steps leads us to lose our balance and stumble. At least the first time.

We can conclude that VR is capable of a physiological and psychological impact on us.[1] This fact makes it a powerful tool that needs to be wielded with great responsibility in what is now seen as a rapidly evolving area in journalism – Immersive Journalism.

This powerful illusion of reality also has another important effect on us – it can influence our emotions. It has already been called the 'ultimate empathy machine', and with good reason.

Modern Immersive Journalism owes a great deal to the work of Nonny de la Pena and her 2012 Sundance Film Festival piece 'Hunger in Los Angeles'.[2] It was a re-creation of an event on the streets of Los Angeles in a food queue where a diabetic man had collapsed, waiting in line outside a food bank.[3] Audiences who experienced the piece were surprised at how much it affected them. One reporter is said to have asked Nonny if the man survived and was relieved to know that he had.

This level of empathy is what Immersive Journalism is capable of generating and is one of the many reasons why news organisations the world over, from the *New York Times*, *CNN*, *BBC*, *Al Jazeera* to India's *NDTV* and *Times NOW*, to name a few, are delving into it.

The technology in which journalists can now tell and present their stories to heighten audience immersion is rapidly changing. Take the case of television. Once it was established as a medium to distribute a story, television mostly evolved on a predictable linear trajectory, adding higher resolution displays and years later, basic user feedback and interaction via remote controls. Not so in today's Immersive Journalism platforms. The technology is exponentially evolving and *shaping* the very ideas about how to present a news piece in an engaging manner to draw the audience into the story. This is what journalists as well as tech manufacturers in the Virtual Reality (VR), and Augmented Reality (AR) hardware and software industry are realising.

Broadly speaking, Immersive Journalism content comprises, VR video, AR and Computer-Generated Imagery. Such an ecosystem plays a unique position in the evolution of this field – it gives us the opportunity to help create the way forward as we discover new inroads into Immersive Journalism. It is from this perspective that this chapter is written, hoping to sow seeds along the way for the enterprising and passionate digital journalists to take the concept forward and expand it.

The Ethics of Immersive Journalism

In the monsoon of 2017, I was invited to Mumbai, India, to set up a pilot Immersive Journalism incubator for a leading news organisation, with a focus on training reporters, crew and camera department professionals in producing compelling Virtual Reality or more accurately, 'immersive' news pieces that would appeal to audiences locally as well as internationally.

One morning I found the city had ground to a halt due to incessant rains during the past forty-eight hours. Civic authorities do their best every monsoon season in Mumbai, yet at times, nature can overwhelming negate all efforts. As I looked out the window of the hotel I was staying in the suburbs, I could see the chaos amid the traffic disruption that the flooding had created.

I realised that this was one of news pieces that could be covered in 360 3D video VR (distinct from 360 video, which we will discuss later).[4] In a few minutes I was wading waist-deep in the water, with the VR camera – a custom-made waterproof rig – looking for an opportune vantage point to place it. That was when, for the first time, the question of ethics in immersive video coverage struck me.

I could place the camera exactly where I was standing, and the audience would see people struggling, holding on to rusty rails by the side of the road to wade forward, while the water level reached over the wheels of the cars parked nearby. In front of me was an overflowing garbage bin and a sewer a little further away was spewing its contents uncontrollably.

However, if I walked about a hundred metres down the main street, the scene was different. There, civic service personnel in fluorescent yellow jackets and citizen volunteers were busy helping people and picture presented was of a resilient city, dealing with a natural calamity bravely and systematically.

Figure 3.1: Clouds over Sidra

Non-biased journalism, whether traditional or VR based, would of course devote equal weightage to both scenarios. In India, there is a concern that news channels are entirely driven by competition, ratings, and sensationalism. If they choose to show government apathy, audiences might see more of the former scene (the overflowing garbage and sewer) and less of the latter. Or vice-versa.

With Immersive Journalism pieces, this can become a critical concern. The reason is that in a Virtual Reality video, there is no 'TV screen' from which the audience consumes content. The audience is 'embodied in the actual location'. If the audience was to look at the immersive news piece shot that day, they could look down and see the murky sewer-mixed flood water flow between their legs and scraps of garbage cling to them before getting swept away by the current.

Looking around and seeing pavement dwellers with young children, uprooted from their homes, can turn up the empathy level a few notches, in most audiences.

The fact that audiences can be put through such an immersive experience from a controlled viewpoint (the location the news editor/reporter chooses) is a cause of serious concern to us when we look at ethics in immersive journalism.[5]

One can see how if the chosen viewpoint was just a hundred metres down the road, the immersive news piece could be a lot less exciting, for lack of a better word, and would act in favour of showing a well-prepared civic system.

We've explored only one such angle of how ethics become a concern. There are far more serious scenarios dealing with, for example, wartime reporting in immersive media and personal privacy both for people featured in a piece being produced, and later for audiences viewing an immersive journalistic piece.

Audience Privacy

To give an example of personal privacy issues that could arise, when a person puts on a headset and is viewing content, everywhere they 'look at' and for how long their gaze lingered can be tracked. These gaze-heatmaps as they are called, can tell a news organisation how a story affected their audience. Thus, an audience-bias map can be built, based on what kind of stories elicit empathy from audiences, and in the case of commercial exploitation of such data, it is plausible to expect commercial brands to place imagery within such pieces during post-production.

Audiences should be rightfully told if their gaze is being tracked. The question is, will organisations and playback platforms prominently make this known, or will it be buried in the general terms of service that people click when installing an app.

Augmented Reality and Audience Immersion

We generally accept there are two related presentation and display technologies when it comes to immersive journalism – Augmented Reality (AR) and Virtual Reality (VR). Let's consider Augmented Reality first, which should set the context for the second.

AR can be explained as the overlaying of digital information and graphics anchored to our view of the real world. The current popular methods for AR are optical see through and video see through.

Optical See Through AR

Microsoft's HoloLens[6] is one of the well-known optical see through AR systems. In this, the wearer can see the real-world though a transparent screen, and within a smaller field of view, a special coating allows for the projection of digital imagery and text, which are 'locked' to real world coordinates. For example, if looking at a 'hologram' of a digitally created person via the HoloLens, the digital person will seem to occupy real world space in a room, allowing us to walk up to and back away from the digital person, as though a real person was in the room. This is done with the aid of Computer Vision (CV) algorithms and physical sensors on the HoloLens device which scan and update the room in the background, along with Artificial Intelligence, to identify real world objects in the scene.

However, such a device is not yet consumer ready in the practical sense. The price point is also high to allow it to attain mass adoption for consumption of Immersive Journalism content.

Video See Through AR

Most medium to high-end smart phones, irrespective of the operating system they run, have powerful processors and sensors. Accelerometers, GPS and other sensors already bundled in these smart phones makes for some powerful AR hardware.

The cameras built into these phones can rival even professional ones. Using the phone's camera to bring in the real world onto the phone's display and then superimposing digital imagery can make for very robust AR systems.

The catch is, of course, that people must hold their hands out in front of them, and 'see' the real world via their phone displays – usually a 6 inch 'portal' into the real world.

Virtual Reality and Audience Immersion

Virtual Reality (VR) systems were previously expensive for a consumer and mostly used only by the military and the scientific community. A few privileged universities also had access to these systems. The availability of affordable VR systems can be attributed to the launch of the Oculus Rift – A VR headset that was intended for immersive gaming but soon made its way into many mainstream industries that have a need for immersive visualisation – from real estate to engineering and even films.

VR headsets contain a high resolution screen and some high-end optics that magnify the field of view to almost near our natural field of view. This is what contributes to such a great sense of immersion when a VR headset is worn. The wearer is visually cut off from the outside world, and the visuals presented within the VR headset become the wearer's 'new world'.

For this illusion to work, very precise sensors which track the wearer's head and position, need to work in tandem with graphics processing chips that can re-draw the virtual world from the tracking data supplied by the trackers. This is done thousands of times per second. The screens, LCD or OLED displays, need to have a fast-enough display refresh rate. If any one of the components in a VR systems lags, chances are that the outcome will have physical implications on the wearer. Nausea is one of the more common side effects.

Today's VR systems are quite capable and even VR headsets driven by mobile phones have become powerful enough to present at least 4k video resolution. They can be used for Immersive Journalism with ease.

A Purist's Definition of Virtual Reality

If we go by the dictionary definition of Virtual Reality,[7] we will fall short of what the video-based VR can deliver as an immersive medium. The dictionary definition of VR will have us only looking at computer generated (CG) reconstructions, or as of the time of this writing, quite crude video-grammetry capture of slices of real life.

'The Hunger' in Los Angeles immersive piece would tick all the boxes in the dictionary definition of VR. We have six degrees of freedom (DOF) to move in – yaw, roll, pitch, forward/back, left/right and up/down – as the VR headset (our position and point of view) is tracked and the CG world is updated to present our current point of view.

But what about immersive journalism pieces that are captured in video, with stereoscopic depth and in 360? Do such stories not qualify as immersive enough? To make an argument that stereoscopic 360 video can indeed be as immersive, we should realise that we still have three degrees of freedom (pitch, roll, yaw) in video-based VR when captured stereoscopically. To lend credence to this argument, imagine an immersive journalism piece where you, the audience, are in a hostage situation, tied to a chair. We've instantly removed three degrees of freedom (you can guess which) and now the only cues for audience immersion are three DOF and the illusion of depth that never fails to fool the brain – stereoscopic visuals.

Therefore, it is important to capture news pieces in stereoscopic 360, not as flat 360 video. You can't cheat the scale in a VR headset. Conflicting cues will arise when viewing a flat 360 video in a VR headset, because you are 'inside' the scene and seeing everything in mono. It is like watching living video wallpaper plastered to the insides of a sphere. Without stereoscopic or binocular cues to aid in our judging of scale and without the benefit of the other three degrees of freedom, our suspension of disbelief in favour of Virtual Reality is arrested.

Mixed Reality and Audience Immersion

Presently (2022), due to the nature and design of AR systems, they can't display high fidelity visuals comparable in quality to that of powerful computer tethered VR systems. AR systems will soon catch up. It's inevitable.

Interestingly, there is a 'game' for the HoloLens which immediately shows the far-reaching potential that AR, or indeed, Mixed Reality, can have in Immersive Journalism. In this game, titled 'Fragments'[8] digital characters occupy real world space in the HoloLens wearer's room. Characters walk around, sit, and gesture at you (!) and other characters in the room when speaking.

Now imagine if this were a re-creation of a real-world crime story about three people in a room, who got into an argument which leads to an assault of one of them. The story could be told in two ways – a diorama like setting, where the scene plays out on a table top, and the audience uses today's AR mobile phone displays. They watch in a God-like fashion, viewing the events from above, as the animated story unfolds.

Or the audience could wear an AR device like the HoloLens. This would afford true real-world scales to be used for the characters and they could 'sit' in the same room as the audience, while the story unfolds in Mixed Reality.

Going a step further, if this were a case in which a jury has to pass judgement in a court, many cues that cannot readily be intuited from a cartoon-like diorama setting, could be observed. For instance, if two of the characters were sitting on a couch when the argument ensued, body language and the tone of voice could show how the argument escalated. Machine learning systems and AI can animate facial expressions like surprise, anger, aggressiveness, etc. from voice inflections.

This also reminds us of the previous topics of ethics and the ability to influence people with the sheer power immersive journalism can wield.

Immersion in VR

> *A couple of years ago I was with the former US President Clinton in a tiny mud hut in Africa. I wasn't physically there with him, but because of the excellent way this immersive journalism piece was produced, it really did feel that way.*
>
> –Inside Impact: East Africa

Inside Impact: East Africa is a masterpiece in immersive journalism using VR.[9]

Why is the immersion so high in that piece? There are multiple factors but what stands out most is the adherence to scale in the VR video and the placement of the VR camera; you casually look over your shoulder and you can 'feel' the textured mud walls of the hut you are in, while a few feet ahead the former president is sitting speaking with the dwelling's inhabitants. In another scene, you find yourself sitting on a tattered green couch placed on an unused railway track – you look towards your feet and you see the shining metal of the track along it are pieces of paper blowing in the wind.

These details are what lend to the sense of realism of being transported to another part of the world and being and immersed in it, while the main narrative unfolds.

Being able to re-create an entire world does give VR certain benefits over AR. In AR, the sense of immersion is diminished because people are looking at a scene through the physical confines of their mobile phone or tablet or a similar device. The effective field of view is so narrow that it does not suspend the feeling of disbelief being aimed for.

In VR, because the audience's entire field of view is only the virtual world, which updates in sync with the audience's head movement, immersion is very high.

Readers are recommended to experience this VR pieces with an Oculus Rift, GearVR or OculusGo headset. VariousVR experiences can be found at https://www.felixandpaul.com/.

Immersive Production in VR

The biggest temptation to journalists starting out in the medium is to buy one of the increasingly growing numbers of the so-called VR cameras. Many mainstream electronics manufacturers already have them available. These are mostly point-and-shoot 360 video cameras, and not the best choice for producing compelling video–VR Immersive journalism content.

During the setting up of an Immersive Journalism incubator at a leading news organisation in India, enthusiasm was high and everyone wanted to go out and shoot VR news segments. However, there is a big difference between shooting and reporting a news piece with a 360 camera, versus producing content that transports audiences and activates their empathy.

For evaluation, we opened the day's newspaper and looked at stories that would justify coverage in VR. A breaking story on demonstrations at a local hospital due to the government contemplating to charge haemophiliac patients for blood packets, stood out. The temptation again, was to gear up a reporter and a VR camera and be in thick of the demonstration, so the chaos could be captured and people's sentiments recorded from the ground. It would put the audiences right in the centre of the news piece.

There is however, so much more to meaningful Immersive Journalism. We reasoned a better way forward was to find one such haemophiliac patient and document what and how the change by the government would affect them and their family. A video could be prepared about a typical day in the life of a haemophiliac patient. It could also document the challenges they and their family face at home, then lead to the hospital and the current situation. This would make a compelling piece of immersive journalism.

Similarly, the Immersive Journalism incubator gave up on an obvious plan of capturing 360 footage of crowds during the Indian festival of Ganesh Chaturthi, where thousands of devotees immerse gigantic idols of the God, Ganesha, into the sea. Instead, they found merit in documenting the festival as it began by visiting a typical home, where a small idol was brought in, prayers offered and then followed the family's journey, a few days later, as they made their way, sometimes on foot to one of the immersion spots dotting the city.

Each immersive journalism piece usually lends itself better to one medium over the other – Virtual Reality or Augmented Reality.

When reviewing the two examples we have considered, it would be obvious that an immersive piece would be better done in video-based VR (versus a CG reconstruction), but would not lend itself well to AR.

However, there is a growing fad of AR teleportation, which might provide a novel experience in, say, the Ganesh Chaturthi festival scenario.

Teleporting in AR

How this works is, the audience or user start their mobile phone AR app, and aim it at the world in front of them. They then see a floating 'orb' with live video of usually another location, playing on the surface of this orb/sphere.

Now, because this AR object is anchored to the real world via AR tracking, the holder of the mobile phone can walk closer and see the orb scale in size as well as the video from the remote location until, at one point, the user 'enters into' the orb and the live video is textured all around him or her, thus blocking out the real-world view that their camera phones are depicting on the phone display. Remember, they are still experiencing all this on a phone display and if they look away the illusion is shattered.

By moving their hands around, while 'inside' the sphere, they can see different slices of the video from the remote location being webcast live (usually). This form of

Immersive Journalism can allow an audience in say, Europe, to teleport to a beach in Mumbai during the Ganesh immersion festival.

Where the power of this format of AR immersive journalism will shine is when optical see-through AR eyewear with a large field-of-view displays come to the market.

Tools for Production of Immersive Journalism

Producing content in VR and AR is usually a department-wide effort in an organisation, much like producing a typical news segment. However, just as traditional news segments can be also be produced solo by enterprising journalists and reporters, so can VR and AR pieces be produced by individuals. Technology is married to creativity today, and there is no clear delineating line between the two; any independent journalist with mastery over both can produce immersive content.

By no means is this supposed to be the definitive guide to tools or producing immersive content. Keeping that in mind, let's start with hardware and software that are readily available today and then move on to production methodology.

VR Cameras

Rather than list out brand names, it would be better to list crucial characteristics that a VR Camera should have:

- Be capable of stereoscopic 360 capture. There are custom-built rigs and all-in-one radial rigs, mostly from China
- Be genlock synced. Be aware, some very popular so-called professional 3D 360 VR cameras are not genlock synced and are being used by big production companies who are unaware of the need for genlock or hardware sync when producing stereoscopic 360 footage.
- There is no one-camera-fits-all formula for immersive content production. The best pieces use a combination of radial 360 VR cameras, matched with stereoscopic 3D cameras for closeups.
- The fewer the cameras in a 3D rig (but with good overlap) the lesser the points of failure and burden of data processing.

VR Camera Accessories

- Sturdy lockable base monopod. This is so that the 'footprint' of the tripod isn't so visible at the nadir (lower/base) of the footage captured.
- Hotshoe/camera mountable LED light panel when needed.
- Audio: an ambisonic-capable microphone is good to have to capture the spatial depth of the location.

VR 3D Reconstruction Software

- For Immersive Journalism pieces where video footage is not available or the whole story is being reconstructed, game engines have become the resource to produce the content. Two popular engines are Unreal Engine and Unity. These engines are used in the re-creation of stories offering full six DOF movement with today's VR headsets. If asked to suggest an engine of choice, I prefer Unity because of the vast developer community, availability of plugins that aid in immersive content production and overall comfort-level in using the software.

- Iclone is a software that will allow for output in Virtual Reality video format.
- Unity Asset Store has realistic human characters for animation, photo realistic digital 'back lots'. Even behaviour AI systems can be bought here and used in projects.

VR Production

VR Post Production

- Mistika VR: Once footage has been shot with VR cameras, which can be four or more, the footage needs to be 'stitched' into one panoramic (and stereoscopic) image before it can be edited into a story. This is where Mistika VR holds its own.
- The popular Adobe Creative Suite CC is already geared for editing in Virtual Reality. Inbuilt plugins and editing while reviewing using a VR headset make immersive content production in the field a viable option.
- Canvas STK: A relatively new plugin system for Adobe after-effects. This plugin is highly recommended when producing stereoscopic 360 VR content.

VR Presentation Platforms

- YouTube is one of the most widely known and easy to use platforms for uploading and presenting video based Immersive Journalism content in VR.
- Google Daydream store: Accessible via Google Daydream VR headsets.
- Facebook and Oculus Video: These are platforms are accessible via the Oculus VR headsets.
- Oculus and Daydream store: These are for CG based Immersive Journalism pieces that allow audience interaction.
- Headsets: Google Cardboard for basic VR consumption, Samsung GearVR, Oculus Rift and Facebook's recently launched Oculus Go headset. There are many other such headsets to experience VR content.

Video-Based VR Production

Video-based VR production usually starts with real-world footage shot with a VR capable camera and audio captured in ambisonic format. The video files from the VR camera rig which can comprise 6–8 individual cameras arranged in a config to capture the entire 360 field of view, now need to be stitched into a panoramic image and any pixel 'seams' need to be cleaned up so as not to distract when the finished footage is viewed in a headset. This is where softwares like Mistika come. With its advanced optical flow algorithms and intuitive interface, Mistika allows rapid output of pristine stereoscopic VR footage (assuming the footage was captured with a stereoscopic VR rig).

The next step for VR production is to import the footage into an editing program such as Adobe Premier CC and import the ambisonic audio footage. Adobe Premier allows mastering of common VR video formats. The full immersive video can be watched in real-time on a headset such as the Oculus Rift, while editing in Premier. Along the way, using Adobe's dynamic link connection to its other software AfterEffects, allows for creation of depth with plugins such as Canvas STK and colour-correcting the footage.

Finally, choosing an immersive output setting and tick marking YouTube VR video and spatial audio, allows the completed video to be output-ready for upload and presentation on VR headsets.

CG-Based VR Production

Producing 'dictionary-compliant' VR involves re-creation of a news or journalistic piece with computer graphics and affording user interaction in the virtual world.

Using the Unity Engine, one can start off by either buying a readymade 'digital set' that closely resembles the setting of the actual stories, and then modifying it to stay as true to the environment the story took place or takes place in.

Locations captured by high-end photogrammetry can be optimised and imported, but often, pre-existing standard 3D models (town, park, houses, furniture) are used.

The story is then authored as a 'cut scene' in game language. Here, timed animations and sound are played back, and the audience, wearing a headset, can enter the scene and interact with objects if allowed to do so by the author of the piece.

Finally, the project is either run directly from the game engine and viewed in a VR headset, or if it is optimised well, the project might run on mobile VR headsets available today such as the Oculus Go, or Samsung Gear VR. The quality of visuals and the experience will be a trade-off between the processor of the mobile phone and the mobile VR headset.

AR Production

The methodology for producing AR content is only slightly different from CG based VR production. Again, the Unity Game Engine will be used (as can Unreal Engine) and importing one of the AR SDKs of choice for the end platform for which you want to develop.

One key difference between AR and VR will now become obvious. Taking the hypothetical scenario mentioned earlier in the 'Mixed Reality and Audiences immersion' section, we had three people in a CG created room. For AR, we would need to lose the walls, the ceiling and floor. We could keep the couch on which the people were sitting when the argument ensued.

Once this AR piece is output and viewed through an AR device, the camera or optical see-through capability of the AR headset would let our real-world imagery come through, get superimposed on the two people and the couch, and get locked to our real-world floor.

This is one of the main differences between AR and VR. In VR you create or re-create the entire world, in AR you usually only create digital elements that need to 'inhabit' ours!

AR Platforms

- Augmented Reality SDKs: Until recently, AR software carried a high price tag and had restrictive usage policies attached. Things changed when both Google and Apple released their AR SDKs (software development kits) in the form of ARCore and ARKit, respectively. For Immersive Journalism, chances are one of these SDKs will be used, though there are others.
- Authoring Platform: Unity Engine, the game engine, shines again. Both ARCore and ARKit work within the Unity platform and the resulting AR content can be an output to popular mobile phones and tablets running android or Apple iOS operating system
- HoloLens Content Authoring: Unity Engine also offers the capability to author content for this AR headset.

Conclusion

As of now (June 2022), Immersive Journalism is a wide-open field, ready to be cultivated by pioneering journalists and students of journalism. Rules and norms have not been set yet, but guidelines for ethics and creation of compelling immersive content are being developed at an exponential pace.

There are issues of fake news, certainly. Because of the immersive nature of these pieces, they can easily influence audiences. For instance, in the president Clinton piece, it is possible, with today's digital imaging manipulation technology, AI and machine learning capabilities, that audiences are subjected to a doctored and polarising piece of content.

In CG re-creations of VR stories, even narrow AI pieces of code can manipulate an audience. For instance, on the Unity asset store is a harmless yet realistic plugin to drive virtual 'eyes' of a character.[10] In other words, to humanise these digital eyes. Sliders allow for semi-automated or user-input driven reactions such as 'stare-factor' or 'look away' threshold and macro-saccades. When combined with real-world audio narrative, it is possible to speculate that such digital replicas of people could influence audiences, intentionally or otherwise.

Yet, the mediums of VR and AR, when used conscientiously, can be powerful galvanisers to motivate change for the better.

This chapter only scratches the surface of what's possible and institutions are encouraged to set up Immersive Journalism sandboxes to help spearhead research and produce graduates who are updated in this evolving world of Digital Journalism.

Tips and Tools

Tips

- Keep Immersive Journalism pieces under 15 minutes if possible. This is to ensure optimum audience ease, taking into account VR headset comfort.
- Aim for maximum immersion and 'presence' with an Immersive Journalism production. This can be achieved, at the very least, by shooting video in stereoscopic 360.
- Use sound as a powerful storytelling tool.

Tools

- Production software such as Adobe CC is indispensable and is VR ready.
- Unity 3D is a convenient game engine for creating hybrid (CG + video based) Immersive Journalism projects.
- An Oculus Rift Headset for previewing while in production can be used.
- Multi-Rig Camera for capture such as the Obsidian-S is useful. Google's Jump system is also recommended.

Questions

1. When producing a VR project, ask the all-important question: What does VR bring to this story that regular video journalism can't?
2. Once the project is complete, take a non-biased look and ask if and how the experience might influence a viewer from an ethics point of view.
3. Ask if the immersive journalism piece has the potential to reach and make a wider global audience care? Strive for that!

Explore More

R.T. Stone, K.P. Watts, P. Zhong, and C.S. Wei, 'Physical and Cognitive Effects of Virtual Reality Integrated Training', *Human Factors*, 16 September 2011, **53**(5), 558-572, http://journals.sagepub.com/doi/10.1177/0018720811413389.

Expert Speaks

Retha Hill is on the faculty of the Walter Cronkite School of Journalism and Mass Communication at Arizona State University where she is the executive director of the New Media Innovation and Entrepreneurship Lab. Hill, an award-winning journalist, is the founder of AncestoriesXR, an extended reality platform that helps families tell their unique genealogy using video game technology and immersive media. Retha Hill was in conversation with Dr Anubhuti Yadav on 29 July 2022.

How do you think newsrooms are utilising the power of AR and VR in journalism?

Most newsrooms are still experimenting with AR and VR. After 2015, many newsrooms thought 360 video would be the next big thing and poured resources into it. Gannett, the owner of the *Arizona Republic* and *USA Today*, for example, launched a weekly show called 'VRtually There', that featured three 360 videos in each episode which were designed to give viewers incredibly rich experiences such as going on a deep-sea dive or flying through the air with a skydiver. The company even came up with something called a 'cubemercial'. But the public did not latch on even though people could access these experiences by popping a late model smartphone into a cardboard viewer and watching the videos. The *New York Times* had successfully demonstrated the effectiveness of such content in 2015 when it launched its first 360 documentary called, *The Displaced.* The news company mailed cardboards to more than a million subscribers. If the recipients could figure out how to assemble the viewer, they could be transported into the world of three refugee children to see what life was like for them in South Sudan, Ukraine and Jordan. The *New York Times* followed up with other documentaries and shorter pieces. *The Times* and other media outlets hoped the interest would kick off mass adoption of the technology. It did not.

Even tech giant Google stumbled when it came to 360 VR. It shuttered the Google Jump program in May 2019 which followed the shutdown of Google Spotlight Studios a few months before. The camera gave creators, such as two of my former students who created a documentary on the US–Mexico border in 360 VR, access to a 16-camera rig that shot beautiful, hyper-realistic high-def video. The studios provided a place for creators to show off their work. But the public did not embrace the technology.

That experience may be partially responsible for newsrooms being more cautious with AR and VR. The bigger or more adventurous newsrooms are still experimenting with AR. The *New York Times* has a section devoted to its efforts.[11] Many are smaller efforts that are more practical such as showing the effectiveness of an N95 face mask. You can see the effects through the Times' Instagram app.

The program also used JavaScript and Webgl to allow people to access the content from their desktop simply by scrolling to look through the page. Another explainer shows the impact of a polar vortex, a natural phenomenon that disperses super cold air to the Northern Hemisphere.

The *Washington Post* launched its first web-based AR story (the industry's first) in 2018 to let people explore the skull of a mysterious dinosaur housed at the Smithsonian Institution. Viewers can look at it via the website,[12] but if they navigate to that page on a smartphone or other enabled mobile device they can point their device at the floor and see the skull come into their own space.

Snap AR provides a way for newsrooms to reach younger, more diverse audiences by creating a Lens. You can create AR using Spark AR, which is the Meta studio, and post your content on your Instagram app.

The bigger newsrooms have or are creating R&D studios. The *New York Times* experiments quite a bit and will create guides such as one on Spark AR or on Photogrammetry to help the rest of us catch up. Their advantage is they have a lab full of engineers and creators where most newsrooms might have one multimedia producer whose main responsibility is posting breaking news updates to the newsroom's website and mobile app.

Can you give some examples of the effective use of AR and VR?

The big takeaway from the 360 experience is to keep experimenting and to create practical 'news you can use' applications. In addition to the N 95 mask AR, the *New York Times* has created other such applications. If you go to the *New Your Times* Instagram page and click the tab denoted by three little stars, you enter into a work of special effects and augmented reality that point to what media companies can do now. One example shows how inflation is shrinking your purchasing power. Once you click on the effect you can wave your phone at the floor and tap. You can then see how inflation has decreased your buying power for gas, for used cars and for other everyday items. Another AR shows an Olympic gymnast on the parallel bars that you can bring into your own space.

Figure 3.2: The New Yourk Times: Instagram

Some content creators make their augmented reality projects available through Snap or they build AR applications that can be accessed from the Apple App Store or Google Playground. An AR app is better for content that connects to a database such a geo-location app that shows places of interest that are triggered by location or a weather app that might display temperature and forecast in AR, again based on geo-location.

Apple's Reality Composer and Adobe's Areo are interfaces that allow people new to AR to quickly build an augmented reality experience. The experience can be created with a late-model smartphone or tablet.

What is your message for the students who are in awe of these new technologies?

Students should ask themselves the same questions as I suggested for media organisations. Does this AR experience enhance understanding or delight news consumers in a way that a photo or video won't? That is a great place to start. Students should always remember that news technologies are tools, and each tool has to be used correctly in order to extract the most value. A hammer is great to pound nails; it is less useful to use as a door stopper or a paperweight. AR is great to help people get info when they need it such as weather and forecasts that might show up through a pair of AR glasses or a quick flash that your commuter train will be at the station in 60 seconds so you might want to run. AR helps to take people where they might not be able to go now such as standing and looking up at an Olympic gymnast perform or standing next to a very tall basketball player or peering into the universe as seen by the James Webb telescope or going back in time to see pioneering women standing at the very places in your city where they once stood. AR is a tool, as is VR, photography, 360 video and illustrations. We should not be afraid of immersive media technology any more than we should have been afraid of those grainy photos that appeared showing the aftermath of a battle during the US Civil War in the 1860s. Photography back then showed people something they were not able to see, like a war -- unless they were there and lived to talk about it. Technology can be abused; videos have been and AR and VR will be. We have to keep reminding people to trust those media outlets with ethical standards or you won't know if what you are looking at is a true reflection of reality.

How do you think media organisations can embrace this?

Newsrooms can start small by creating a page on their Instagram account. They can build a simple effect such as fireworks going off at midnight on 31 December. Then they can progress from there. Content creators should ask themselves if a display is best shown as an augmented reality, rather than a photograph or video. People who use Instagram a lot would probably look at the effect if it is highlighted on a reel and is interesting to look at. Instagram reaches different news consumers than TV, print or website content. Know your audience and know why you are creating something in augmented reality. The questions to ask is, will this give news consumers something surprising or useful, such as showing how N95 mask traps particles, or perhaps an AR of the latest basketball recruit to the local team to show just how tall the new guy is. Experiment, understand what works and what is engaging audiences, then build from there, such as creating an augmented reality app for the smartphone or tablet. The cost of building these apps has come way down from what it was when I built my first AR app in 2010.

Notes

1. '"It Can Have Lasting Psychological Effects": The Ethics of Virtual Reality', *CBC Radio*, 6 October 2017, http://www.cbc.ca/radio/tapestry/keeping-it-real-in-virtual-reality-1.4328289/it-can-have-lasting-psychological-effects-the-ethics-of-virtual-reality-1.4330169.
2. N.D. Pena, 'Hunger in Los Angeles – Immersive Journalism', Sundance Film Festival 2012, *Emblematic*, http://emblematicgroup.com/experiences/hunger-in-la/.
3. 'Hunger in Los Angeles - Immersive Journalism', *YouTube*, 10 January 2013, https://www.youtube.com/watch?v=SSLG8auUZKc.
4. 'Clouds Over Sidra', *YouTube*, 28 January 2016, https://www.youtube.com/watch?v=mUosdCQsMkM.
5. Hollis Kool, 'The Ethics of Immersive Journalism: A Rhetorical Analysis of News Storytelling with Virtual Reality technology', *Intersect: The Stanford Journal of Science, Technology, and Society*, 2016, **9**(3), http://ojs.stanford.edu/ojs/index.php/intersect/article/view/871/863.
6. Microsoft, 'Microsoft HoloLens 2', https://www.microsoft.com/en-us/hololens.
7. Merriam Webster, https://www.merriam-webster.com/dictionary/virtual%20reality.
8. Asobo Studio, http://www.asobostudio.com/games/fragments.
9. Felix and Paul Studios, https://www.felixandpaul.com/?insideimpact.
10. Tore Knabe, 'Realistic Eye Movements', *Tore Knabe's Blog*, http://tore-knabe.com/unity-asset-realistic-eye-movements/.
11. 'Immersive', *The New York Times*, https://www.nytimes.com/spotlight/augmented-reality.
12. Bonnie Berkowitz, Seth Blanchard, Gabriel Florit and Youjin Shin, A mystery dinosaur in the nation's basement', *The Washington Post*, 17 September 2018, https://www.washingtonpost.com/graphics/2018/national/smithsonian-dinosaur-augmented-reality/?utm_term=.fe3c8765938f&itid=lk_inline_manual_4.

Chapter 4

Data Journalism

Dr Anubhuti Yadav

Information is the oil of the 21st century and analysis is the combustion engine.

–Peter Sondergaard, Gartner Research

Data driven journalism is the future. Journalists need to be data savvy. It used to be that you would get stories by chatting to people in bars, and it still might be that you'll do it that way sometimes. But now it's also going to be about poring over data and equipping yourself with the tools to analyze it and pick out what's interesting. And keeping it in perspective, helping people out by really seeing where it all fits together, and what's going on in the country.

–Tim Berners-Lee, founder of the World Wide Web

When the information was scarce, most of our (journalists) efforts were devoted to hunting and gathering. Now that information is abundant, processing is more important.

–Philip Meyer

Introduction

Data journalism has become a buzzword both in the newsrooms and media education institutes. While there is a great deal of conversation around data journalism but in reality, in India, we have very few experts in data journalism in the industry as well as in academia. Though at the time of the Covid-19 pandemic we witnessed several stories based on data, there is still a long way to go. In this chapter, we will learn what data journalism is, why it is important, how to get data online, data scraping and data visualisation.

Journalists across the world have been using data to tell stories that are more interactive, engaging and meaningful.[1] We shall also discuss some of these stories and the process followed by the journalists to cover the stories.

'Data Is the New Oil' is the catch-phrase coined in 2006 by Clive Humby, a British mathematician and data scientist. Since then this phrase has been used innumerable times in conferences in the field of Marketing, Advertising, Public Relations, Journalism and so on. Search for #dataisnewoil on Twitter to know the popularity of this term and how experts the world over are quoting it. Humby explains it further, 'It (oil) is valuable, but if unrefined it cannot really be used. It has to be changed into gas, plastic, chemicals etc to create a valuable entity that drives profitable activity; so must data be broken down, analyzed for it to have value.'

This applies to journalists – for any data-driven story, the data has to be broken down, analysed, and visualised for the people to understand. In India, the biggest problem is the lack of credible data. During the launch of the India Data portal, a one-stop open-access portal for journalists to access, interact with, and visualise information data, and knowledge related to agriculture and financial inclusion, Ms Ritu Kapur, co-founder of the *Quint* said, 'No news organization currently has pockets deep enough to do large-scale surveys. . . . We need credible data considering the amount of under-reporting and misreporting that has come to the fore.'

For journalists, data can come in many forms. It is not just structured data that is organised in columns and rows in a spreadsheet format – it can also be unstructured text, photos, audios or videos. Such databases can help journalists a great deal but a database alone is not journalism. It is a field of information that needs to be harvested carefully with insight and caution. It needs to be compared and augmented with observations and interviews.

What Is Data Journalism

Several terms are used interchangeably when we talk about data journalism. These are Computer-Assisted Reporting, Precision Journalism, Computational Journalism and, of course the most popular, data journalism.[2]

Computer-Assisted Reporting

As the name suggests, this is the use of computer software for reporting. It is an organised, systematic approach to collect and analyse data to improve the news. It was used for the first time in 1952 by *CBS* to predict the results of the US presidential elections. Since the 1960s, journalists have sought to independently monitor power by analysing databases of public records with scientific methods.[3]

Precision Journalism

This term was popularised in 1973 by Phillip Meyer, who is considered the father of computer-assisted reporting, through his book *Precision Journalism*. Precision Journalism, according to Meyer, is applying techniques used in social science research to analyse data and present precise information in easily understood ways. Using computers and statistics software adds depth to reporting and improves its accuracy. Meyer first used Precision Journalism in determining the underlying causes of the 1967 riot in Detroit, USA, which contributed to a Pulitzer Prize for the Detroit Free Press.

In an interview with *Investigating Power*, while responding to the question that some people think that they don't need journalism anymore because everybody can just dip into the never-ending digital stream and take out what they want, he said you needed journalism more than ever before to organise all that information that's correct. Only organised information can be of any value and there are two ways to organise it – one is with narrative storytelling and the other is with the scientific method of hypothesis testing and theory building. If you can combine these two skills, then you have something that people will pay attention to and something that would be very influential.

Computational Journalism

Computational Journalism means the use of computational methods and approaches for journalism. This includes research, reporting and production of content in a wide variety of forms. The terms Computational Journalism and Computer assisted reporting are used interchangeably.

Data Journalism

While there are debates and discussions on the difference between all these terms amongst scholars but the emergence of the label 'Data Journalism' at the beginning of this century indicates a new phase wherein the sheer volume of data that is freely available online combined with sophisticated user-centric tools, self-publishing tools and crowdsourcing tools enables more people to work with more data more easily than ever before.[4]

Here is how experts in the field of Data Journalism explain the concept based on their experience:

> *Gathering, filtering and visualising what is happening beyond what the eye can see has a growing value.*
>
> –Datajournalism.com

> *Gathering, cleaning, organizing, analyzing, visualizing and publishing data to support the creation facts of journalism.*
>
> –Aron Pinofer

> *Data can be the source for Data Journalism or it can be the tool with which a story can be told – or it can be both.*
>
> –Kuek Ser Kuang

> *The crux of the story would not exist without data. The discovery of the story would not have happened without data. It is the root of the story or it is what holds the story together.*
>
> –Gurman Bhatia

CAR (Computer-assisted reporting) does not refer to journalists sitting at the keyboard writing stories or surfing the web and social media. It refers to downloading or building databases and doing data analysis that can provide context and depth to daily stories. It refers to techniques of producing tips that launch more complex stories from a broader perspective and with a better understanding of the issues.

–Brant Houstan

History of Data Journalism

Data journalism has caught the attention of all in the field of journalism, especially during the Covid-19 pandemic. Indian news media also engaged with it in large numbers meaningfully during this time. For international media the concept is not new and there are many media houses like the *Guardian* and the *New York Times* which have established themselves as newsrooms with expertise in data journalism. The roots of data journalism can be found in the stories covered by these media houses.[5]

According to the literature available on data journalism, the first data-based story was published on 5 May 1821 by the *Guardian*, then known as *Manchester Guardian*. It was a part of the report of leaked data about the cost and quality of schooling for the working classes in Manchester.[6]

Another very famous and most quoted visualisation was the one developed by Florence Nightingale, known for her contribution to the healthcare of army troops. Her night rounds to aid the wounded established her image as the 'Lady with the Lamp'. She published the data visualisation of the increasing death toll among British troops in Crimea. Caused by infectious disease, she covered two periods, April 1854 to March 1855 and April 1855 to March 1856. The visualisation shows the difference in the number of deaths after the basic cleaning measures were put into place. With this infographic, Nightingale was able to show the impact of sanitation in controlling diseases.

These stories were done when computers were not used in journalism. The earliest example of computer-assisted reporting or precision journalism is the story done by *CBS* in 1952 to predict the result of the US presidential elections. In this a UNIVAC (Universal Automatic Computer) was used to predict a landslide victory for the Republican, Gen. Dwight D. Eisenhower. However, *CBS* decided not to air the projection as the prediction seemed too unlikely. Eventually, UNIVAC was only 3 per cent off the actual result.[7] Late at night, Collingwood, correspondent *CBS*, made an embarrassing confession to millions of viewers, *'Univac had made an accurate prediction hours before, but CBS hadn't aired it'*.

In 1967, Philip Meyer, author of *Precision Journalism*, used a mainframe to analyse a survey of Detroit residents for understanding and explaining the serious riots that erupted in the city. Philip Meyer advocated the use of database analysis and social research methods and reporting which was used by a few journalists till mid-1980s.

In 1989, US journalism professor recognize the value of computer-assisted reporting when a Pulitzer Prize was given to the *Atlanta Journal* for its stories on racial disparities in home-loan practices. This was the year when Elliot Jaspin established the Missouri School of Journalism, which is now known as the National Institute for Computer-Assisted reporting. The years 1980–90 were the years of seminars and conferences by several institutions and organisations to popularise data journalism. Some of these institutions and organisation were:

Investigative Reporters and Editors (Missouri, United States, https://www.ire.org/)

Missouri School of Journalism (Columbia, United States, https://journalism.missouri.edu/)

The Global Investigative Journalism Network (Maryland, United States, https://gijn.org/)

NetMedia (Kolkata, India, https://netmedia.in/)

Danish International Centre of Analytical Reporting (Copenhagen, Denmark, https://laegemiddelstyrelsen.dk/en/about/organisation/name/)

World Press Institute (Minnesota, United States, https://worldpressinstitute.org/)

Hack and Hackers (London UK, https://www.hackshackersldn.co.uk/)

The European Journalism Centre (The Netherlands & Belgium, https://ejc.net/)

Dataharvests Centre for Investigative Reporting (Amsterdam, Netherlands, https://dataharvest.eu/)

Investigative Reporters and Editors (IRE) and NICAR,

Missouri School of Journalism

The Global Investigative Journalism Network

NetMedia

Danish International Centre of Analytical Reporting

World Press Institute

Hacks/Hackers

The European Journalism Centre

Dataharvest Centre for Investigative Reporting

The field of data journalism is flourishing. After over fifty-five years of journalism using data, it is clear that data is not only a routine part of journalism but also a driving force for stories (Brant Houstan, Knight Chair in Investigative Reporting, University of Illinois).[8]

Indian media is way behind its global peers in data journalism. Popular media surveys started in 1980s when Prannoy Roy conducted opinion polls during elections to find the mood of Indian voters. The rapid growth of electronic media in 1990s made the election surveys and exit polls popular in India and since then it became regular feature.[9]

This was limited during elections to opinion poll surveys and exit poll surveys. In a country so socially, economically, culturally and politically diverse one would assume that statistics would be a crucial component of news as a way to ensure truthful and insightful coverage. Sadly, realities on the ground paint a different picture, and the media seem to be largely indifferent to the lure of data journalism, that is claiming global media houses.[10]

One of the earliest initiatives of using open data to inform the public on a range of issues was taken in 2011 by Govindraj Ethiraj, a television and print journalist. He founded IndiaSpend, an agency of record in data and facts on Indian social, political, and economy, which has completed eleven years. It was started to address the lack of data and evidence-led journalism in India. IndiaSpend also has a section called 'Data Gaps' where they highlight the data that is not shared publicly and raise question about it.

From 2016 to mid-2018, excellent data-based stories came from the *Hindustan Times*. Journalists like Samarth Bansal. Gurman Bhatia and Harry Stevens did bring to the fore data journalism in Indian newsrooms. Some of the interesting stories are:

1. 'Despite the Myth, Mitron Is Not Modi's Favourite Word: An analysis of PM's Speech'.[11] In this story, PM Narendra Modi's speeches were analysed to find out the more frequently words used by him to address the audience.
2. 'At Death's Door' was an investigative story about capital punishment in India. The story was an analysis of the criminal justice system of India. It was a six-part story. Part 1 was about how trial courts in India sentence hundreds of convicts to death but executions are rare. Part 2 was on 'Justice Delayed' and Part 3 addressed how nobody knows how many people in India have been executed or the identity of those who are on death row. Part 4 and 5 are about mercy petitions and the quality of mercy and Part 6 debunked the myths about the death penalty.[12]

In 2002 Open Government Data Platform (www. data.gov.in) was launched to facilitate access to government-owned shareable data. The idea was to promote wider accessibility and application of government owned data and unlock the potential of data for national development. There are at present 571,499 resources, 12,822 catalogues, from more than 180 departments available on the portal. Data is available department-wise and sector-wise. For Covid-19, the latest statistics are available, along with the visualisations. The website is a gold mine of data that journalists can use for a variety of stories.

According to Samarth Bansal (www.bansalsamarth.com),[13] we are not yet ready to institutionalise this kind of work (visual journalism). Cash-constrained Indian newsrooms neither have the resources to hire the talent nor the imagination to nurture it. Yet, things have to start somewhere, but I don't see that time now.

When data journalism abroad was gaining respectability as a form of journalism, the Indian media was undergoing a transition away from serious informational and critical journalism to one with a greater focus on soft stories needing less reader or viewer attention.[14]

The impediments as described by Rajesh Mahapatra in the article 'India's Media Missing the Data Journalism Revolution' by Priya Rajasekar are Financial Constraints, high attrition, and challenges of prioritisation.[15]

Despite these challenges and lack of technical resources and skilled staff, there are some organisations and individuals who are doing excellent work. Their work that can inspire others and put India on the world map in data journalism. Here is a list of these organisations:

DataLEADS

IndiaSpend

India Data Portal

Economic and Political Weekly

Where to Find Data and How

For any data journalist, the most important resource is data. This data could be open data that is available freely and we do not have to ask the copyright holder for permission to use it. Or it could be proprietary data where we have to buy or take permission to use it. The data can come from a variety of sources like government organisations and portals, industry bodies, international data portals, NGOs, websites and so on. In this section we will try to find out what the various sources of data are and what skills one must have to locate data which can be used.

As mentioned earlier there are many sources of data from where journalists can take it and use it in their stories. Before we delve into data sources for media, we must understand that data journalism is not just about using data for building stories but is also about questioning the available data. Not all data sets are credible and the journalists must ask questions like who collected that data, how it was collected, what was the sample size, how did they determine who should be included in the sample, was there anything excluded from the data and so on. Also, we must always look for any parallel data available which may have been collected by some other organisation.

Some Sources for Data

- Arms Transfers Database (SIPRI): https://www.sipri.org/databases/armstransfers
- Asian Development Bank Data Portal: https://data.adb.org/
- Climate Data Online (NOAA): https://www.ncdc.noaa.gov/cdo-web/

- Data Is Plural's list of Datasets/newsletter: https://www.data-is-plural.com/archive/
- Extractive Industry Data (EITI): https://eiti.org/
- Foreign Lobbyists (Open Secrets): https://www.opensecrets.org/fara
- GitHub (Open Data): https://github.com/collections/open-data
- Global Fishing Watch: https://globalfishingwatch.org/
- Global Forest Watch: https://www.globalforestwatch.org/
- ILO: https://www.ilo.org/global/lang--en/index.htm
- IMF Data Portal: https://www.imf.org/en/Data—Investigative Dashboard: https://aleph.occrp.org/
- OECD Data Portal: https://data.oecd.org/
- Open Corporates: https://opencorporates.com/
- Organized Crime and Corruption Reporting Project (OCCRP): https://www.occrp.org/en
- Search Earthquake Catalog (USGS): https://earthquake.usgs.gov/earthquakes/search/
- Transparency International: https://www.transparency.org/en
- UN Comtrade: https://comtrade.un.org/
- UN Data Portal: https://data.un.org/
- UNHCR Data portal: https://www.unhcr.org/data.html
- WHO Data Portal: https://www.who.int/data/gho
- UNICEF Data Portal: https://data.unicef.org/
- UNODC: https://www.unodc.org/
- WEF Reports: https://www.weforum.org/reports/
- World Bank Databank: https://databank.worldbank.org/home.aspx
- WTO: https://www.wto.org/

How to Find Data: Mastering Some Digital Skills

In addition to these data sources, there is a lot of data available on the web. To find the data relevant to the story, we need to develop digital research skills.

Search Engines

Google is a robust search engine, but it is not the only search engine. There are number of other search engines like Yahoo, Bing, Baidu and so on. In June 2022, online search engine Bing accounted for 8.92 per cent of the global search market, while market leader Google had market share of 83.89 per cent. Yahoo market share was 2.54 per cent during that period. In India, the market share of Google search engine in June 2021 was over 95 per cent.[17] Some regional alternatives for Google are Yandex (Russia) and Baidu (China). If someone wants to remain anonymous while searching then DuckDuckGo is an option.

Searching content on a search engine is not as easy as it appears. When a search query is typed, there could be millions of web pages that might have content that matches your query. The Google Search Index contains hundreds of billions of web pages and is well over 100,000,000 gigabytes in size. It's like the index at the back of a book – with an entry for every word seen on every web page that we index. When we index a web page, we add it to the entries for all the words that it contains. What we get depends totally on how have we searched. To get the relevant results we have to search smartly. The best way to get the most relevant results from the search engine is use of advanced search.[17]

Advanced search helps in narrowing down your search, making it more specific. For example, we can search for specific words and phrases. Advanced search also allows us to exclude certain words and phrases from your search. The results can also be narrowed down by language, region and filetype. Since journalists are interested in topical content, they can also find pages updated recently or they can also customise the time range. Journalists can also filter the content by usage rights. This allows them to find content that they can easily use, edit and remix without getting into copyright infringement issues.

Like Google search engine, Bing also offers advanced search and works on similar lines. In addition to the advance search, there are certain Boolean queries that we must master.

Boolean Queries

Boolean Queries are strings of words that allow us to cut through the usual social media chatter by upgrading a default search to a multifaceted, specific search to find more precise snippets of information.[18]

Boolean search queries can be used for search engine in addition to their own feature of advanced search and also for social media.

Some of the common Boolean queries that journalism students and journalists should master are:

AND

Use of AND limits the results. Search by 'Russia AND Ukraine' will retrieve results where both the terms are used.

OR

Use of OR expands the results. For example, search by 'War OR Russia' will retrieve all results where either the word 'War' or 'Russia' was used.

NOT

Use of NOT allows us to exclude terms we don't want to appear in the search results. For example, search by 'War NOT Afghanistan' will show results which contain 'war' but not 'Afghanistan.

QUOTES '…'

Using '...' allows us to search for a specific word combination, or an exact phrase match.

For example, search by 'Digital Newsroom' will show only results which have both these words.

BRACKETS OR PARENTHESES

Brackets or parentheses are used to group multiple terms or search operators to control how the search is executed. For example, ('Geyzer' OR 'gizer') NOT ('Havells' OR 'Havils').

Searching During a Certain Timeframe

These operators help in finding content within a certain timeframe:

since:

until:

before:

after:

For example, 'Farmers Protest' AND 'tractor rally' since:2021-01-25 (year-month-day)

Advanced Search

The advanced search function is also available in Twitter, Google and YouTube where there is also a possibility of defining a custom range.

- https://twitter.com/search-advanced
- https://www.google.co.in/advanced_search
- https://www.youtube.com/watch?v=P5eGdeCIZiM

Search by filetype

This operator helps us in searching for a certain filetype like, PDF, CSV. DOCX, TXT, PPT and so on. For example, we can search 'Media and Entertainment' filetype:pdf.

Search by Site

This is used if we want to search for content within a specific website. For example, we can search 'Covid19 Misinformation' site: who.int.

All these operators do not guarantee that we will get what we want. What it guarantees is that a lot of time will be saved in searching.

Data Visualisation

Visualising data is the most exciting part of data journalism. Data visualisation presents data in such a Covid-19 form that it becomes easy for the audience to understand the numbers. Data journalists can make use of tables, graphics, charts, WordClouds, maps, timelines, pictures and so on to present data. Some examples of data-based stories are:

Figure 4.1: History of Pandemics

Source: Visualcapitalist, https://www.visualcapitalist.com/history-of-pandemics-deadliest/.

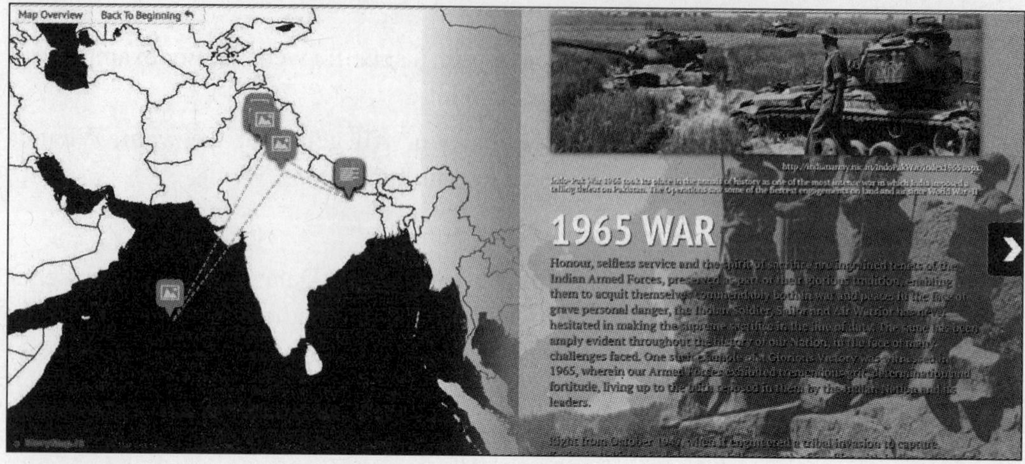

Figure 4.2: StoryMap

Source: StoryMap created by Anubhuti Yadav, https://storymap.knightlab.com/edit/?id=1965-war.

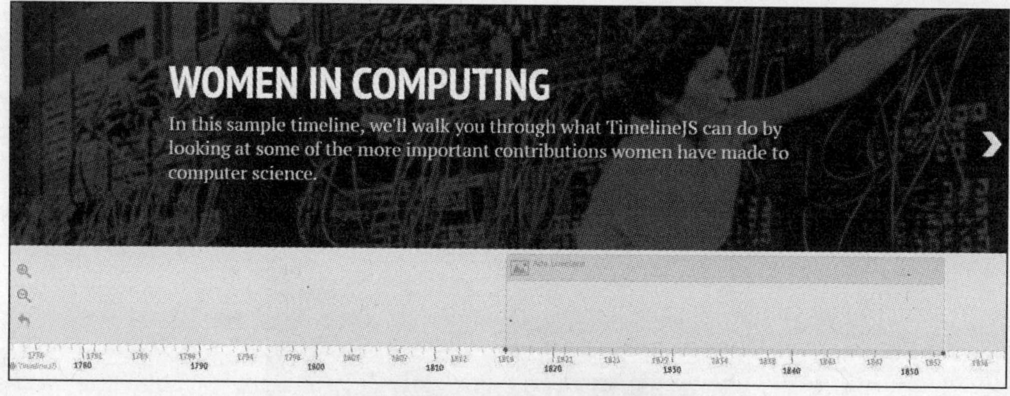

Figure 4.3: TimelineJS

Source: Timeline JS, https://timeline.knightlab.com/#examples.

Tools for Data Visualisation

- Infogram[19]
- Flourish[20]
- Timeline JS[21]
- StoryMap JS[22]
- DataWrapper[23]
- Canva[24]
- Tableau[25]

Summary

With so much data generated every second, it is important to make sense of data. Journalists should know how to access data, analyse it and visualise it for its audience. It is important for the journalists to adopt scientific methods for searching content online. Mastering Boolean queries can help them a great deal in finding the relevant content quickly efficiently. Journalists should also upskill themselves and learn data visualisation tools.

Questions

1. Search for a data-based story from India and try to find out the data visualisation tools used to develop the story.
2. Find out a data-based story which is done using government data. How would you do that story differently?
3. Discuss the examples of Boolean queries – AND, OR and Parenthesis.
4. Search for a data set on the topic of your choice and write a data-based story.

Expert Speaks

Mr Shajan Kumar is the Head, Data Visualisation and Fact Check at the *Mathrubhumi*. He was in conversation with Dr Anubhuti Yadav.

Data Journalism is growing in India. The mainstream newspapers have started creating special news desks to work on serious data stories. Journalists are trained in data mining, cleaning and analysing. Numbers are making all the difference in storytelling. More care is now on data visualisation too. And readers are liking it. It's very easy to manipulate data the way you want.

And thus comes the need of ethics in journalism. Data needs to be handled with care and concern. And that is the one reason we at the *Mathrubhumi* clubbed it with fact check. A lot of fact checking is required in Data Journalism. Data Journalism is bringing back the good old grassroots journalism practices to our news desks. Sometimes it moves to Investigative Journalism and Solutions Journalism.

Well, there are too many challenges in Data Journalism. The availability of updated data has always been a problem. You need to collect the latest data from different parties. And then compile it for use. While doing it, authorities will start asking, what are we going to do with the data? They will give you their side of the story to protect their actions.

We need more skilled people to work on Data Journalism—people with a blend of arts and science. Those who use both sides of their brain. Data visualisation must also move from just graphs and tables. Interactive infographics is the trend. The four things I look at a Data Journalist while recruiting is common sense, confidence, courage and lot of patience. If a person has these qualities, it is easy to train him or her in Excel, Flourish, Python, R and Tableau.

Notes

1. 'How the *Hindustan Times* Is Introducing Indian Readers to Interactive Stories', *Storybench*, 9 June 2017, https://www.storybench.org/hindustan-times-introducing-indian-readers-interactive-stories/.
2. Liliana Bounegru, 'Data Journalism in Perspective', *DataJournalism.com*, https://datajournalism.com/read/handbook/one/introduction/data-journalism-in-perspective.
3. Liliana Bounegru, Lucy Chambers and Jonathan Gray, *The Data Journalism Handbook, European Journalism Centre*, 2012, https://s3.eu-central-1.amazonaws.com/datajournalismcom/handbooks/The-Data-Journalism-Handbook-1.pdf.
4. Liliana Bounegru et al., *The Data Journalism Handbook*.
5. Brant Houston, 'Fifty Years of Journalism and Data: A Brief History', *Global Investigative Journalism Network*, 12 November 2015, https://gijn.org/2015/11/12/fifty-years-of-journalism-and-data-a-brief-history/.
6. Emily Turner, 'From Florence to the Machines: The Evolution of Data Journalism – in Pictures', *theguardian.com*, 13 August 2021, https://www.theguardian.com/gnmeducationcentre/gallery/2021/aug/13/the-evolution-of-data-journalism-in-pictures.
7. Emily Turner, 'From Florence to the Machines'.
8. Brant Houston, *Data for Journalists: A Practical Guide for Computer-Assisted Reporting* (New York: Routledge, 2019).
9. Praveen Rai, (2014). 'Fallibility of Opinion Polls in India', *Economic and Political Weekly*, **49** (18), 3 May 2014, pp. 13–17, http://www.jstor.org/stable/24480214.
10. Priya Rajasekar, 'India's Media — Missing the Data Journalism Revolution?', *Global Investigative Journalism Network*, 21 July 2014, https://gijn.org/2014/07/21/indias-media-missing-the-data-journalism-revolution/.
11. Samarth Bansal, 'Despite the Myth, "Mitron" Is Not Modi's Favourite Word: An Analysis of PM's Speeches', 28 March 2017, *Hindustan Times*, http://www.hindustantimes.com/interactives/modi-mitron-speech-analysis.
12. 'At Death's Door: An investigation into capital punishment in India', *Hindustan Times*, https://www.hindustantimes.com/static/deaths-door/.
13. Samarth Bansal, Thoughts and observations on data journalism in India', *Samarth's Notes*, 1 January, 2021, https://listed.to/@bansalsamarth/21352/3-thoughts-and-observations-on-data-journalism-in-india.
14. Priya Rajasekar, 'India's Media — Missing the Data Journalism Revolution?'
15. Priya Rajasekar, 'India's Media — Missing the Data Journalism Revolution?'
16. 'Worldwide Desktop Market Share of Leading Search Engines from January 2010 to June 2022', *Statista*, https://www.statista.com/statistics/216573/worldwide-market-share-of-search-engines/
17. 'Advanced Search', Instructor Vincent Ryan, *DataJournalism.com*, https://datajournalism.com/watch/google-search-for-journalists/advanced-search/advanced-search-1.
18. Lydia Morrish, 'Boolean Basics: How to Write a Search Query for Newsgathering That Works' *First Draft*, 10 June 2019, https://firstdraftnews.org:443/articles/boolean-basics-how-to-write-a-search-query-for-newsgathering-that-works/.
19. 'How to Create Charts, Reports, and Infographics with Infogram', *YouTube*, 11 April 2017, https://www.youtube.com/watch?v=NdnroM2bbAk.
20. 'Flourish Tutorial: Part 1 – Introduction to Flourish for Data Visualization', *YouTube*, 7 February 2018, https://www.youtube.com/watch?v=cN1Q9MusZbc.
21. 'Timeline JS Intro Tutorial', *YouTube*, 29 April 2016, https://www.youtube.com/watch?v=ZUVUjt7jd1c.
22. 'StoryMap: Maps That Tell Stories', *knight lab*, https://storymap.knightlab.com/#examples.
23. 'Welcome to the Datawrapper Academy!', *Datawrapper*, https://academy.datawrapper.de/.
24. 'How to Use Canva for Beginners', *YouTube*, 7 January 2021, https://www.youtube.com/watch?v=un50Bs4BvZ8.
25. 'Tableau Tutorial for Beginners', *YouTube*, 20 August 2018, https://www.youtube.com/watch?v=fO7g0pnWaRA.

Chapter 5

Social Media and Journalism: Opportunities and Challenges

Sonia Bhaskar

Humans were always far better at inventing tools than using them wisely.

–Prof. Yuval Noah Harari

Historian, Philosopher and Bestselling Author

Introduction

There has been a fundamental change in journalism because of the social media and its use in journalism. From research to news gathering to its dissemination functions, all are impacted by the social media. Social media is used to crowd-source ideas for the stories, to monitor what people are talking about and to find what is trending on social media which can be newsworthy. It also helps is disseminating content to different audience using a wide variety of platforms like Facebook, Instagram, Twitter, WhatsApp and so on. Not only this, social media can play very important role in personal brand-building for the journalists. It has become crucial for journalists to engage with their target audience and create communities not only around their news organisations but also around themselves as journalists. This allows journalists to connect with their audience in a number of ways like personal chats, open and closed groups and also by broadcasting live from the site where some event has taken place. In this chapter we will discuss how social media is used in the field of journalism, what opportunities it offers to journalists and news organisations, and what challenges it throws up in journalism.

'I have been in this mask for the last 15 hours and it's not over yet!' said my colleague on WhatsApp at 9 p.m. as Bihar election results were still see-sawing with no decision in sight. As a part of the digital team, we had been working from home since March 2020 and only interacted via emails, doing edit meetings via Microsoft Team and predominantly using WhatsApp for most inter-departmental coordination. Even by November, the Covid-19 pandemic showed no signs of letting up after all these months. But Bihar elections meant that some core-team members had to step out of the security of their homes and actually go to work.

The day, 10 November 2020 was going to see the culmination of a hard-fought election for 243 seats of the Bihar State Assembly. These were the first polls to be held since the Covid-19 pandemic hit with full force. On one side of the battle was the ruling coalition National Democratic Alliance (NDA) with Bhartiya Janta Party (BJP) and Janata Dal United (JD-U), and on the other side was Mahagathbandhan (MGB) or the grand coalition led by Rashtriya Janata Dal (RJD) and Indian National Congress (INC). The fight was between the sixty-nine-year-old Chief Minister Nitish Kumar aiming for a fourth term and Tejashwi Yadav, the debutant scion of the prominent political family of Laloo Yadav. Tejashwi turned thirty-one just the day before the counting.

That day began at 6 a.m. for most newsrooms. Like every election verdict day, results were expected to come in thick-and-fast once counting started at around 8 a.m. With Electronic Voting Machines (EVMs), normally the leads come in quickly and within a few hours the election can be called; by evening all the results get closed. The common joke doing the rounds was we may close Bihar long before America wrapped up its marathon election counting. Though this proved to be true, Bihar was quite tricky too.

A cliff-hanger of a contest, it went down to the wire where fortune switched sides faster than anyone could keep track of – a seat like Hilsa was won by just twelve votes. The Election Commission was not taking chances, and held as many as four press conferences through the day and even after the day got over, to keep everyone posted and generally assure everyone that 'all is well'![1]

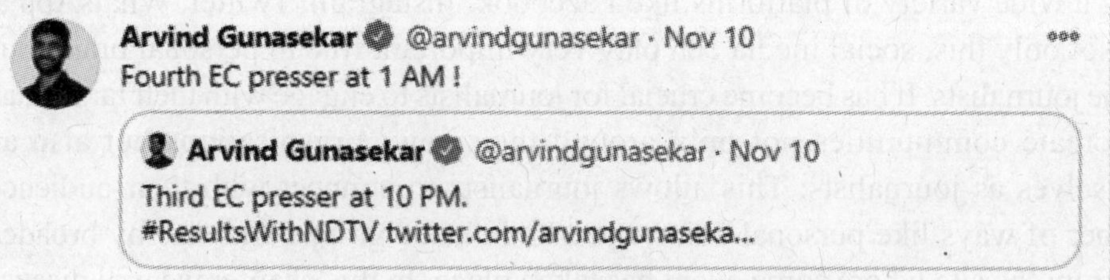

Figure 5.1: Twitter

Source: https://twitter.com/arvindgunasekar/status/1326223052380778496?s=20

But even as journalists on ground and in the newsrooms worked tirelessly to report the blow-by-blow account of every twist and turn of the battle for Bihar, the cliff-hanger, first claims of victory came on social media, between 11.30 and 11.45 p.m., in the tweets of BJP President J.P. Nadda, Home Minister Amit Shah and Prime Minister Narendra Modi. The BJP top brass claimed victory even as counting was on.[2] The final results were confirmed almost three hours later.

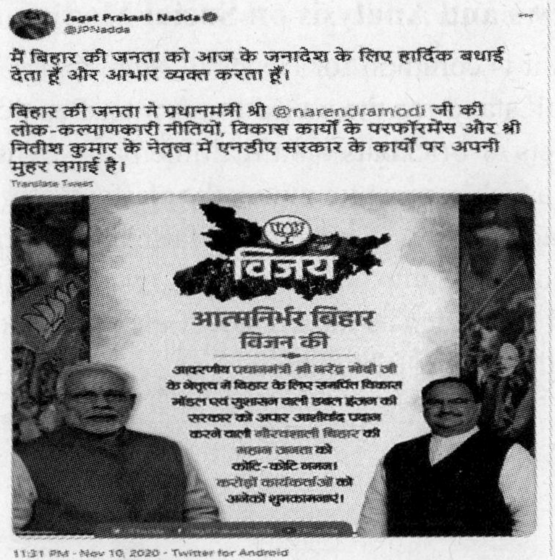

Figure 5.2: Twitter

Source: https://twitter.com/JPNadda/status/1326223374566137856

Figure 5.3: Twitter

Source: https://twitter.com/AmitShah/status/1326222000524832768

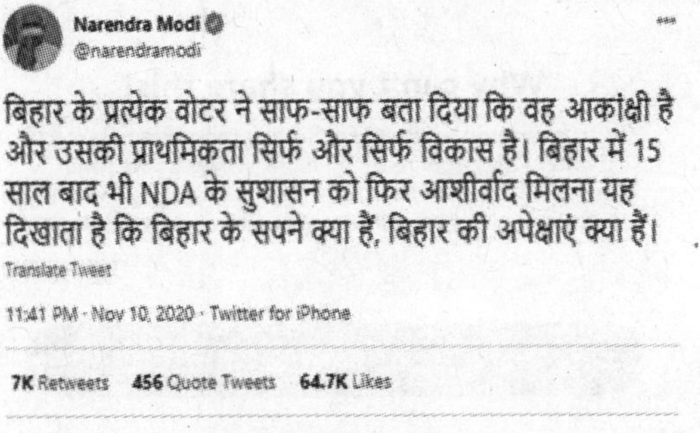

Figure 5.4: Twitter

Source: https://twitter.com/narendramodi/status/1326225944172965888

Breaking News, Views and Analysis on Social Media

We live in times when it is common for Heads of State to use social media platforms to put out their 'official' stand for the world to react to. People from across the globe can either offer bouquets or brickbats on a realtime basis. What is not so widespread yet but may soon be, is a tech company running the platform flagging a piece of content, even if it is from a Head of State, as potentially false and flouting their rules. We saw it with US President Donald Trump and his defiant tweets in 2020 against the election results, which declared Joe Biden as the President-elect after he won enough electoral votes to take him past the crucial 270 mark.

Figure 5.5: Twitter

US President Donald Trump's tweet after the Election results were called in favour of his opponent, Democratic candidate Joe Biden

Source: https://twitter.com/realDonaldTrump/status/1325099845045071873?s=20

(Since the account has been suspended by Twitter, the tweets are no longer accessible.)

Figure 5.6: Twitter

President Trump claimed rigging of the electoral process in a series of tweets on November 7, 2010, which were blocked by the platform to prevent the spread of what the platform felt was misleading content

Source: https://twitter.com/realDonaldTrump

(Since the account has been suspended by Twitter, the tweets are no longer accessible).

So even as the platforms decided to block these posts or flag them, reactions flowed in from both ends of the spectrum. People either ridiculed the Head of State with a meme, video or a gif or lent him words of support with just a text message. Reactions to the tweets poured in from both sides of the divide.

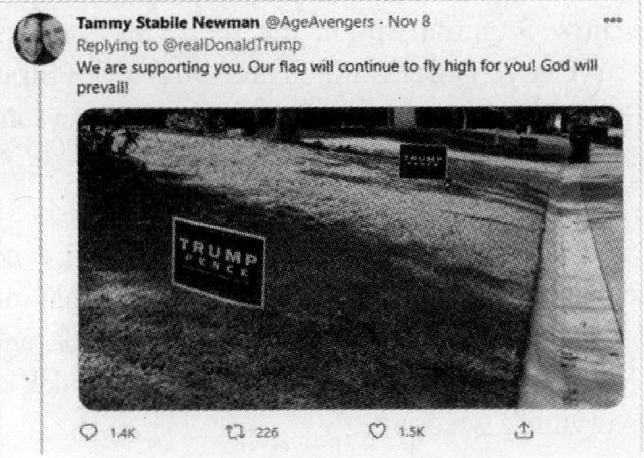

Figure 5.7: Twitter

Source: https://twitter.com/AgeAvengers/status/1325208477568913408?s=20

(This page has since been removed from Twitter)

Figure 5.8: Twitter

Source: https://twitter.com/DanielNewman/status/1325146371368906752?s=20

Even as all of these actions keep happening on social media, journalists and media organisations are constantly weighing the consequences of reporting these 'official' posts and review the pros and cons. They also consider how the original post should be reported, whether it is still in public domain or not. But the action on social media is quite independent of the workflow and best practices of journalism. While in a news organisation a reporter's story will go through multiple layers of checks and reviews for approvals, editing, fact-checking and copy editing before getting published, on social media there are no such filters or editorial controls that process the information that goes through.

Describing this scenario in the book *More News Is Good News: Untold Stories from 25 Years of Television News*, on the occasion of broadcaster NDTV's twenty-fifth anniversary, this is how Suparna Singh, the then CEO of NDTV (also Head of Convergence at NDTV Convergence Limited and Director of Strategy, NDTV Group) who has worked with NDTV since 1994 in various capacities, wrote in the chapter titled 'The Digital Newsroom: Who's Really in Charge Here?'

> What *is* clear is that 140 characters have become a massive equaliser in a space where expertise and gatekeeping were invited, coveted and, consequently, hard won. Today, everyone is a news editor. You choose the topic that interests you, shortlist your sources for that information, collate what you track, and ignore everything else. Welcome, Myopia. We feed only on subjects that we like, exercising monk-like abstinence for everything we don't.[3]

On Social Media, Who Is In-charge?

The unique dynamic of the social media platforms is that there are no restrictions as to who can post and what they can post. Often it is more about quantity rather than quality of the information. This is completely in contrast with how information has been put out in public domain by mainline newspapers or television channels. If there is an error that creeps into any report despite the due processes being followed, there is an editorial procedure to address it. The scale of the error determines how the channel chooses to inform the public and explain what the mistake was and issues a correction. In 2015, during the counting of votes of the Bihar elections, the early trends were overwhelmingly in favour of a particular alliance, which turned out to be erroneous data from the agency providing it. This agency was providing data to multiple organisations and many channels ended up transmitting incorrect information. Dr Prannoy Roy, one of the pioneers of election coverage in India, decided to put out the details of what caused the error on-air. The clarification video was put out across all NDTV platforms, with a detailed explanation.[4]

Apologising, accepting and clarifying errors is not just good ethics, it is also a way to build credibility as a journalist and as a journalistic organisation. Social media is where criticism comes first and very quickly, so these platforms can be used to inform the readers, connect with them and put out clarifications or the correct version of the story.

However, when information floated on social media is not bound by any common norms and guidelines, then where does the onus lie to ensure quality of content and verified facts? And when things go wrong, then who should take immediate corrective action? Is it the responsibility of the people who uploaded content or the platforms themselves? In his book, *The Networked Public – How Social Media is Changing Democracy*, lawyer Amber Sinha argues:

> The more significant interchanges of ideas and the shaping of public consciousness may now be occurring over social media. Yet, overall, courts globally have been resistant to accord the same status to the public forums on these platforms. The primary reason is that these remain privately owned platforms. They have their own community guidelines.[5]

Amber Sinha explains this by pointing out the difference between a public park or a street and a hotel or any other commercial establishment which is privately owned. A public park or a street are public spaces and hence accord the privilege to people to assemble, discuss and debate issues. However, in a privately owned establishment, the owner has the discretion to decide what is permitted or not permitted on their premises.

So apart from President Trump's tweets which were flagged by Twitter on multiple occasions in 2020 for spreading misinformation, former Malaysian Prime Minister Mahathir Mohamad's tweets were deleted over his outburst following what the French President Emmanuel Macron described as an 'Islamic terrorist attack' in Nice in October.[6] Just a few days prior to the Nice incident, where a violent knife attack had killed three people, a school teacher was beheaded in Paris for showing a cartoon of Prophet Mohammad in class. President Macron criticized radical Islam for the Paris incident that drew outrage from across the globe, online and offline.[7]

In this backdrop, the remarks of the Malaysian leader on Twitter where in one of his tweets he said, 'Muslims have a right to be angry and kill millions of French people for the massacres of the past,' were seen as intended to incite violence. What was missed was that this particular tweet of ex-PM Mahathir was a part of a series of thirteen tweets which talked about things like, 'By and large the Muslims have not applied the "eye for an eye" law.' He went on to say, 'Muslims don't. The French shouldn't. Instead, the French should teach their people to respect other people's feelings.'[8]

This is an example where the platform decided that the content posted flouted its own rules and guidelines and hence needed to be removed or flagged. This is in line with the point Sinha was trying to make about public park versus private hotel. Applying the same argument, by virtue of their private ownership the Facebooks and Twitters of the world need to take responsibility for what is uploaded on their platform. But they have been inconsistent about this role by citing that they are technology companies not content publishers, and their offering is for people to express themselves freely, irrespective of where they stand on issues, their caste, creed, race, gender. They claim they are a democratic space where freedom of expression and free speech is of paramount importance.

This is something that the Facebook founder and CEO, Mark Zuckerberg has reiterated many times and cites the following reason for taking a hands-off approach to act more rigorously against problematic content:

> So once we're taking this content down, the question is: where do you draw the line? Most people agree with the principles that you should be able to say things other people don't like, but you shouldn't be able to say things that put people in danger. The shift over the past several years is that many people would now argue that more speech is dangerous than would have before. This raises the question of exactly what counts as dangerous speech online.[9]

Zuckerberg made this point during his address at Georgetown University in 2019, titled 'Standing for Voice and Free Expression'. This sounds more like the issues newsrooms grapple with in their edit meetings daily, about what content to prioritise and publish and what to discard. This overlap between social media platforms and traditional media houses, is at the core of why social media is the biggest challenge facing journalism. It impacts every aspect of journalism, from content creation, distribution to monetisation.

Personalised Newsfeed: Boon or Bane?

> *Once these algorithms know you better than you know yourself, they can control and manipulate you, and you won't be able to do much about it. You will live in the matrix, or in The Truman Show.*
>
> –Prof. Yuval Noah Harari
>
> Historian, Philosopher and Bestselling Author

The technology deployed by most of the social platforms controls what content appears on a user's timeline and is visible to him or her. So if a news organisation with a million followers publishes a piece right now, that piece will not be seen by these million people right away. In fact, most of them will never get to see it. The platform's algorithm will decide when, where, how and most importantly who gets to see what. The decision doesn't rest with the user who has chosen to follow a certain publication nor does it rest with publication which is merely using the platform to distribute its content to a captive audience.

In its Initial Public Offering (IPO) filing document in 2012, describing its product Facebook stated:

> The Facebook News Feed is the core feature of a user's homepage and is a regularly updating list of stories from friends, Pages, and other entities to which a user is

connected on Facebook. It includes posts, photos, event updates, group memberships, app updates, and other activities. Each user's News Feed is personalized based on his or her interests and the sharing activity of the user's friends. Stories in a user's News Feed are prioritized based on several factors, including how many friends have Liked or Commented on a certain piece of content, who posted the content, and what type of content it is. News Feed is a key component of our social distribution capability.[10]

In this description lies the core concept of the platform and the biggest cause of disruption, debate and discussion.

Social Media Rules

The impact of social media on journalism has been as great an upheaval as any other in the history of the industry.

–The Platform Press: How Silicon Valley Reengineered Journalism[11]

The sheer dominance of social media platforms stem from the unbeatable size of the user base. In a world of 7.98 billion people, by July 2022 there were 5.03 billion internet users and the total number of active social media users was a staggering 4.70 billion, according to the Digital 2022 July Global Statshot Report – produced in partnership with Hootsuite and We Are Social.[12] Just in 2019, 453 million social media users were added, leading to a growth of 12.3 per cent since 2019. The Covid-19 pandemic gave a further boost to social media usage. More than 180 million more people used social media between July and September 2020 compared to the previous three months, equating to an average increase of almost 2 million users per day. By 2020, the world was spending more than 10 billion hours per day using social media, which equals to more than 1 million years of human existence![13]

Social platforms provide a tempting proposition to publishers looking to scale up reach, grow their audience and create an opportunity for their content to be accessed and consumed in a manner that was traditionally not possible. So the numbers that these platforms are reporting and the growth these are clocking offer an attractive, even if not a lucrative, proposition for media organisations.

A report published in November 2020 on the 'Sustainability of Journalism' by House of Lords Communication and Digital Committee says:

> Although online platforms have created new opportunities for publishers to distribute content, they have challenged established funding models and disrupted the relationship between publishers and consumers. There is a fundamental imbalance of power between platforms and publishers. Publishers need platforms far more than the platforms need them; and publishers are disadvantaged by a dysfunctional online advertising market.[14]

News outlets are reeling under pressure to fix their revenue models and reduce their dependence on advertising as the predominant source of revenue. The Covid-19 pandemic has adversely hit the advertising spends globally, putting a huge financial strain on journalism establishments, with many shutting down or cutting salaries or laying off staff to survive. Subscription models have had limited success on online platforms where most people expect everything to be free and hesitate to pay money for news. Social media platforms are furthering this tendency to get information for free. Publishers are being forced to make their content available on these platforms for free or on a revenue sharing basis that may not always be viable for the publisher.

Platforms like Facebook and Instagram also have a feature called 'Boost Post' which prompts publishers to pump in money to increase the reach of their post among a larger audience, even among those outside the followers of their current social media handles. Similar provisions to promote tweets or even hashtags to appear in the trending list also exist on platforms like Twitter; YouTube has its own provisions for improving the visibility of promoted content on their platform. So while organically generated posts hit the algorithm's barrier in terms of reach, these platforms hope to make money by distributing the content created by the publishers who have already invested time, effort, talent, resources to produce it.

The House of Lords Committee adds:

> There is a fundamental imbalance of power between news publishers and platforms. Due to their dominant market position, Facebook and Google can stipulate the terms on which they use publishers' content. This includes whether and how much they pay for news appearing on their platform, which news sources their algorithms rank most highly and how much notice they give publishers of changes to these algorithms. Algorithms are a product of the human value judgments of their designers, but there is a lack of transparency about them and designers' possible biases.[15]

What Happens in a Minute on Social Media

It boggles the mind to see the sheer volume of what happens in a minute in the world of social media. Before the COVID-19 Pandemic, in 2019, every minute users:[16]

- Sent 575,000 tweets
- Watched 4,500,000 videos on YouTube
- Posted 277,777 stories and 55,140 photos on Instagram

When it comes to Facebook, in 2020 every minute saw users:

- Share 150,000 messages
- Upload 147,000 photos

And if that seems staggering, then observe this – in 2020, 41,666,667 messages were shared every minute on WhatsApp! [17]

After one year of the pandemic, by 2021 not only did existing platforms see a jump in usage, but people were also spending more time on additional platforms like Zoom, Teams, Slack.[18]

- Zoom: Hosts 856 minutes of webinar
- Slack: Users send 148,000 messages
- Teams: Connects 100,000 users
- Facebook: Users share 240,000 photos and Live receives 44 million views
- Twitter: Users post 575,000 tweets
- YouTube: Users stream 694,000 hours
- Instagram: Users share 65,000 photos

It almost seems strange that not many foresaw that social media will turn into this gigantic force within just few years. In his 2018 book, *Breaking News: The Remaking of Journalism and Why It Matters Now*, Alan Rusbridger, who was editor-in-chief of Guardian News and Media from 1995 to 2015, talked about how in the early days of social media in 2007-2008, it was getting popular but those in the news business, Rusbridger included, 'couldn't see that it had anything to do with news business.' He wrote, 'Editorially, our own writers were far from convinced that Facebook would work.'[19]

That was not so long ago. Since the advent of these platforms, in a span of little over a decade half the world's population are on these platforms. By the start of a new decade in 2020, just Facebook had 2.7 billion users. If one looks at the other platforms that are a part of the Facebook stable like Facebook Messenger (1.3 billion users), Instagram which it acquired in 2012 has 1.2 billion users and WhatsApp, which it acquired in 2014 has 2 billon users. That is a lot of users and their data, that this one company has accumulated. It gives it a massive control of the world of communication, information and media.

Something that was highlighted in the 2017 report published by The Tow Centre for Digital Journalism based at Columbia Journalism School, went on to explain:

> The principles of the open web, which held promise for citizens and journalists alike, have given way to an ecosystem dominated by a small number of platform companies who hold tremendous influence over what we see and know. The internet we see today, one largely controlled by two to three companies, is a far cry from the open web of Tim Berners-Lee.[20]

Facebooks and Twitters of the world have acquired a proportion and scale we never imagined and are proving to be one of the biggest disruptive forces of our times, affecting every aspect of human life and society, with unparalleled consequences.

Journalism is not alone to adopt, adapt and bear the positive and negative consequences of these disruptive forces. But it is telling how social media has strengthened and also exposed chinks in the armour of journalism as it has been practised for decades and in case of print, for centuries.

Adapting to the New World: BBC Experience

On a cold April morning in 2019 in Belfast, Northern Ireland, seventeen journalists from South Asia were rushing through the different floors and corridors of Hotel Holiday Inn towards the buffet breakfast. The bunch of journalists was running late and had an appointment to keep. They had all arrived in the late evening the previous day from London for a one-day field trip to BBC Northern Ireland. It was part of their Chevening Fellowship programme organised by the British Foreign and Commonwealth Office for select South Asian journalists. It had drizzled all night and there was a nip in the air. It was a 300 metre walk to their destination. As the bunch rushed through Bruce Street and then took a left turn to Dublin Road, the imposing historical building at Ormeau Avenue emerged, home to BBC Broadcast House of Northern Ireland since 1941. The structure was similar to the BBC's London Headquarters that this group of journalists had visited few weeks earlier. The resemblance was apparent but the Belfast Broadcast House has a formidable history of its own. The building suffered substantial damages when it was bombed in 1974, during the violent Irish crisis and legend has it that the organisation continued its broadcast operations uninterrupted all through the attack.

I was a part of this bunch and reached just in time to keep to the packed schedule planned for us. The experience of the day was unlike anything I had earlier. To be inside BBC, get a glimpse of its operations and talk at length to the editors, anchors and production team members was truly an enriching event. But the experience I would like to share here is about the edit meet, the first thing on our time table that morning. It was an august gathering of twenty of BBC Ireland's senior-most editorial staff and correspondents. We were told that the meeting would normally be held in the middle of the news floor, with participation from everyone. That day, since we were also joining in, it was being held in a more controlled setting of a conference room. But even in this select gathering there were key people from TV, Radio (which is still a huge component for BBC in UK) and the digital team were present. So for each story and show being planned for the day, be it Brexit follow ups to Game of Throne finale season launch that was two days away, each of the verticals presented their plan and not just their plan but how each of the stories could be used across platforms. So they discussed what TV could take from Radio and what digital teams could pick up from each of the verticals in terms of existing content and repurpose or create fresh pieces of content for each of the digital platforms – website, podcast and social media platforms.

It was interesting to watch how social media and digital platforms were being treated as equal stake holders. In some cases, digital even took over the lead for generating extra content to reach newer audiences and drive engagement.

We met Darwin Templeton who had just taken over as Assistant News Editor – Digital at BBC Northern Ireland after almost twenty-eight years in Print. According to him, newspapers thought that digital would be the saving grace and advertisements from digital would make up for the falling circulation, but Google and Facebook changed that. 'So earlier it was about increasing pageviews, click bait headlines and get the story out first, but BBC adopted the approach of using social media to reach out to new audiences, new sections of the population in the age of 16 to 35, whom you can't reach out through TV.'

Over seven thousand kilometres from Belfast, in BBC's Delhi office, in the heart of the city, a similar meeting convenes every morning. In 2016, BBC decided to foray into four new language services in India – Gujarati, Marathi, Telugu and Punjabi, which had a combined potential reach of 250 million in India. This expansion made Delhi the largest bureau for BBC outside London.[21] Each of these new language services, in addition to the established services like Hindi, Tamil, Bangla and Urdu, were to be mainly available online and on social media, with some presence on TV.[22] By 2022, Director General of BBC, Tim Davie 70 million Indians were accessing BBC's language services.[23]

Mukesh Sharma, who has been with the BBC for close to two decades in different capacities, was heading its Hindi language service at the time I interviewed him for this book. He explained to me how the daily morning ritual of the edit meet is the backbone of an integrated multimedia newsroom to plan and coordinate 360-degree coverage across platforms and ensure that editorial policy and guidelines are adhered to, whether it is a fresh story for broadcast or website or a post on Facebook, Twitter or Instagram. He says:

> What happens in the morning edit meeting, every language service has their own edit meeting first. And the morning edit meeting has social person, video person, the people present on the desk and the editors, everyone joins the meeting in the morning. That's where all the ideas are discussed, people are encouraged to come up with anything – no idea is a bad idea. Because we've tried to build a multimedia Newsroom, so a reporter who was probably doing a long form text piece yesterday is probably going to work on a video story today, although the approval in terms of storyboard and stuff would come from the video team or the editors. They approve it so that it's properly done in a video format the way it should be done. So we may agree or disagree that 'no, instead let's do it in a video for that story may be better or maybe let's do both with you know apart from video, let's do a text also', so that's where the agreement happens then we have a central meeting, where representatives from all the languages come and whatever they've gathered from their own meetings, of course there could be certain things which are very local so they just leave that out and then they share what is not very local and what should be mentioned in the editorial meeting for everyone to know that this is happening.

So while the decision making and commissioning is centralised, the execution is done at individual team level. This centralised system ensures synergy between teams and enables smooth day-to-day functioning with full awareness of which team is doing what, for which platform and in what format.

Think of the sheer number of platforms – Facebook, Twitter, Instagram, YouTube, Facebook Messenger, WhatsApp, Telegram, to name a few. If an organisation decides to be on all platforms, then populating each of these is a task in itself.

The Tow Centre for Digital Journalism based at Columbia Journalism School conducted more than seventy interviews over twelve months in 2017 and concluded:

> In the past two years alone, the integration between the news business and social platforms such as Facebook, Twitter, Snapchat, and Google has accelerated. Globally there are well over 40 different social media sites and messaging apps through which news publishers can reach segments of their audience. Facebook operates at a scale hitherto unseen. No publisher in the history of journalism has enjoyed the same kind of influence over the news consumption of the world.[24]

Different Newsrooms, Different Strategies

For any journalist today or anyone aspiring to be one, understanding the ecosystem of social media is very important. As per the Internet Adoption in India report published jointly by Internet and Mobile Association of India (IAMAI) and data analytics firm Kantar, based on an ICUBE 2021 study, there are 622 million active internet users (AIU) in India out of a total population of 1.4 billion. 82 per cent of the AIU (that is over 510 million users), use it for accessing social media and 100 per cent of the active internet users opt for mobile phones to access internet.[25]

So any content being generated needs to adopt a mobile-first strategy. But there is more. It is important to understand how people are consuming news now in India. Even before the COVID-19 Pandemic, according to the Reuters Institute India Digital News Report, 2019 found:

> Among our respondents, direct discovery of news (where users go directly to a news organisation's website or app) is seen as far less important than various forms of distributed discovery (where users discover and access news through a variety of digital platforms). Search is an important gateway for many users, and as audiences have embraced social media like Facebook and Twitter, publishers have begun sharing breaking news and features on these platforms. At the same time, messaging apps like WhatsApp are now being used by millions to get online news, and by publishers sending news directly to subscribers.[26]

Other findings of the Reuters survey in terms of how respondents got their news pre-Covid include:

- 52 per cent from Facebook and WhatsApp
- 26 per cent from Instagram
- 18 per cent from Twitter
- 16 per cent from Facebook Messenger
- 5 per cent from Snapchat

But one of the key takeaways of the survey even back then was that online news generally (56 per cent), and social media specifically (28 per cent), have outpaced print (16 per cent) as the main source of news among respondents under 35, whereas respondents over 35 still mix online and offline media to a greater extent.[27]

Some of these trends have only intensified post Covid. According to the Reuters Institute India Digital News Report, 2022,[28] 'More widely, this year's data confirm how the various shocks of the last few years, including the Coronavirus pandemic, have further accelerated structural shifts towards a more digital, mobile, and platform-dominated media environment, with further implications for the business models and formats of journalism.'[29]

Another key takeaway from the report, 'Across all devices, our data show direct access to apps and websites becoming less important over time and social media becoming more important, partly due to their ubiquity and convenience. At an aggregate level, we have reached something of a tipping point this year, with social media preference (28%) surging ahead of direct access (23%).'[30]

And the report reiterates the importance of mobile for accessing news in the Indian context, where the report found, 'India is a strongly mobile-focused market, with 72% accessing news through smartphones and just 35% via computers.'[31]

The *Indian Express*, a publication that has been around for ninety years, publishes over a thousand posts a week across different social media platforms. Three members of the online team, spanning almost three different generations of journalists, shared their viewpoints during an interview for this book. Nandagopal Rajan, online editor of *Indian Express* has about twenty years of experience across print and digital media, bulk of it with *Express*; Aaron Pereira, has spent about half a decade with *Express* and has an overall experience of ten years in the industry with some experience in Print, but bulk of the working years have been spent with digital platforms. Pereira works with the web team but coordinates with Print correspondents across India. And finally, Mansi Dua, who may have about five years of experience but these have all been spent managing social media platforms, so she has a good amount of first-hand experience of managing content on these platforms.

Explaining the change in the way social media was being handled by *Express*, Rajan says:

> We used to have a very decent decentralized system of social media. It's like, you know, I edited a copy I will post it. It used to be like that. We are now slowly going away from it now primarily because we want a little bit of uniformity and similar language to develop which is becoming very difficult, as our team becomes larger, people are all over the place, like especially since the lockdown, I don't know how many people we have in Delhi now, we are spread out all over the place. So there are coordination issues and that starts showing up on the timeline also. So that is

> one of the reasons why we are now sort of getting to funnel the posting process and sort of figuring things out slightly differently.

For the *Quint*, a news and opinion website which is a part of a digital media organisation, 'Social media has been a CPU of sorts!' (CPU or the Central Processing Unit or brain of a computer).

According to Medha Chakrabartty, associate editor, audience engagement:

> We've built a reach of millions on Facebook and we're constantly striving to crack each new challenge that platforms like Instagram and Snapchat bring to the mix. Currently, Instagram is something we are focusing on and the returns have been great so far because Instagram allows us to not just focus on a social verse that primarily depends on rich, informative visual content but also one which is constantly evolving with respect to product innovations and story-telling formats.

The social media driven approach of the *Quint* newsroom is clearly visible from the volume of posts across different platforms per week, according to the figures shared by Medha:

Facebook: 600

Twitter: 600–700

Instagram: 65–70

YouTube: 40–50

Telegram: 45–50

WhatsApp: A chatbot fetches in the latest stories

LinkedIn: 40–50

Facebook Messenger: 25–30

Each platform has its own features and functionality and one size doesn't fit all or rather, the same content doesn't fit all. Explains Medha:

> When it comes to formats, each platform is of course conducive to a different one. Facebook, for example, is a link-based ecosystem that allows publishers to redirect readers to their websites; Instagram, on the other hand, has always been wary of links – it is a platform where links don't work, come what may! So our focus is always to break information down into snackable bits and make them as easy as possible for consumption while sticking to facts, research, and corroborated figures. For Twitter, the approach has always been a real-time, round-the-clock, hands-on one, since the Twitter algorithm will always prioritise new posts over old ones. So, while an Instagram is better at resurfacing a 2-day old post that's a timeless op-ed, Twitter is better at surfacing instant news updates that will get dated in an hour.

Taking the example of Bihar Elections, Mukesh Sharma explains how BBC Hindi service created different types of content for different social media platforms:

If we look at video then what we've commissioned are few basic explainers just in order to explain to people what Bihar election means, why it matters and what are the myths around Bihar election; it will generally work well for Facebook and Instagram. These work better there compared to YouTube where we've seen more traffic coming around the story of the day or around a search if people are actively looking for something where the traffic is YouTube coming. So it's more sort of news driven. So if Tejashwi has spoken or Nitish has said something or Prime Minister Modi has said something in Bihar and we are creating a video package out of it, that would work better on our YouTube channel as well as Facebook because on Facebook we have a lot of people from these states – Uttar Pradesh and Bihar – from the Hindi speaking areas, and we get good results, but we also get good results on YouTube. Compared to myths about what will work well on Facebook and Instagram, for Instagram, because there is a younger audience and for them, they actually want issues to be explained in quite simple language. Very basic stuff works on Instagram. For Twitter, we've seen least engagement but, if there is a ground report coming out of Bihar, that gets more engagement on Twitter because the influencers or common people retweet and they show that okay, this is the reality which BBC is bringing.

So maximising each piece of content for as many platforms as possible is the new norm.

Gone are the days when once an interview was canned, the job was over. Today the same content needs to be milked to break down the news point or points into different formats and templates to suit different platforms and their requirements. So from articles and long-read analytical pieces to photo galleries (if the story has strong visual elements that may narrate the story through pictures), quote graphics to sum up the main points made, and then of course videos, everything needs to be done to increase reach.

Constant Learning, Unlearning, Re-learning

In terms of video content, the other format that most social media platforms offer is live streaming. So be it YouTube or Facebook, Twitter or Instagram, users can go live from the mobile app itself or patch the channel feed through the developer section of these platforms.

Figure 5.9: Go Live Feature Built into Social Media Apps

In case of YouTube and Facebook, users can also get notified, if the settings allow, once a channel they have subscribed goes live with a broadcast.

Figure 5.10: Livestreaming on YouTube

Source: https://www.youtube.com/watch?v=WB-y7_ymPJ4

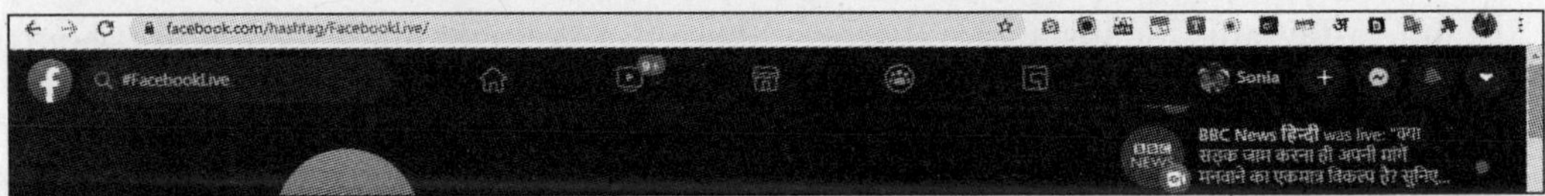

Figure 5.11: Facebook Live Notification

In August 2020, Instagram launched a short-video upload feature called Instagram Reels, which had inbuilt basic editing tools, audio, Augmented Reality (AR) effects and made creating and uploading videos from the phone itself easy.[32]

Prior to Reels, Instagram had launched another video app IGTV. But unlike Reels which was for short format video, IGTV was meant to be for long format videos. Apart from a separate app, IGTV was also integrated with the Instagram app to view longer duration videos that got uploaded on the platform.[33]

While most platforms are pushing for video content to drive engagement, not all organisations have the capability or can afford to get into video production. For *Indian Express*, given they are a print organization, 90 per cent of what they post on social media are articles with minimal video content.

Explaining the reason, Rajan says:

> It is more about distribution for us. I don't know how much of engagement happens on a lot of these platforms, right? Everybody talks about engagement. We also know engagement is important, but see, you either get engagement or you get traffic. I don't really believe that engagement sort of drives up traffic. We have tried all of that. So I don't know how do you get engagement competing with news organizations, which have 80% of the content going out in the form of video. For us 10 percent of the content is video. How do we compete in that case? ROI (Return on investment) problem would be when we burn money to create so much video content so that it creates engagement on Facebook. So if a few videos get lots of views, you will get what maximum thousand dollars which won't even suffice for one person's salary. So how does it work out?

There is another side to this distribution channel aspect of social media. Most social media platforms offer native solutions to posting content on their platform, which means that the user can consume the article posted on Facebook, for example, within Facebook's ecosystem without having to visit the publisher's website or app. The native solution that Facebook offered was called Facebook Instant Articles[34] which was launched in 2015 with a focus on mobile experience and promised faster loading speeds. But more importantly it offered a 70/30 revenue share with publishers if Facebook sold the ads against articles.[35] The trade-off, of course, was that the user got the content from a news organisation without visiting their digital properties. Here too the Tow Centre report found news organisations opting for different strategies depending on their own subscription models and what worked for them financially.[36]

Instant Articles is just one of the native offerings, Instagram as a platform is geared towards native consumption of the content posted and doesn't allow for posting link backs to the publishers' website from its platform. Snapchat Discover is also a similar native offering, as is Stories and Twitter Moments.

'Story' format is another common feature for many of these platforms on mobile. Instagram has it. Facebook added it. All these enable a snappy message to be assembled with a picture, text, some filters and basic effects to be posted via mobile, which disappear in twenty-four hours, unless archived. It is a feature borrowed heavily from Snapchat which originally came up with this template and this continues to be its USP (Unique Selling Proposition).

On Instagram and Facebook, within the 'story' format there are features to add countdowns, Q&A and swipe up feature linking the story back to the publisher's website.

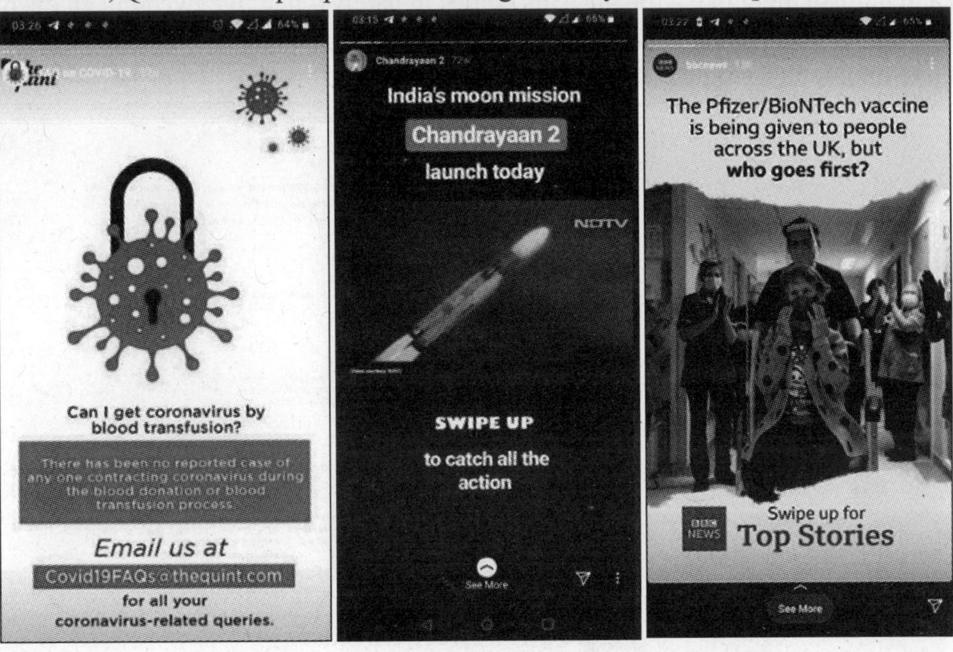

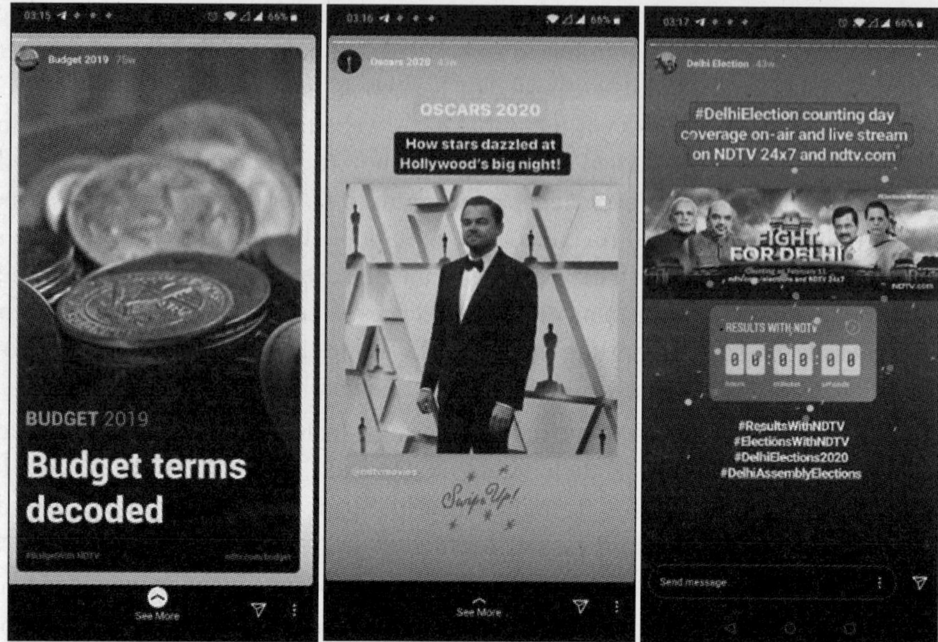

Figure 5.12: Examples of 'Story' Format Used by Different Publications

Even the established platforms are constantly undergoing change. Twitter emerged in 2006 as a microblogging site and the world learnt to communicate in just 140 characters. It took eleven years for Twitter to increase the character limit to 280. Like all platforms, Twitter has seen many tweaks. Now one can add multiple tweets at one go and publish them like a thread. This comes in handy when live tweeting an event or tweeting about different aspects of a story, presenting different angles or arguments around a topic in a single chain of conversation.

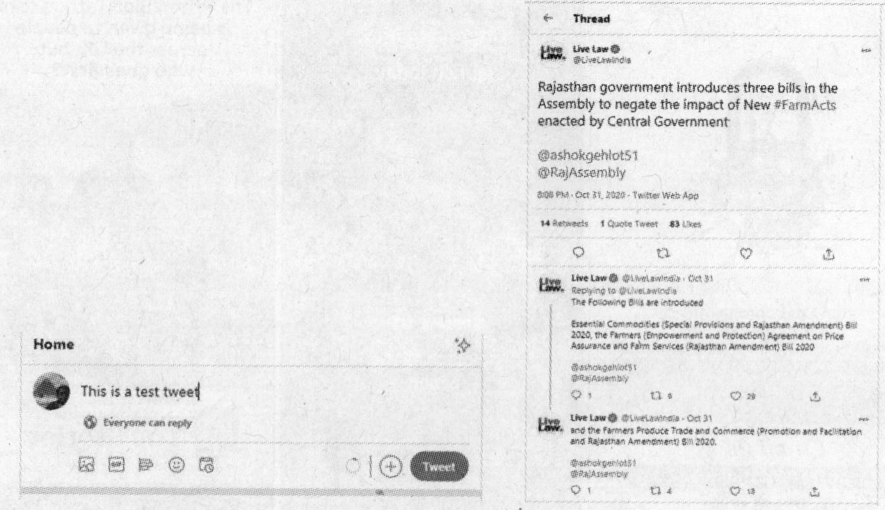

Figure 5.13: Tweet Threads

Twitter also popularised the use of hashtag, which enabled conversations to be organised around a topic, made search on a certain interest easy, but more importantly, it collated the trending topics based on the volume of tweets around a particular hashtag. The trends can be tracked at all India level, at city level, even at global level and also genre-wise under News, Sports and entertainment. There is also a personalised trending list which is collated based on a surfer's usage patterns.

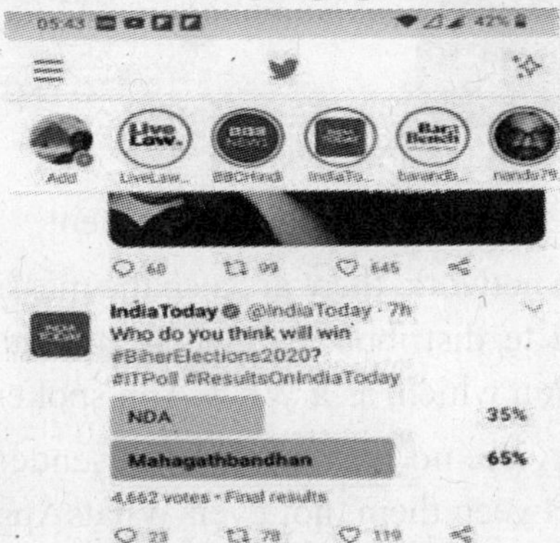

Figure 5.14: Example of a Poll in Twitter

There are also nifty tools like Poll that can be used as an interactive feature to engage and elicit responses from people on the platform.

Twitter has a provision to curate stories around a certain topic under an umbrella where all the coverage can be showcased using a feature called Twitter Moments. So highlights around an event, say Bihar elections, can be presented in one place by aggregating relevant tweets made through the day. 'Moments' can be created by clicking on the lightning icon, when 'Moments' option is selected from the dropdown menu. And then individually, the tweets can be manually added to the Moments.

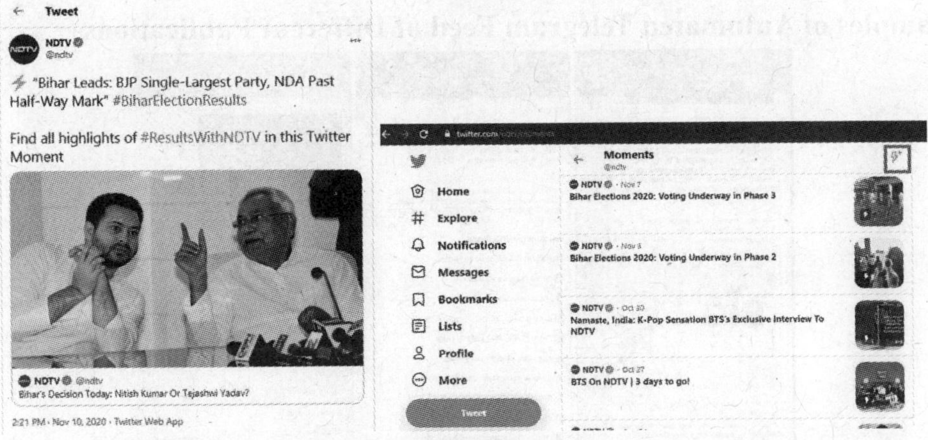

Figure 5.15: Twitter Stories

Source: https://twitter.com/ndtv/status/1326085089692848128

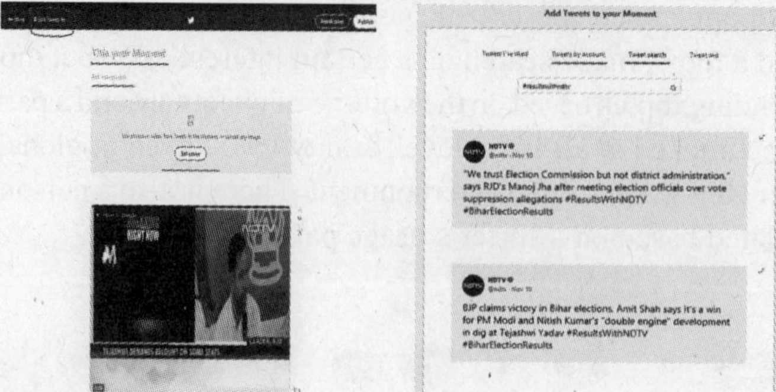

Figure 5.16: Twitter Moment

Apart from social media network, there are also the messaging apps like WhatsApp and Telegram that are used to distribute content by media houses. These platforms provide end-to-end encryption which, as a WhatsApp spokesperson explained:

> Being an encrypted service, no one, except the sender and a receiver can read messages exchanged between them, not even WhatsApp. WhatsApp's end-to-end encryption ensures only you and the person you're communicating with can read what's sent, and nobody in between, not even WhatsApp. Messages sent on WhatsApp are secured with locks, and only the recipient and sender have the special keys needed to unlock and read your messages. All of this happens automatically and there is no need to turn on settings or set-up special secret chats to secure your end-to-end encrypted messages.[37]

Most media houses have automated the feed for these messaging platforms, so once someone subscribes to the messaging group, they can either opt for the categories for which they would like an update or the automated feed can send a notification every time there is an update.

Examples of Automated Telegram Feed of Different Publications

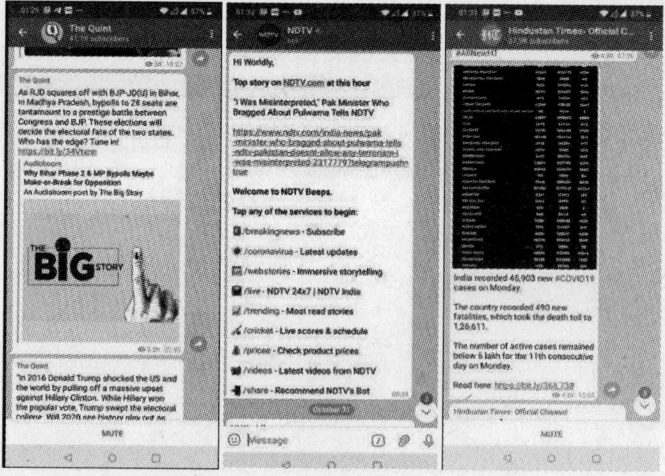

Example 5.17: Automated WhatsApp feed of The Quint

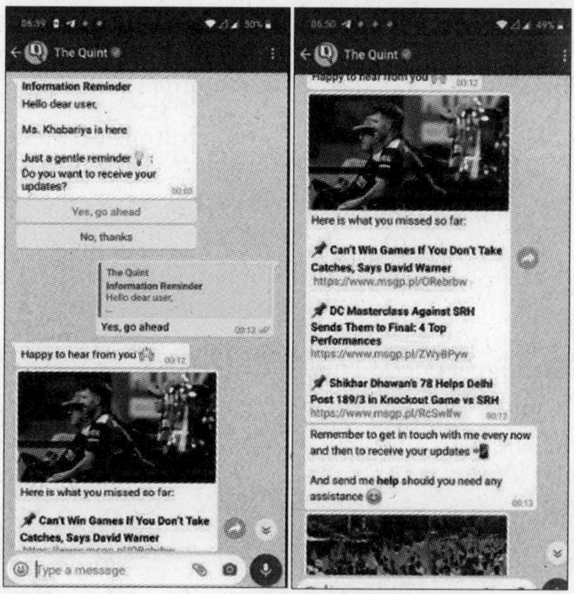

Figure 5.18: Automated WhatsApp feed of The Quint

The latest platform to try to woo publishers to get on it in India, is Snapchat, with NDTV being one of the first news organisations to be signed as partner.

Snapchat, the Hugely Popular Messaging App, Has Chosen NDTV as News Partner in India

NDTV will provide customised news for the 30 million users of Snapchat in India. NDTV will also offer other premium content including information that can help Snap users identify the cheapest products they are allowing for as well as train tickets and much more.

By Jagmeet Singh | Updated: 22 October 2020 15:31 IST

Share on Facebook | Tweet | Snapchat | Share | Reddit | Email | Comment

Figure 5.19: Snapchat–NDTV

Source: https://gadgets.ndtv.com/apps/news/snapchat-india-150-percent-daily-active-users-india-ndtv-partnership-2313655

What it all means for journalists is that they should keep their eyes and ears open to capitalise on the opportunities that these platforms offer. Apart from learning to innovate and amplifying their content by reaching out to newer audiences, journalists also need to be more open than they have been in the past to adapt to an ever-changing situation where what exists today may not be there tomorrow or may exist in a form that is not yet known.

'It takes a lot of resources and we are investing and it is always a learning game. So you can't really have a strategy when you get into it. But you build on it and learn as and when you go about it,' says Mansi Dua of *Indian Express*.

Another thing to remember is some platforms that exist today may cease to do so at some point and sometimes without notice. The 200 million who had signed up on

TikTok in India, being a case in point for being one of the fifty-nine Chinese apps, the Government of India decided to ban in retaliation to the simmering border tensions between India and China that escalated in June 2020.[38]

The tech companies are feeling the heat from multiple quarters. While TikTok was a casualty of a tense and still emerging geo-political situation, Twitter had to apologise on 18 November, 2020 to the government for showing Ladakh as a part of China, after an explanation was sought in the form of an affidavit with a stern message that 'it amounted to treason and it was a criminal offence that questioned the sovereignty of the country.'[39]

So even as everyone gears up to build their presence on these platforms, they need to be mindful of the transient nature, frequent updates and modifications and the unpredictability of which platforms may exist and in what form in future, how they will be regulated and what will be the legal framework adopted. All these will be things to watch out for in times to come.

Like Rajan says:

> Earlier, I would say I would have been a social media evangelist in a way, you know, but now I am more or less not keen on these platforms because they don't really look out after the publishers in that sense. If you depend on them too much right, like say you have 50 percent of your traffic coming from Facebook, their algorithm change would happen because of something they want to do . . . and how that impacts a publisher who has bet on social media, is a problem. So if you take them too, seriously, it's a problem.

Navigating the New Information Ecosystem

The other danger of social media is 'the information chaos', as Rusbridger calls it. He explains it as:

> But if facts were elusive, the digital world had transmitted half-truths and lies at a speed and scale that would have been unimaginable a decade earlier. The patient work of journalists to take time to discover what actually happened was buried in the avalanche of rumour – and then invisible except to the relatively tiny minority who still cared enough for old fashioned facts to pay for them.[40]

So newspapers need subscriptions, news channels could be paid but a WhatsApp forward in a family group is free and, additionally, may be considered more trustworthy than traditional media as it comes from someone known. Internet on fingertips, thanks to mobile phones availability,[41] has meant that more people have access to the internet without the media literacy to critically think, analyse and put a context to all the information and content they suddenly have access to.

An example of this was in view in full force in February 2019, when a brazen suicide attack on a Central Reserve Police Force (CRPF) convoy in Pulwama in Jammu and

Kashmir (J&K) killed forty soldiers. As anger and passions ran high, especially on news channels rushing to break the news, social media was flooded with manipulated images and videos claiming to be of the blast site. One of the images that got circulated showing the dead bodies of the soldiers killed was actually from a Naxal attack that took place in Dantewada, Chhattisgarh, in 2010, almost ten years ago.[42] So while the image was genuine, it was repurposed to fuel anger at a tense time. Similarly, when the Indian Air Force undertook the air strikes in Balakot in Pakistan Occupied Kashmir (POK) in retaliation to the Pulwama terrorist attack, a viral video claiming to be footage of the strike turned out to be from a video game.[43]

Pandemic brought with it its own set of misinformation and disinformation and some stemming from the political leaders themselves. Researchers from Cornell University, after analysing 38 million pandemic related English language articles, identified 11 topics of misinformation, including conspiracy theories and concluded, 'President Trump was the largest driver of the "infodemic".' Of the 38 million content pieces, the study found about 1.1 million provided Covid-19 misinformation (a little under 3 per cent of the Covid-19 conversation). But of this misinformation conversation, 37.9 per cent were around Trump mentions, making him the centre of the infodemic. Fact checking comprised just 16.4 per cent of the conversation, too small a part to make a difference to the larger problem.[44]

From miracle cures (which made up 26.4 per cent of infodemic discussion online according to Cornell study[45]), suggesting injecting bleach in humans (which President Trump later played down as a joke) to propagating hydroxychloroquine as a cure and posting or retweeting conspiracy theories, Trump was guilty as charged on most of these accounts and more. Social media platforms like Facebook and Twitter were forced to act by flagging and removing some of the President's posts.

Snapchat, the Hugely Popular Messaging App, Has Chosen NDTV as News Partner in India

NDTV will provide customised news for the 30 million users of Snapchat in India. NDTV will also offer other premium content including information that can help Snap users identify the cheapest products they are allowing for as well as train tickets and much more.

By Jagmeet Singh | Updated: 22 October 2020 15:31 IST

Share on Facebook | Tweet | Snapchat | Share | Reddit | Email | Comment

Figure 5.20: Misinformation

Source: https://www.scientificamerican.com/article/covid-misinformation-is-killing-people1/

In fact, the extent of the misinformation around Covid-19 pandemic seemed to shake the social media platforms out of their inertia, to finally act in some ways to strike out false information, and present verified and authoritative sources of content on their platforms in a more prominent manner. It may not be enough. But it was definitely a start and some of these actions got extended to the US elections as well.

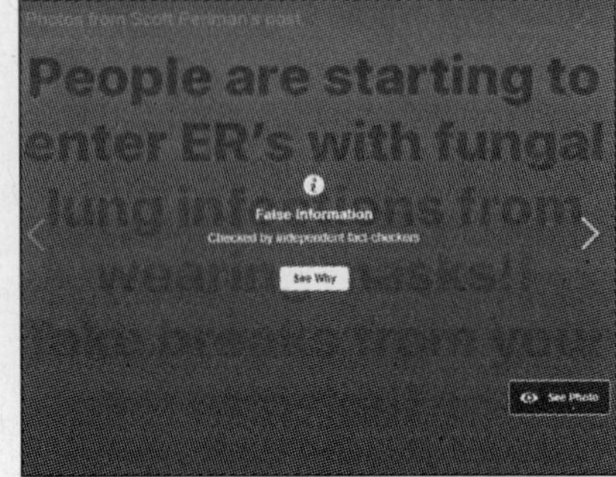

Figure 5.21: Example of Content Flagged by Facebook

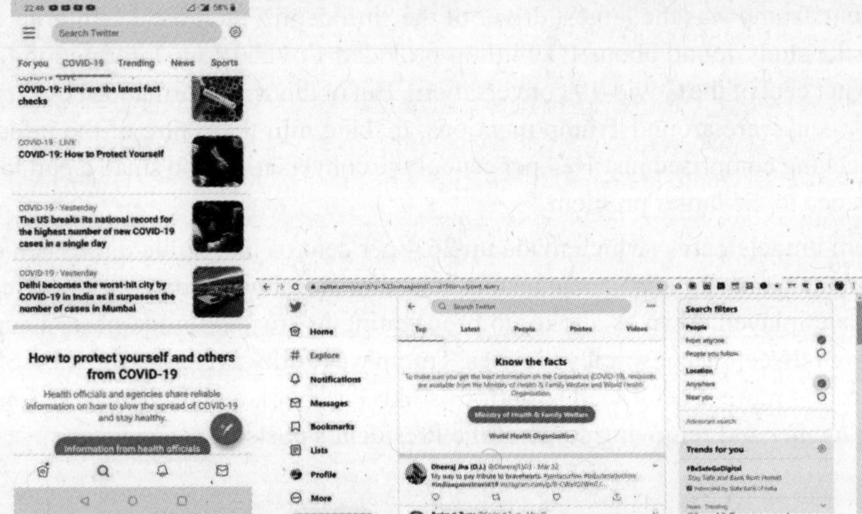

Figure 5.22: Example of Verified Covid-19 Related Content Highlighted by Twitter

Losing Control of the Narrative

It's one thing for Zuckerberg to build the world's biggest microphone and then choose to rent that microphone to liars, authoritarians, professional propagandists, or anyone else who can afford to pay market rate. It's another, more galling thing for him to claim that he is doing so for everyone's benefit.

–Andrew Marantz

Andrew Marantz is a staff writer at the *New Yorker* and the author of *Antisocial: Online Extremists, Techno-Utopians, and the Hijacking of the American Conversation.*[46]

Already, social media platforms have been forced to do what Zuckerberg expressed reluctance to get into – restrict or censor content. The horrors of the hands-off approach and acting as just a technology company, not taking responsibility of what transpires on the platforms owned by them, unfolded for the world to see in March 2019 when a man in Christchurch, New Zealand, went berserk and started firing at people gathered in two mosques to offer Friday prayers and streamed it live on Facebook. According to a report in BBC, the video was viewed 4,000 times before it was removed by Facebook. 'Fewer than 200 people had watched it live and the first user report of the video had come 12 minutes after it had ended,' said the report quoting Facebook.[47]

Though Facebook removed the clip fairly quickly once it was reported, the same BBC report states that, 'And within 24 hours, it (Facebook) had blocked 1.2 million copies at the point of upload and deleted another 300,000.'[48] But by the time Facebook got to it, the clip had also been shared on other platforms like Twitter, YouTube and so on. Not just that, many news organisations picked up the video and used it to file their stories. So even after the main video was deleted, the clip found a life of its own on the internet.

It was an act of terrorism that saw fifty people being killed and an almost equal number wounded. It showed how the platforms could be dangerously misused. It is not just acts of violence, also rampant on social media are hate speech and targeted trolling of people, be it from certain community, ideology, location, race or gender. The platforms have a checkered record in moderating these regular occurrences which have grave impact on people and society. It is now hardly a secret on how an industry has developed and is flourishing around spinning a narrative and populating the social media platforms with divisive content and taking advantage of the huge user base that these platforms have amassed, to repeatedly feed an agenda to try to indoctrinate the unsuspecting millions.

In case of the Christchurch attack video, many news organisations were called out for not removing the videos from their online stories even after the social media platforms deleted it. This is something that journalists and editors need to be mindful of before picking up content from the internet for filing stories.

It is also their job to document and report on the threats that these platforms pose if left unmonitored. A big scandal involving Facebook was the Cambridge Analytica expose in 2018. It was the result of some painstaking work put in by Carole Cadwalladr, a journalist in UK publication *Observer* (a sister newspaper of the *Guardian*). Cambridge Analytica was a British political consultancy firm that was found to be harvesting personal data of 87 million Facebook users to politically target them during the 2016 US elections and also the Brexit referendum. In his book, Rusbridger writes:

> At one level, many Facebook and Google users knew that their ability to use free email, search and messaging services came at a price – the surrender of quite significant amounts of their personal data. But the arithmetic of the harvesting – as many as 87 million profiles of friends and friends of friends – suddenly made Facebook look creepy. In the words of one Google artificial intelligence expert, not only could the platform be used as a totalitarian Panopticon, it was also a 'psychological control vector'.[49]

A *Wall Street Journal* article alleged that Facebook India was going soft on hate speech targeting Muslims by ruling party members on its platform.[50] It pinned the blame on company's top public policy executive Ankhi Das and used a trail of her internal communications to establish her partisan views.[51] Other media houses were quick to pick up the story and even as the issue was being examined by a Parliamentary committee, the mounting pressure made Ankhi Das's position untenable within the company and she was forced to step down, two months after the controversy broke in August 2020. The Ankhi Das episode highlighted yet again the threat of what happens when power, instead of being equally distributed, gets concentrated with a few. In the absence of a strong, independent regulatory mechanism and lack of digital media literacy among the bulk of the users of these platforms, ensuring checks and balances and accountability becomes tough.

This is something that journalists need to look out for as big tech domination and profiteering from personal data is a threat looming large. Journalists should closely monitor this space.

In October 2020, Mumbai Police's Cyber Unit filed a report that over 80,000 fake accounts were created on various social media platforms following the death of the young, promising actor, Sushant Singh Rajput on 14 June 2020.[52] Rajput had been found dead in his Mumbai residence. The police declared it to be death by suicide and though no suicide note was recovered, there were reports that the actor was undergoing treatment for clinical depression, something the police planned to investigate while looking into cause for death.[53] But even as the Mumbai police was investigating, a parallel narrative started to unfold on social media and on certain news channels. From conspiracy theories about murder to botched up post-mortem report to involvement of people known and unknown were floated and reiterated day in and day out. The narrative cast doubts on Mumbai Police, the hospital that conducted the post-mortem and the people the actor worked with or had professional fallout with. There were so many versions and theories floated that eventually the tragic death was relegated to trending hashtags and prime time debates, with each day either throwing up a new character with unknown credentials or claims being made by unidentified sources adding a new twist to an already twisted tale.

These instances highlight a dangerous phenomenon that endanger the very existence of an informed society. It distorts reality to an extent that it becomes impossible to know what is true and what is false. Its impact on society and especially democratic systems and institutions is far reaching. Our survival as an informed society is at stake – a society that takes decisions on the basis of facts and not on the basis of emotions stirred up in an echo chamber of WhatsApp groups, Facebook feeds or Twitter timelines, where being a contrarian is seen as a threat, to be squashed rather than being given the respectful patient consideration, as part of the evolution process. This, 'my way or the highway' filter that social media has created, needs to be busted to restore some order in this information chaos.

What Role Can Journalists Play in Fixing This Chaos?

The most important thing for journalists is to do their job and do it impartially. At no juncture should journalists be seen taking sides, let alone fanning the flames of bigotry. To counter 'fake news' – not an apt term as it has been misused to target credible media reporting that has not found favour with the powers at the helm – good journalism is needed more than ever before. Journalism needs to rise above the crisis it faces to do the hard job of reporting the truth.

Dedicated fact-checking organisations are a product of the information ecosystem that has emerged. These organisations track online platforms and messaging services for content that is going viral or has the potential to cause some serious damage, verify the source and content, and debunk any claims found to be manipulated or misrepresented. Some of these organisations do the fact checking in multiple languages. India has about seventeen signatories to the International Fact-Checking Network's (IFCN) code of principles.[54] IFCN is globally recognised body for verifying credentials of fact checking organisations. Platforms like Facebook and Google are increasingly looking to upfront and prioritise fact checked content to counter the deluge of the fake, unverified content that threatens to undo their achievements of the past and leave a lasting blot on their legacy.

WhatsApp with over 400 million monthly active users in India plays an important role in the current information ecosystem. Since it is a closed network and hence difficult to track and verify content that is getting shared, the platform itself has taken some measures to check the spread of misinformation.

A WhatsApp spokesperson explained the steps the platform had taken:

> WhatsApp has made significant product changes and worked with partners across civil society, engaged with relevant government authorities and other technology platforms to help address the harmful consequences of misinformation. While there is no single action that can resolve the complex challenges contributing to misinformation, we are committed to helping do our part to ensure that WhatsApp continues to be a force for good in India. In April (2020), we announced limiting 'highly forwarded messages' to one chat only. As a result of this new limit, we witnessed a 70% reduction in the number of highly forwarded messages sent on the platform, globally.'[55]

In addition, WhatsApp is working on closely with some newsrooms and fact-checking organisations,

> Over the course of 2020, the WhatsApp API solution has been offered to a total of nine Indian fact-checking organisations[56] – all of whom are accredited to the International Fact Checking Network. This allows them to manage incoming messages and queries at scale, as well as automating a lot of the responses by sharing fact-checks they have already done. The longer-term aim is to build a common fact-check library that can be used across WhatsApp and enable fact-checked content to be shared at scale.

Journalists Are Not Immune to Pitfalls of Social Media

On 17 June 2020, just two days after a serious flare-up on the Line of Actual Control (LAC) between China and India that killed twenty Indian soldiers, *Times Now* anchors read out a list of thirty Chinese soldiers who they said were killed in the 15 June incident. The information was attributed to *Global Times*, a Chinese publication. This news was broadcast on the basis of content floating on social media platforms, without verifying from any official sources. The anchors did, after some time, say that this could be fake news, but many fact checking organisations and publications pointed out that this tantamounted to propagation of unverified news by mainstream channel which was expected to follow multiple checks before putting out any information – filters that are missing on social media.[57]

Information from social media should also be scrutinised like information from any other source. As mentioned earlier, news can break on social media from the official handles of heads of states, ministries, politicians, institutions, journalists themselves or ordinary people. Mainstream news organisations should be sceptical and apply all filters of editorial judgement before publishing any piece. Says Aaron Pereira of the *Indian Express*:

> We just tend to hold onto a story until we properly get a verification on something that's happening, especially if it's controversial or if it involves lives so we are not always going to be the ones to break the story first on Twitter and then have to delete it. You always make sure that whatever you're putting out goes to a little process of verification and fact checking before it goes out, so that happens. So the good part there is we have reporters on the ground, we don't always rely on what is breaking on television. We do a double confirmation with our reporters and correspondents from across the country and it is only then that we put out the story.

Beware of Personal Threats in Social Media

A woman television news anchor filed a complaint in Mumbai against a forty-year-old man from West Bengal for sending her obscene messages on Facebook. The man was arrested.[58]

As journalists working in an era of the internet, it is a professional hazard even if not a personal necessity to be on these social media platforms. But these platforms can also be the source of harassment and trolling, which at times can get serious and spill over from online to the offline world. According to an international survey of women journalists conducted by the International Federation of Journalists in 2018, 64 per cent had suffered online abuse.[59]

In another report, 'Online Harassment of Journalists: The Trolls Attack' by Reporters Without Borders (RSF) it was found:

> The perpetrators may be ordinary 'haters' (individuals or communities of individuals hiding behind their screens) or 'troll armies' of online mercenaries created by

> authoritarian regimes. In both cases the goal is the same, to silence journalists whose reporting annoys, often using exceptionally abusive methods.

The report goes on to quote freelance journalist from India, Rana Ayyub, who is also the author of a book on 2002 Gujarat riots:

> I've been called Jihadi Jane, Islamo fascist [and] ISIS sex slave. My face has been superimposed on a naked body and my mother's photograph has been taken from my Instagram account and photoshopped in the most objectionable manner possible.[60]

The RSF report also has some specific dos and don'ts for journalists to protect and prepare themselves against online attacks and trolling. The action points include prepping in advance by adopting certain digital security practices like two-step authentications for email accounts, not sharing private information online and journalists who are being harassed should take steps like taking screenshots, collecting evidence, informing co-workers and continuously blocking accounts sending abusive messages.[61]

But there are other threats too to journalists using social media platforms. Journalists like Kishorechandra Wangkhem from Manipur[62] and Prashant Kanojia[63] have been arrested for their posts on social media. Wangkhem was charged with sedition. Both Kanojia and Wangkhem have faced the wrath for their posts on more than one occasion. At a time when India has been sliding in the Press Freedom Index (Sri Lanka, Nepal, Afghanistan and Myanmar rank better than us)[64] social media posts by journalists are proving to be another way to damn them.

Many media organisations have come up with a social media policy, defining what their staff can and cannot post on their individual handles. For instance, one of the key provisions of the *New York Times* social media policy states:

> In social media posts, our journalists must not express partisan opinions, promote political views, endorse candidates, make offensive comments or do anything else that undercuts The Times's journalistic reputation.

BBC, too, lists down the rules to follow by individuals on social media. One of the points in that exhaustive document states, 'If your work requires you to maintain your impartiality, don't express a personal opinion on matters of public policy, politics, or "controversial subjects".' In another point it says, 'Do think about what your likes, shares, retweets, use of hashtags and who you follow say about you, your personal prejudices and opinions.'

What journalists say, like or share should not reflect their opinion or preferences for a certain side. Journalists need to be objective and factual in reporting a story. Voicing an opinion or supporting a certain side can raise doubts about their objectivity and by extension may also imply that the organisation has a tilt towards one side over the other. This can impact the credibility of the news organisation.

BBC has many more points in their social media guidelines for individuals, here are some significant ones:

> Even if you are posting in what appears to be a 'private' group, or you have locked down your privacy settings on your accounts, do apply the same standards as if you were posting publicly. Do be aware that there is no difference between how a personal and an 'official' account is perceived on social media: disclaimers do not offer protection. . . . Do remember that your personal brand on social media is always secondary to your responsibility to the BBC.

The jury is out on whether such policies curb an individual journalist's freedom of expression. *India Today* faced criticism about its social media policy, which was seen as an imposition as it forbade its employees to post their personal political views on their handles and also directed them to post only *India Today* content from their handles.

Some other organisations like the *Quint* don't have documented guidelines on social media usage by their employees but, like their associate editor Medha Chakrabartty says, 'We don't have any mandate that censors self-expression via personal handles but there is an expectation from team members, by virtue of association, to not put out any content that can be construed as inflammatory/incendiary/hate speech.'

If there is a genuine error made by the individual while posting, it is critical to update, correct and apologise, if need be, for the mistake made. When former President of India Pranab Mukherjee was critically ill in August 2020, prominent journalist Rajdeep Sardesai tweeted the news of his demise as 'Big Breaking', except that the news was not true. Sardesai was quick to put out a tweet apologising for that. Acknowledging a mistake shows that to err is human and correcting it, a sign of credibility.

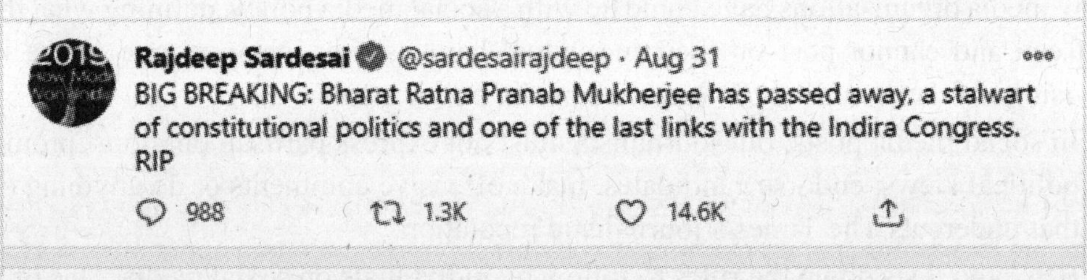

Source: https://twitter.com/sardesairajdeep/status/1300410115992895488?lang=en

Figure 5.23: Apology on Twitter

Source: https://twitter.com/sardesairajdeep/status/1293759013742510080?lang=en

The Future

We are living through unprecedented times. If a private company has to block channels of communication of a Head of State to ensure peace, sanity and truth prevails, imagine the extent of the problem. Also understand the scale of concentration of power with these big tech companies in controlling the information highways of the world. The way forward seems uncertain and ominous. But there is little doubt that the world needs good journalism more than ever before. There cannot be any shortcuts or cutting of corners in restoring faith in what journalism was always meant to do – inform, educate, empower.

What about social media, going forward? It is currently anybody's guess what path these platforms will take to rectify the inherent issues. What is clear is that they have an important role to play. From the Arab Spring revolutions to #MeToo movements to #BlackLivesMatter campaigns and, closer home, the agitation against Citizenship Amendment Act and other protests have all gained traction and momentum thanks to social media. The benefits cannot be denied, just as the evils cannot be ignored.

The job of journalists was never easy and the challenge is only getting harder. In the world we live in, social media and technological disruptions are a reality. More than ever before, following the basic tenets of journalism is the need of the hour. The doomsday predictions of dystopia may not be far-fetched; at stake is the very foundation of an informed society, which is at the core of a successful democracy. A society has to be based on facts with systems in place to prevent falsehoods from taking hold of rationality and running amok. It is time to check the unbridled spread of conspiracy theories, propaganda and fake narratives. To fight them we need to strengthen the crumbling pillars of journalism by addressing the challenges, bolstering trust and supporting its independence.

As for journalists, more than ever, it is time to go back to the basics and report the events as they unfold, objectively, from all sides – being the voice of the voiceless and holding those in power accountable by asking the right questions, being transparent, responsible and factual. There is no silver bullet.

Tips and Tools

Social Media Monitoring Tools

- CrowdTangle
- Who posted what?
- Facebook Graph Searcher
- Graph.tips
- LookupID
- Spoonbill
- TweetBeaver

- Foller.me
- TweetDeck
- GoogleTrends
- Answer the Public
- Klout
- Social mention
- Twazzup
- TweetReach
- Meltwater

Explore More

Social Media and Journalism: How to Effectively Reach the Public: https://sproutsocial.com/insights/social-media-and-journalism/.

Journalism in The Age of Social Media: https://reutersinstitute.politics.ox.ac.uk/our-research/journalism-age-social-media.

What Social Media Needs to Learn from Traditional Media: https://www.wired.com/story/what-social-media-needs-to-learn-from-traditional-media/.

How Journalists Use Social Media: Gathering and Developing the News: https://www.coursera.org/lecture/gathering-the-news/how-journalists-use-social-media-x8Hgw.

How Social Media Is Changing the News: https://www.youtube.com/watch?v=Puro_L7O4eY.

Questions

1. What are the major challenges thrown up by social media when it comes to journalism?
2. Pick a story and come up with a coverage plan for different platforms and content formats.
3. What are the pros and cons of the personalized news feed determined by algorithms?

Notes

1. A. Vaidyanathan, Reporter, edited by Chandrashekar Srinivasan (with inputs from PTI), *Bihar Election Results Will Come Late Night, Says Poll Body*, *NDTV Elections*, 10 November 2020, https://www.ndtv.com/india-news/bihar-election-results-will-come-late-night-says-poll-body-2323408.
2. 'Bihar Election 2020: BJP Claims Victory before Results were announced, *National Herald*, 11 November 2020.https://www.nationalheraldindia.com/india/bihar-election-2020-bjp-claims-victory-before-results-were-announced.
3. Suparna Singh, edited by Ayesha Kagal, 'The Digital Newsroom: Who's Really in Charge Here?' in *More News Is Good News: Untold Stories of 25 Years of Television News* (HarperCollins, 2016).
4. 'We Apologise for Bihar Results Confusion, Says Prannoy Roy', *NDTV* 8 November 2015, https://www.ndtv.com/video/news/news/we-apologise-for-bihar-results-confusion-says-prannoy-roy-390118.
5. Amber Sinha, *The Networked Public - How Social Media Is Changing Democracy*, (New Delhi: Rupa, 2019), pp. 179–181).

6. ANI, 'Twitter Deletes Ex-Malaysian PM's Tweet for Glorifying Attack in France', *NDTV*, 30 October 2020, https://www.ndtv.com/world-news/twitter-deletes-former-malaysian-pm-mahathir-mohamads-tweet-for-glorifying-violence-2317871.
7. AFP, 'France's Macron to Muslims: I hear Your Anger, but Won't Accept Violence', *The Hindu*, October 31, 2020, https://www.thehindu.com/news/international/france-seeks-to-uncover-attackers-links/article32992923.ece
8. Katie Collins, 'Twitter Removes Tweet by Former Malaysian Leader for Glorifying Violence', *CNET*, 29 October 2020, https://www.cnet.com/news/twitter-removes-tweet-by-former-malaysian-leader-for-glorifying-violence/.
9. 'Standing for Voice and Free Expression', *Meta*, 17 October 2019, https://about.fb.com/news/2019/10/mark-zuckerberg-stands-for-voice-and-free-expression/.
10. Facebook Inc., 'Form S-1 Registration Statement Under the Securities Act of 1933', Washington, D.C. 20549: As filed with the Securities and Exchange Commission on 1 February 2012, p. 82, https://www.sec.gov/Archives/edgar/data/1326801/000119312512034517/d287954ds1.htm#toc287954_10.
11. Emily Bell and Taylor Owen with Pete Brown, Codi Hauka, and Nushin Rashidian, 'The Platform Press: How Silicon Valley Reengineered Journalism', *The Tow Center for Digital Journalism at Columbia Journalism School*, 26 May 2017, DOI https://doi.org/10.7916/D8R216ZZ.
12. (KEMP, 2022)
13. Simon Kemp, 'Digital 2020: October Global Statshot', *Datareportal*, October 2020, https://datareportal.com/reports/digital-2020-october-global-statshot.
14. 'Communications and Digital Committee Breaking News? The Future of UK Journalism', www.parliament.uk, 1st Report of Session 2019-21, 27 November 2020, HL Paper 176, https://publications.parliament.uk/pa/ld5801/ldselect/ldcomuni/176/17602.htm.
15. 'Communications and Digital Committee Breaking News? The Future of UK Journalism'.
16. 'Data Never Sleeps 7.0', *DOMO*, https://www.domo.com/learn/data-never-sleeps-7.
17. 'Data Never Sleeps 8.0', *DOMO*, https://www.domo.com/learn/data-never-sleeps-8.
18. 'Data Never Sleeps 9.0', *DOMO*, https://www.domo.com/learn/data-never-sleeps-9.
19. Alan Rusbridger, *Breaking News: The Remaking of Journalism and Why It Matters Now* (Edinburgh, Great Britain: Canongate Books, 2018).
20. Emily Bell et al., 'The Platform Press: How Silicon Valley Reengineered Journalism', p. 17.
21. Hasit Shah, 'India's Digital Future Isn't Just in English: BBC Launches 4 Indian Language Services', *NiemanLab*, 16 November 2016, https://www.niemanlab.org/2016/11/indias-digital-future-isnt-just-in-english-bbc-launches-4-indian-language-services/.
22. Rupa Jha, 'BBC World Service in India', *BBC Blog*, 5 October 2017, https://www.bbc.co.uk/blogs/aboutthebbc/entries/90812dad-ab15-456d-a877-692f603000b4.
23. Gaurav Laghate, 'We're Only Just Warming Up Our Engines in India, Says BBC's Tim Davie', *The Economic Times*, 7 April 2022, https://economictimes.indiatimes.com/industry/media/entertainment/media/were-only-just-warming-up-our-engines-in-india-says-bbcs-tim-davie/articleshow/90695857.cms?from=mdr.
24. Emily Bell et al., 'The Platform Press: How Silicon Valley Reengineered Journalism'.
25. 'Internet Adoption in India: ICUBE 2020', *Kantar*, https://images.assettype.com/afaqs/2021-06/b9a3220f-ae2f-43db-a0b4-36a372b243c4/KANTAR_ICUBE_2020_Report_C1.pdf.
26. Zeenab Aneez, Taberez Ahmed Neyazi, Antonis Kalogeropoulos and Rasmus Kleis Nielsen, 'Reuters Institute: India Digital News Report', *Reuters Institute for Study of Journalism*, January 2019, p. 10, https://reutersinstitute.politics.ox.ac.uk/sites/default/files/2019-03/India_DNR_FINAL.pdf.
27. Zeenab Aneez et al., 'Reuters Institute: India Digital News Report', p. 8.
28. Nic Newman with Richard Fletcher, Craig T. Robertson, Kirsten Eddy and Rasmus Kleis Nielsen, *Reuters Institute Digital News Report 2022*, https://reutersinstitute.politics.ox.ac.uk/sites/default/files/2022-06/Digital_News-Report_2022.pdf/.

29. Nic Newman et al., *Reuters Institute Digital News Report 2022*, p. 10.
30. Nic Newman et al., *Reuters Institute Digital News Report 2022*, p. 23.
31. Nic Newman et al., *Reuters Institute Digital News Report 2022*, p. 134.
32. 'Introducing Instagram Reels', *Instagram*, https://about.instagram.com/blog/announcements/introducing-instagram-reels-announcement.
33. Kevin Systrom, 'Welcome to IGTV, Our New Video App', *Instagram*, 20 June 2018, https://about.instagram.com/blog/announcements/welcome-to-igtv.
34. 'Instant Articles', *Meta*, https://www.facebook.com/formedia/solutions/instant-articles.
35. Emily Bell et al., 'The Platform Press: How Silicon Valley Reengineered Journalism'.
36. Emily Bell et al., 'The Platform Press: How Silicon Valley Reengineered Journalism', p. 21.
37. WhatsApp, 'About End-to-End Encryption', https://faq.whatsapp.com/general/security-and-privacy/end-to-end-encryption.
38. Tasneem Akolawala, 'TikTok Goes Completely Offline in India, Says "It's Complying with Government Directive" ', *Gadgets360*, 30 June 2020, https://gadgets.ndtv.com/apps/news/tiktok-offline-india-app-website-not-working-government-ban-chinese-apps-2254631.
39. PTI, 'Twitter Apologises for "Ladakh in China" Map Error, Promises to Correct It, Says Panel, *The Print*, 18 November 2020. https://theprint.in/india/twitter-apologises-for-ladakh-in-china-map-error-promises-to-correct-it-says-panel/547058/.
40. Alan Rusbridger, *Breaking News*, p. xvii.
41. Pramit Bhattacharya, '88% of households in India have a mobile phone', *Mint*, 5 December 2016, https://www.livemint.com/Politics/kZ7j1NQf5614UvO6WURXfO/88-of-households-in-India-have-a-mobile-phone.html.
42. Swasti Chatterjee, 'Old Photo from 2010 Dantewada Attack Resurfaces as Pulwama'. 17 February 2019, https://www.boomlive.in/old-photo-from-2010-dantewada-attack-resurfaces-as-pulwama/.
43. Deeksha Bhardwaj, 'Viral Video of IAF strike on Balakot Is Actually from a Video Game', *The Print*, 26 February 2019, https://theprint.in/hoaxposed/viral-video-of-iaf-strike-on-balakot-is-actually-from-a-video-game/198217/.
44. Sarah Evanega, Mark Lynas, Jordan Adams and Karinne Smolenyak, 'Coronavirus Misinformation: Quantifying Sources and Themes in the COVID-19 "infodemic" ', p. 4, https://allianceforscience.cornell.edu/wp-content/uploads/2020/09/Evanega-et-al-Coronavirus-misinformationFINAL.pdf.
45. Sarah Evanega et al., 'Coronavirus Misinformation', p. 5.
46. Andrew Marantz, 'Facebook and the "Free Speech" Excuse', *The New Yorker*, 31 October, 2019 https://www.newyorker.com/news/daily-comment/facebook-and-the-free-speech-excuse.
47. 'Facebook: New Zealand Attack Video Viewed 4,000 times', *BBC News*, 19 March 2019, https://www.bbc.com/news/business-47620519.
48. 'Facebook: New Zealand attack video viewed 4,000 times'.
49. Alan Rusbridger, *Breaking News*, p. 358.
50. Horwitz Purnell, Jeff Horwitz and Newley, 'Facebook Executive Supported India's Modi, Disparaged Opposition in Internal Messages', *The Wall Street Journal*, 30 August 2020. https://www.wsj.com/articles/facebook-executive-supported-indias-modi-disparaged-opposition-in-internal-messages-11598809348.
51. Newley Purnell and Jeff Horwitz, 'Facebook's Hate-Speech Rules Collide with Indian Politics', 14 August 2020, https://www.wsj.com/articles/facebook-hate-speech-india-politics-muslim-hindu-modi-zuckerberg-11597423346?redirect=amp#click=https://t.co/PXPLwnBs1a.
52. Suraj Ojha, edited by Sparshita Saxena, 'Sushant Singh Rajput Death Case: Over 80k Fake Accounts Created to Discredit Mumbai Police Probe', *Hindustan Times*, 5 October 2020, https://www.hindustantimes.com/mumbai-news/sushant-singh-rajput-death-case-over-80k-fake-accounts-created-to-discredit-mumbai-police-probe/story-qjpqRUsgC95wBwshReLiyI.html.

53. Mrityunjay Bose, 'Sushant Singh Rajput's Suicide Case: Depression, Manager's Death Being Looked Into', *Deccan Herald*, 14 June 2020, https://www.deccanherald.com/entertainment/entertainment-news/sushant-singh-rajputs-suicide-case-depression-managers-death-being-looked-into-849502.html.
54. 'Verified Signatories of the IFCN Code of Principles', https://ifcncodeofprinciples.poynter.org/signatories.
55. WhatsApp, 'Safety in India', https://faq.whatsapp.com/general/safety-in-india.
56. The Fact-checking organisations include: NewsChecker: +91 99994 99044; India Today: +91 73700 07000; Vishvas News (Dainik Jagran): +91 95992 99372; Boom Live: +91 77009 06588; Factly: +91 92470 52470; Fact Crescendo: +91 90490 53770; The Quint/Webqoof: +91 96436 51818; NewsMobile: +91 11 7127 9799; AFP India: +91 95999 73984.
57. Pooja Chaudhuri, 'Times Now Falls for Fake WhatsApp Forward Listing names of 30 Dead Chinese Soldiers', 17 June 2020, *Alt News*, https://www.altnews.in/times-now-falls-for-fake-whatsapp-forward-listing-names-of-30-dead-chinese-soldiers/.
58. PTI, 'Man Held for Sending Lewd Messages to Woman TV News Anchor', *Business Standard*, 14 July 2019, https://www.business-standard.com/article/pti-stories/man-held-for-sending-lewd-messages-to-woman-tv-news-anchor-119071400669_1.html.
59. 'IFJ Global Survey Shows Massive Impact of Online Abuse on Women Journalists', *International Federation of Journalists*, 23 November 2018, https://www.ifj.org/media-centre/news/detail/article/ifj-global-survey-shows-massive-impact-of-online-abuse-on-women-journalists.html.
60. Reporters Without Borders, 'Online Harassment of Journalists: Attack of the Rolls', July 2018, https://rsf.org/sites/default/files/rsf_report_on_online_harassment.pdf.
61. Reporters Without Borders, 'Online Harassment of Journalists', pp. 33–34.
62. 'Manipur Scribe Held Again for Sedition, This Time for FB Post Slamming Insult to Tribal Woman', 8 October 2020, *The Wire*, https://thewire.in/rights/manipur-journalist-kishorechandra-wangkhem-arrest-facebook-meitei-maram-facebook.
63. 'India: Uttar Pradesh Police Arrest Journalist for Social Media Posts', *International Federation of Journalists*, 20 August 2020, https://www.ifj.org/media-centre/news/detail/category/press-releases/article/india-uttar-pradesh-police-arrest-journalist-for-social-media-posts.html.
64. 'Modi Tightens His Grip on Media', *TSA*, 26 April 2021, https://thesecondangle.com/modi-tightens-his-grip-on-media/.

Chapter 6

Cyber Harassment and Digital Abuse

Dr Parry Aftab

Almost two-thirds of women journalists polled have experienced intimidation, threats, or abuse in relation to their work. More than 25 percent of 'verbal, written and/or physical intimidation including threats to family or friends' took place online.

–International Women's Media Foundation and the International News Safety Institute, December 2013

Introduction

More and more often journalists are faced with incidents of trolling, cyber-harassment and digital abuse. Sometimes it is directed at them, motivated by real or perceived personal or professional harm. Sometimes they are targeted for their political positions or national origin or religious beliefs. Sometimes they were just in the wrong place at the wrong time. In addition, often journalists are reporting and covering cases where others are targeted by digital abuse, trolling, and cyberbullying. These cases may involve minors or adults, political leaders, business persons or even common persons and may falsely accuse the target of crimes or acts of moral turpitude or expose secrets and very intimate information.

To be able to honestly and fairly report news, journalists must feel safe. They must feel supported by their peers and their agencies. They must feel free to speak the truth and follow their investigations and reporting wherever and to whomever they lead or point out. Threats against journalists are not new. But digital attacks on their reputations are. This is where journalistic standards become crucial and where truth and justice can be defeated or succeed, often based on how the issues are addressed and how the journalist responds.

The Network of Women in Media, India (NWMI), a dynamic and credible forum for women in media in India, intervened several times in *combating sexual harassment and online abuse of women journalists.* NWMI demanded that social media platforms like Twitter, Facebook and Instagram should stop enabling intimidation, harassment, misinformation and violence, and take swift action when complaints are made.[1]

Trolling, as the journalist becomes better known and handles more controversial reporting, may not be avoidable. But teaching the targets how to not make things worse, to avoid 'feeding the trolls' and how to be more secure online and offline will be important to protect them. Their publishers must take the journalists' safety seriously, protect their data and location, screen those having direct digital access to the journalists and avoid making matters worse, as well.

The more journalists can appreciate how cyberbullying works, the better prepared they will be if cyber-harassment or trolling occurs.

I have practised cyberlaw for twenty-four years and for twenty-three years I have run the world's first cybersafety and help group, founded in the US and operated globally by thousands of unpaid volunteers from seventy-six countries around the world. I hope my insights will help keep all journalists, and everyone else, safer online and preserve their safety and reputations in the 'real world.' But before we begin, we have to define some of the common terms.

Some Common Terms

Cyberbullying: As defined by StopCyberbullying Global, it is between or among minors, is intentional, and uses (at least in part) digital technology to harm the target.

Cyber-harassment: As defined by WiredSafety, it is the use of digital technology to intentionally harm someone (it is the adult equivalent of cyberbullying).

Cyberstalking: As defined by WiredSafety, it is tracking and following someone online to gather the information that can be used to cyber-harass them or otherwise harm them or help the stalker gain dominance over the target.

Trolling: This is when someone who is not personally acquainted with the target uses digital technology to attack, threaten or otherwise damage the reputation of their target individual, group or community. This may be motivated by, among other things, boredom, hate, bigotry and bias, righteous indignation, jealousy or political differences. This is almost always conducted anonymously or with attempts to impersonate someone to have them implicated falsely in the trolling.

Bystanders: As defined by StopCyberbullying Global, they are individuals who are connected to or personally know the target or the abusers, witness the digital abuse and take no action to report it, support the target or stop it.

Facilitators: They are friends, supporters, or acquaintances of the abuser or members of their digital community who 'like', 'share', comment on or otherwise support or spread the digital abuse. They fall into several categories, from 'instigators', to 'posses', to 'drama queens', among others. But all fall under the general definition of 'facilitators'. They may do so unintentionally, merely by reacting to the post or message, but without them, most cyber-harassment and cyberbullying dies a quick death.

Next, recognise that not everything that is rude or mean or that hurts someone's feelings is digital abuse. Cyber abuse, cyber-harassment, and cyberbullying must be either repeated or serious. Posting a comment about your weight or complexion one-time doesn't qualify. Even posting it twice or even three times, may not qualify. But posting it twenty times or fifty times, or sending you ten WhatsApp messages saying the same thing may qualify as cyber abuse, cyber-harassment or cyberbullying. But a death threat, threat of serious bodily harm, sharing of intimate images or photoshopping your head onto someone else's nude body doesn't need to be repeated to qualify as digital abuse.

Many books have been written about these kinds of digital abuses. In this article we will focus on what you need to know to better arm yourself when digital abuse is directed at you, as a journalist, and how to effectively report on incidents of digital abuse when cyberbullying occurs.

Six Tips

These apply equally to both cyberbullying and digital abuse. Ignore them at your peril.

1. *Stop, Block and Tell:* If you are targeted or are advising someone who has been targeted, the first thing to be done is to 'Stop' and not react, respond or do something to make it worse. The abuser wants a reaction. Don't play into their hands. The digital advice 'don't feed the trolls', stems from this. Then 'Block' the abuser, their accounts and their ability to contact you. Finally, 'Tell' someone you trust, the authorities, or if the target is a minor, a trusted adult.
2. *Take 5!:* While it is easy to tell someone not to react or lash out when they are abused online, being able to control the reaction and natural impulse to respond isn't easy. 'Take 5!' means to step away from all digital devices and find something that will help you find balance, calm down and take control. It might be reading a book, going for a jog, doing yoga or deep breathing, having a cup of tea or something stronger to drink, cuddling with your pet or child, taking a bath or shower – the possible Take 5 activities differ for each person. By turning to something that gives you peace, calmness and strength, it is less likely that you will make the situation worse.
3. *R-E-S-P-E-C-T Yourself and Others:* The ideal way to address digital abuse is to avoid it entirely. The best way to do that is to be honest, maintain your integrity and not do anything digitally that you wouldn't do face-to-face. Follow the golden rule of internet – treat people the way you want to be treated online. Following this traditional 'golden rule' both online and offline is a good idea.
4. *Use the Right Medium for the Message:* Some things are better done in RL (real life) in person. Some things are appropriate for texting, WhatsApp, posting online or email. Breaking up with someone by text or WhatsApp isn't appropriate. Long nuanced discussions on politics or human values require more than an email. By

giving thought to the right medium for the message being delivered, many instances of perceived harassment will be avoided.

5. *Take It Offline!* Misperceived offensive communications or actions (as mentioned in the previous point 'right medium for the message') applies equally to other misunderstandings or miscommunications where, because of the nature of digital communications, bad jokes, irony, sarcasm and emotionally-charged messages are often misunderstood and are treated by the recipient as harassment. Sometimes misdirected messages arrive in the wrong inbox and the recipient feels offended. Sometimes a crucial word (whose meaning the sender misunderstands) or an auto-correct changes the nature of the message unintentionally. StopCyberbullying Global calls this kind of digital abuse 'accidental cyberbullying' or 'accidental cyber-harassment.' It is an exception to the 'all cyber-harassment or cyberbullying must be intentional' rule (more details are provided later). In addition, some abuse occurs with the abuser masquerading as the real target, doing or saying something for which the target will be blamed. The only way to know what is meant or who is actually behind the screen is to communicate offline, face-to-face.
6. *Take Digital Threats Seriously:* The adage of 'sticks and stones' no longer applies. In this digital age, words online are equivalent to actions that can, in turn, motivate further actions and can have long-lasting ramifications. Any indications of threats to the target, their friends or family, their pets or their property should be taken seriously and reported to the authorities. Your safety begins with you and you have to be vigilant.

What Is Cyberbullying?

The short definition of cyberbullying is:

> When a minor uses technology as a weapon to intentionally target and hurt another minor, it's cyberbullying.

The long and more comprehensive definition of cyberbullying is:

> Any cyber-communication or publication posted or sent by a minor online, by instant message, e-mail, website, diary site, online profile, interactive game, handheld device, cellphone, game device, digital camera or video, webcam or use of any interactive digital device that is intended to frighten, embarrass, harass, hurt, set-up, cause harm to, extort, pose as or otherwise target another minor.

With one exception, all cyberbullying must be intentional. It requires that the cyberbully intends to do harm to or annoy its target. In the one exception to this rule, the student is careless and hurts another's feelings by accident. This is called 'inadvertent cyberbullying' or 'accidental cyberbullying,' because the target feels victimised, even if it is not the other student's intention. Since it often leads to retaliation, traditional cyberbullying, and cyber warfare, it is considered one of the five main types of cyberbullying, but addressed differently.

Cyberbullying needs to have minors on both sides, as targets, and as a cyberbully. If there aren't minors on both sides of the communication, it is considered 'cyber-harassment', not 'cyberbullying'. When a student harasses a teacher, it falls under cyber harassment.

How Prevalent Is It?

With our increased reliance on technology, incidences of cyberbullying are growing everywhere. StopCyberbullying.org visited schools around North America (primarily in the U.S.) and polled the students in each session. Over a year they polled approximately 45,000 students in middle school and early high school, as well as sixth-graders in some grammar schools. They listed the kinds of things that typically constitute cyberbullying (there are over 84 identified by students over the years) and asked the students to raise their hands if any of those things had happened to them in the last year.

They never had fewer than 85 per cent of the students admit that they had been targeted at least once in the last year. In an affluent county outside of New York City where most students have multiple devices with Internet connections, 97 per cent of the middle schoolers polled admitted to having been cyberbullied. And in one boarding school in Canada, 100 per cent of the students responded that they had been cyberbullied. (The 24/7 campus-life increases both the interactivity and harassment.)

In a school located in Bengaluru, in 2016, over 50 per cent of the girls out of an audience of 1,200 girls 13–15 year-olds admitted to having been cyberbullied at least once in the previous year. Shockingly, 8 of the girls said they had been sextorted or received blackmail related to a morphed image, where their face had been superimposed on an intimate image. This far out-distanced the number of sextortion or morphing victims from a similar group in North America.

When contrasted with their counterparts in the West, fewer Indian students said they would tell their parents if they were targeted by cyberbullying or other digital abuse than. The Indian students explained that their parents were very negative about any non-academic digital use and would be less supportive because of their general suspicions about all digital use. Western students of the same age said that they feared their parents would either over-react or under-appreciate any cyberbullying or fail to understand what it even meant.

In addition to the general reasons for not confiding in their parents about cyberbullying, their reasons for hiding it from their parents ranged from general embarrassment, fear of being blamed, not wanting to 'tattle', being afraid of retaliation and having their friends blamed unfairly.

Almost half of the Indian students, like their Western counterparts, have had their passwords guessed, stolen or their accounts accessed without their consent. About 20 per cent of Indian students polled and 40 per cent of Western students polled have either had their password stolen and changed by a cyberbully (locking them out of their account) or had communications sent to others posing as them. And these numbers are increasing, not improving, globally.

In the West, cyberbullying begins as early as second or third grade (7–8 years of age), depending on the age when mobile phones, virtual worlds, and internet use begin. It peaks in fourth grade and again in seventh and eighth grade (12–14 years). The US fourth graders' favourite form of cyberbullying is extortion. 'If you don't do . . ., I will . . .' Interestingly, expatriate populations and schools where expatriate students predominate in India report the same patterns and frequency of cyberbullying as their US, Canadian and UK counterparts. Government schools in India have a much lower percentage of cyberbullying incidents, largely because of the lack of digital accessibility and data accounts in their mobile phones. However post pandemic the susceptibility to cyberbullying increased. According to the research, 'Has the Covid-19 pandemic affected the susceptibility to cyberbullying in India', there was a noticeable increase in the factors affecting cyberbullying susceptibility during the Covid-19 pandemic as a result of an increase in social media and online gaming activity.[2]

I rely on face-to-face conversations and admissions of students globally to determine patterns and prevalence of cyberbullying. Academic surveys, sadly, often fail to disclose the true extent of cyberbullying for several reasons. Sometimes the researchers go through the parents or schools to reach the students and students want to hide the truth. Sometimes the researchers and the students have a problem agreeing on definitions. The definition-disconnect is a common problem. 'Cyberbullying' is often in the eye of the student beholder. What one thinks requires death threats to qualify as 'cyberbullying', another may think that calling someone a name will suffice. Parents think the use of lewd or inappropriate language is sufficient to constitute cyberbullying, while many students use those kinds of words online without reservation. That's why we highlight the research conducted by my expert young volunteers and my face-to-face polls.

In addition, comparing statistics across different cultures is a problem. Cultural and societal values and differences can take what might be considered an innocent remark in one community and make it a serious reputational disaster in another.

Cyber Harassment in Journalism

Cyber harassment has become rampant in the past few years. Journalists across the world are at the receiving end. A survey conducted by the editor of *Newquest Oxfordshire*, Samantha Harman, revealed that more than 80 per cent of the regional journalists felt the problem of online abuse has become significantly worse since they began their careers. The majority of the respondents said they encountered general abuse online every day with 40 per cent spending more than an hour each week reading and dealing with it. The most common platform according to the survey was Facebook with 89 per cent of respondents receiving abuse on this platform. For Twitter, it was 67 per cent. Some 80 per cent said they received abuse in the comments section of their websites.[3]

In a research conducted by United Nations Educational, Scientific and Cultural Organisation (UNESCO) and the International Centre for Journalists (ICFJ) 73 per cent of women journalists said they had experienced online violence in the courses of their work.

Online violence is the new frontline in journalism safety, and it is particularly dangerous for women. Just like elsewhere in the society, women experience higher levels of online harassment, assault and abuse in their daily lives. Women journalists are also at much greater risk in the course of their work, especially on digital platforms. In the online environment, we see exponential attacks – at scale – on women journalists, particularly at the intersection of hate speech and disinformation.[4]

In India, the Editor Guild of India, a forum established in 1978 with the twin objectives of protecting press freedom and raising the standards of editorial leadership of newspapers and magazines, in a statement in January 2021 condemned the online harassment and organised trolling of women journalists and demanded the government take urgent steps to dismantle such misogynistic and abusive digital ecosystem when the images of some women journalists and professionals were posted online, putting them 'up for auction'.[5]

Internet Trolling

Using the internet in destructive ways in a social setting with no apparent instrumental purpose are termed Internet Trolling. The purpose and intent of trolls, their psychology, and their process of creating chaos online is an important area of study keeping in view the drastic increase in the number of such cases the world over. A closer look at the trolls and their comments shows a pattern. From a person seeking attention by being disruptive to the one enjoying hurting others and displaying sadism to the one taking advantage of being anonymous online, internet trolls can be categorised in many ways.

Who Are Internet Trolls?

Internet trolls are the individuals on the web who connect to create chaos. According to Dr Claire Hardaker, an academic researcher, a troll is 'a computer user who constructs the identity of sincerely wishing to be part of the group in question . . . but whose real intention is to cause disruption and/or trigger conflict for their amusement.'

Dr Claire categorised the trolls into following according to their intent and the people or issues they target:

1. RIP trolls, who spend their time causing misery on memorial sites.
2. Fame trolls, who focus all their energies on provoking celebrities.
3. Care trolls, who purport to see abuse in every post about children or animals.
4. Political trolls, who seek to bully MPs out of office.

and many others.

Helen Lewis, in her article, 'Who Are the Trolls' published in *New Statesman* added two more categories:[6]

1. Subcultural trolls or 'true' trolls, who troll forums full of earnest people and derail their conversations with silly questions.
2. Professional trolls or 'trollumnists', who are writers and public figures whose media careers are built on their willingness to 'say the unsayable', or rather, they say something which will attract huge volumes of attention (albeit negative) and hits.

To this can be added one more category called 'anti women trolls' who draw more pleasure in harassing women, especially the women who are more vocal, particularly feminists. There has been an increase in the cases of stalking, hate speech, bullying and death threats against more vocal women. In fact, on some online forums anonymity combined with misogyny can make for an almost a gang rape-like mentality.

Reasons for Internet Trolling

US researcher Alice Marwick gives the following explanation for Internet Trolling:[7]

> There's the disturbing possibility that people are creating online environments purely to express the type of racist, homophobic, or sexist speech that is no longer acceptable in public society, at work, or even at home.

Anonymity, thus, is the biggest reason for Internet Trolling. This anonymity leads to online disinhibition which is one of the characteristics of Internet Trolling. According to the psychologist John Suller,[8] some people self-disclose or act out more frequently or intensely when they are online. He explored six factors that interact with each other in creating this online disinhibition effect – dissociative anonymity, invisibility, asynchronicity, solipsistic introjection, dissociative imagination and minimization of authority. Personality variables also will influence the extent of this disinhibition. Rather than thinking of disinhibition as the revealing of an underlying 'true self', we can conceptualise it as a shift to a constellation within the self-structure, involving clusters of effect and cognition that differ from the in-person constellation. All these factors described by Suller trigger Internet Trolling.

What Motivates Cyberbullying and Cyber Harassment?

When it comes to cyberbullying, people are often motivated by anger, revenge or frustration. Sometimes they do it for entertainment or because they are bored and have too much time on their hands and too many tech toys to play with. Many do it for laughs or to get a reaction. They may do it because they think it's fun or it will make them more popular. And a growing number do it to make a point to others, to improve their profile or their videos' page views and get attention for their '15 megabytes of fame'.

Summary

What we have covered in this chapter is only a sample of what journalists should understand about cyberbullying and digital attacks. Understanding what cyberbullying and internet trolling is, how it works and the devastating effects of it has on people is important for journalists to know. This trend is likely to increase as more of India is connected and data plans become still more affordable and wi-fi is more accessible. Adults need to understand more about how they are targeted by cyber-harassers, who are intent on destroying their reputations and personal lives. They also need to understand the motives of their harassers and ways to reduce the risk of cyber-harassment abuse. Arming journalists with information and the facts about how digital abuse works, how it is perpetuated and wife how it can move into Real Life and back into cyberspace will help create a more digitally-aware and cyber-safe population.

Questions

1. What is the difference between cyberbullying and cyber harassment?
2. Have a look at the Twitter handles of some female journalists and see how they are trolled. Discuss the reasons why are they being trolled.
3. What is online disinhibition? Discuss the factors that lead to online disinhibition.

Tips and Tricks

Disengage: DO NOT respond to the trolls

Protect your accounts

Turn on two-factor authentication for all your accounts

Check if your email or phone number is in a data breach at https://haveibeenpwned.com/

Create long passwords with a mix of numbers, symbols and letters

Do not use the same password for all your accounts

Explore More

Digital Safety Kit: https://cpj.org/2019/07/digital-safety-kit-journalists/.

Cyber Security Training for Journalists: https://europeanjournalists.org/blog/2015/01/22/cyber-security-training-for-journalists/.

https://ideas.ted.com/smart-ways-to-handle-snark-and-trolls-on-social-media/.

https://www.journalismfestival.com/programme/2017/managing-gendered-online-harrassment.

References

'Adult Cyber-Harassment and Cyberstalking', *Wiredsafety*, https://www.wiredsafety.com/adult-cyber-harassment-and-cyberstalking.

Affairs (ASPA), A. S. for P. (2019a, September 24), *Bystanders to Bullying* [Text], StopBullying.Gov, https://www.stopbullying.gov/prevention/bystanders-to-bullying.

Affairs (ASPA), A. S. for P. (2019b, September 24), *What Is Cyberbullying* [Text], StopBullying.Gov, https://www.stopbullying.gov/cyberbullying/what-is-it.

Claire, 'The anti-social network: Tracking the trolls', *Dr Claire Hardaker, 1 May 2015,* https://wp.lancs.ac.uk/drclaireh/2015/05/01/the-anti-social-network-tracking-the-trolls/.

S. Jagtar, K. Paulette, H. Esther and A. of Civilizations, *Media and Information Literacy: Reinforcing Human Rights, Countering Radicalization and Extremism (The MILID Yearbook, 2016),* UNESCO Publishing.

'Psychology of Cyberspace: The Online Disinhibition Effect', truecenterpublishing, https://truecenterpublishing.com/psycyber/disinhibit.html.

Notes

1. 'NWMI Demands That Social Media Platforms Stop Enabling Intimidation, Harassment, Misinformation and Violence', *NWMI*, 4 February 2022, https://nwmindia.org/statements/nwmi-demands-that-social-media-platforms-stop-enabling-intimidation-harassment-misinformation-and-violence/.
2. Ojasvi Jain, Muskan Gupta, Sidh Satam, and Sibal Panda, Has the COVID-19 Pandemic Affected the Susceptibility to Cyberbullying in India?' *Computers in Human Behavior Reports*, 2, 100029, August–November 2020, https://doi.org/10.1016/j.chbr.2020.100029.
3. 'Revealed: The Onslaught of Online Abuse and the Toll on Regional Journalists', *Society for Editors*, 28 September 2020, https://www.societyofeditors.org/soe_news/revealed-the-onslaught-of-online-abuse-and-the-toll-on-regional-journalists/.
4. Julie Posetti, Nermine Aboulez, Kalina Bontcheva, Jackie Harrison and Silvio Waisbord, *Online Violence against Women Journalists: A Global Snapshot of Incidence and Impacts, United Nations Educational, Scientific and Cultural Organisation*, 2020, https://unesdoc.unesco.org/ark:/48223/pf0000375136.
5. Editors Guild of India, https://editorsguild.in/; 'Global Research Project Investigates Violence against Women Journalists', *International Women's Media Foundation*, 2 December 2013, https://www.iwmf.org/2013/12/global-research-project-investigates-violence-against-women-journalists/.
6. Helen Lewis, 'Who Are the Trolls?' *New Statesman*, 29 July 2013, https://www.newstatesman.com/science-tech/2013/07/who-are-trolls.
7. Helen Lewis, 'Who Are the Trolls?'
8. Mary Ann Liebert, 'Cyberpsychology & Behavior: The Impact of the Internet, Multimedia and Virtual Reality on Behavior and Society', *Researchgate*, https://www.researchgate.net/journal/Cyberpsychology-behavior-the-impact-of-the-Internet-multimedia-and-virtual-reality-on-behavior-and-society-1557-8364.

Chapter 7

Mobile Journalism: The Power of Communications Technology

Himanshu Shekhar

Mobile journalism is not just an emerging form of media with the use of decentralized newsrooms. MOJO is now established and indispensable.

–School of Journalism, UK

Introduction

It was a wintry morning sometime in February 2017 when I was handed over an Apple iPhone 6s mobile phone with a 12-megapixel camera, two new sim cards, a hotspot, a tripod, a lapel microphone and a few transfer cables, connectors and adapters and told to leave for Uttar Pradesh. The official assignment was to shoot a series of special ground reports on the election campaign during the assembly elections in India's biggest and politically most important state. I had to criss-cross several districts in central Uttar Pradesh, shoot special stories in both urban and rural assembly constituencies and transfer the story feed to our Delhi office daily through the mobile apps on my iPhone. I had just a day to learn how to professionally shoot with an iPhone 6s, check the compatibility of the other equipment with it, learn how to safely store the footage, and install and learn to use the mobile apps through which the video footage was to be edited and sent to NDTV's Delhi office.

As a TV news journalist groomed in the conventional environment for seventeen years, this appeared to be the toughest assignment of my professional career in broadcast journalism. The prospect of travelling alone on an official assignment and managing all the logistics of election coverage seemed daunting. I set out with loads of questions in my mind about the feasibility of professionally shooting with a mobile phone instead of the usual camera I was used to. The coverage plan included shooting in rural areas, especially backward villages where internet and mobile connectivity, at times, would be a logistical challenge.

As I grappled with the hundreds of apps on my mobile phone, I was nervous at the prospect of working without any assistance or professional help. It reminded me of my visit to Uttar Pradesh during the 2004 general elections as a young TV news reporter. That was thirteen years earlier, when I had travelled there with two Outside Broadcast (OB) Vans for a live broadcast of important political rallies and special election programmes. During those days, every OB Van had a crew of four professionals – a broadcast engineer, a cameraperson, a camera assistant and a driver. In addition, I had a separate cameraperson with me for shooting special stories and interviews. So, I had the privilege to travel with a team of nine professionals. Now thirteen years later, in 2017, the change was remarkable. I was a one-person team. The nine professionals were all gone. The advancements in the internet and communication technology had completely transformed my professional world. I was in the world of MOJO – mobile journalism.

Reporter as a Cameraperson

As I began shooting with my mobile phone, it marked the beginning of my new journey as a TV news journalist. The first few days of MOJO were marked with apprehension and fear – Was I shooting in the right camera mode? Was my camera angle and frame in the right place? What was the quality of the footage I was recording? Was there adequate light in my shoot frame? Was the audio of the soundbites I was recording up to the mark? How feasible would it be to send a twenty-minute news feed to the Delhi office? What if the MOJO experiment failed? After every day of shooting in the field, I chose to spend a couple of hours assessing the quality of the camera footage I had shot with my iPhone 6s.

With every day, my degree of confidence increased. The first experiment with MOJO turned out to be a great learning experience. The introduction to the new world of MOJO seemed exciting yet challenging at the same time. I realised it needed an important structural change in my approach to work. Apart from reporting, I needed to develop the imagination of a camera person too. I had to start thinking about the story pictorially, and plan my frames and camera angles accordingly while shooting a news story. This was an additional skill I needed to develop as a TV news professional.

In the new world of MOJO, apart from the editorial content, the reporter is responsible for shooting the primary video footage, fix the interview frame, ensure good audio quality and manage the entire process of transferring the story feed to the news headquarters. In a way, it allows reporters to shoot a story according to the planned script. It brings them much closer to the news story. The goalposts of success have changed too – the degree of success a reporter can achieve in the world of MOJO is entirely dependent on how well he or she can learn the art of shooting with a mobile phone camera. MOJO has transformed the entire newsgathering process conventionally associated with TV News Media. The reporter has to work on inventory management, too. Once the shoot is over for the day, the reporter has to charge both the mobile phone and the power backup systems, test the quality of the video footage shot during the day and ensure that all the MOJO equipment is ready for the next day's shoot.

MOJO makes it easy to access and disseminate news and video content. New mobile technologies have played an enabling role in this structural shift in the world of broadcast journalism. Importantly, as I took my first steps in MOJO, local journalists working in faraway districts were of immense help in the initial days. Some of them had already experimented with MOJO and had a lot of practical information and exposure to the world of mobile apps.

As I experimented with different options to send video feed from different districts, it exposed me to the advancements in internet and communication technologies which were gradually transforming the world of broadcast journalism. In the new world of MOJO, it was equally important for a reporter to acquire knowledge about communication technologies, which was hitherto the domain of OB Van engineers and the technical team which accompanied the news team in the field. The degree to which a reporter can professionally use mobile technologies depends on the level of adaptability, that is, the extent to which the reporter is willing to learn the power of smartphones and adopt the new developments in mobile and communication technologies. With requisite training, a mobile journalist can work on all aspects of news production in the field – from newsgathering to shooting to video editing and uploading the feed on the news server.

Breakdown of Technological Barriers

MOJO has redefined the way television news journalists work. It has given reporters autonomy to shoot but also increased their accountability and responsibility in the news gathering process. They are free to use portable devices like smartphones, digital cameras and tablets for newsgathering purposes and broadcast news directly from the scene of action. Smartphones have removed the technological barriers that existed between the reporter and the consumers of news. The continuous advancements in mobile and communication technologies are giving a fillip to this transformational change in the world of broadcast journalism.

All this is also gradually changing the broad structure of news organisations as they take the next step in adapting to this larger change which is redefining the contours of broadcast journalism. Reporters now have a more direct interface with the news production team in the office. They shoot and directly transfer the story feed to the office. The story is then downloaded by producers for final editing and production work. This has reduced the role of engineers and technical teams in transmitting the story feed to the office. This has helped news organisations significantly reduce their cost of operations and cut costs on inventory management and workforce.

Mobile journalism is not just about creating videos using smartphones. It is much beyond that. Of course, the main device for mobile journalism remains the smartphone with its feature of internet connectivity, but it is not just about using it for videoing stories. It is about using it for research and for developing stories in a variety of formats like infographics, audio, video and live broadcast with 360-degree coverage. It is also about the distribution of stories with mobile messaging applications like WhatsApp, Facebook, Telegram, Instagram and so on. It is also about interacting and engaging with the audience.

Mobile Journalism is a form of digital storytelling where the primary device used for creating and editing images, audio and video is a smartphone. In a fully MOJO newsroom, this can break down the silos between different departments such as the social media desk and the video production desk.[1]

Roots of MOJO

In terms of the scale of change and impact brought in by Mobile Journalism, it is similar to the advent of Leica 1 camera designed in 1913 by Oskar Barnack which revolutionised the twentieth century photojournalism.[2] It allowed, for the first time, a cameraperson to shoot out of their studios. Camera professionals began to shoot outdoors and captured moments as and when they happened. The new developments in internet technologies expedited the advent of mobile journalism at the global level.

The first recorded instance of MOJO dates back to February 2004 when a corporate executive working for a mobile phone company clicked a photo that was published on the front page of the *New York Times*. As author Stephen Quinn wrote in his book titled 'MOJO – Mobile Journalism in the Asian Region':

> On 17th February 2004, *The New York Times* published, for the first time on page one, a photograph taken with a mobile phone. It was an image grabbed at the formal signing of the merger between two mobile phone giants, Cingular and AT&T Wireless in New York the previous day. Joseph McCabe Jr., AT&T's Chief Financial Officer, snapped Cingular Chief Executive Officer, John Zeglis signing the document. The photograph was pretty ordinary. But it marked a milestone in the use of the mobile phone for newsgathering.[3]

Quinn went on to say that the first recorded incident of MOJO in Television News happened more than five years later in New Mexico. He wrote:

> Five and a half years after the still image taken with a mobile phone appeared on the front page of The New York Times, television reporter Jeremy Jojola filed a live report using only a mobile phone and free web-based software called Qik. On 20th August 2009, Jojola used an I Phone and Qik Software . . . to cover a story for KOB-TV in Albuquerque, New Mexico.[4]

The first phone equipped with a built-in camera was PHS VP-210.[5] Launched by the Japanese company Kyocera in July 1999, it marked a watershed development in mobile technology. It became a precursor of MOJO in many ways. The gradual advancement of mobile technologies has created space for mobile journalism, which in turn is reshaping the broad contours of the Television News industry. Convergence of technologies, advancement in mobile technologies, and new developments in broadcast and wireless telephone technologies have created a conducive environment for the emergence of Mobile Journalism. The world's first fully commercial third-generation (3G) mobile phone network was launched in Tokyo in October 2001 by Japanese NTT DoCoMo.[6] Wireless connections allowed mobile phone users to send and receive videos. Almost a decade later, Nokia and Reuters launched perhaps the first experiment in MOJO in the world involving a leading multinational mobile company and a global news agency. A small group of reporters was given Nokia N95 Smartphone, a tripod, and a few other equipment. They covered the New York Fashion Week, the Edinburgh TV Festival and Olympic Games in Beijing. This experiment sparked interest in MOJO and played a signal role in popularizing this idea at the global level.[7]

The convergence of mobile and communication technologies has enabled international news networks to create their apps to streamline the MOJO operations. BBC has developed its app known as Portable News Gathering (PNG). It is designed to help reporters in recording, editing and sending videos and photos to BBC's news production rooms.[8]

Incognito Reporting

MOJO provides greater accessibility to a reporter in a given news zone to a news object. Unobtrusively, a reporter can go closer to the subject of his or her news without being noticed. This enables them to work with anonymity if they so desire. In certain emergencies, it would allow the Reporter to work incognito, move easily in a crowd or a disturbed zone as a commoner, recording stealthily the subjects of their story. MOJO enables the reporter to avoid public glare and shoot stories and record developments with stealth.

MOJO and Social Media

Mobile Journalism has completely transformed the way journalists interact and communicate with the world. It has made the news dissemination processes faster as reporters increasingly share news and information on both conventional and social media news platforms with hundreds of millions of customers. Technological advancements and increasing competition in the telecom sector are making smartphones cheaper and better, the cost of data transmission is going down and it is becoming easier to access and transmit information through mobile platforms.

The rise of MOJO has accompanied the phenomenal increase in use of social media platforms. This helps journalists create both news and video content at short notice and share them on social media platforms like Twitter, Facebook, YouTube and so on, apart from TV, radio and online websites. MOJO is a valuable aid in helping journalist share live video and content about a developing breaking news story on both conventional and social media platforms. Anthony Adomato has described this new world in his book *Mobile and Social Media Journalism: A Practical Guide*. He writes:

> When covering news in real-time, there are three tools you should consider: A combination of live-tweeting, live streaming and live blogging can keep the audience informed during breaking news and other types of ongoing news events...Streaming video through Facebook Live or Periscope can bring people to the screen in ways other social media posts can't.[9]

MOJO: Challenges and Limitations

The first big challenge I faced while shooting with iPhone 6s in Uttar Pradesh was in recording the sound bites. The Talkback cable I initially used for recording the sound bites of news subjects turned out to be ineffectual, especially in open market spaces or along the highways where the natural background sound level was high and the recording absorbed a lot of ambient sounds, too. Shooting indoors in a controlled environment was relatively easier but recording in the open, crowded space proved to be difficult. We soon found a way to address this issue. Our engineering department gave me a gun mike which was formatted for use with a mobile phone and had a heavy windshield to keep the ambient noise out.

Covering big political rallies was the other big challenge as iPhone 6s had a limited optical zoom facility. Security agencies and organisers often asked reporters to stand far away from the main dais when high-profile political leaders came to address election rallies. It was also difficult to shoot late in the evening or at night as the quality of the recorded footage was not of a good quality. There were also concerns about the safety of the tripods and other MOJO equipment while shooting in crowded places. A conventional news team has at least two members – a reporter and a cameraperson – who helped each other in keeping an eye on the camera equipment. But shooting alone in political rallies attended by tens of thousands of people was problematic as I had to be attentive on several fronts – listening and taking notes of the speech made by political leaders, constantly checking the quality of the audio and video recording on the mobile phone, keeping an eye on the battery and ensuring the safety of the MOJO equipment. I realised that using a normal tripod in heavily crowded places like an election rally or a political roadshow, where a reporter had to constantly move with the subject he or she was covering, was a difficult task.

In fact, during crises, MOJO works both as an opportunity and a challenge. It allows the reporter to start broadcasting live from ground zero and transmit feed and audio content to news networks at short notice. But it can also become a handicap in circumstances where the mobile connectivity is exceptionally poor or has collapsed, for example, during a natural disaster. In a disaster-hit zone, if the mobile communication towers have collapsed, it significantly impairs the ability of reporters to work on the

MOJO platform. The mobile internet connectivity would be lost for days and it would be impossible to transmit any information to the newsroom. Excessive exposure to heat, especially during outdoor shoots in peak summer, can also badly affect the ability of smartphones to function for long hours. Some hi-tech smartphones are even designed to stop functioning once the handset gets heated beyond a specified temperature. In such situations, reporters have no option but to wait for the handset to cool down, which slows down the pace of work in the field.

MOJO: The Road Ahead

Smartphones are among the fastest-selling gadgets in the world. According to the Gartener Inc Smartphone sales grew six percent in 2021.[10]

While the sales were low during the Covid-19 pandemic because of component shortages and supply chain issues, the time spent mobile increased significantly. According to an App Annie (renamed as data.ai) report titled 'State of Mobile 2022', people spent a whopping 3.8 trillion hours on mobile phones in 2021. In the top 10 mobile markets globally, users spent 4.8 hours a day on mobiles. Led by TikTok (which witnessed an increase of 90 per cent globally outside of China), 7 of every 10 minutes was spent on either social, photo and/or video apps.[11]

According to InMobi's 'State of Programmatic Mobile Video Advertising in India' report, there are 356 million mobile video viewers in India and videos have emerged as the most preferred form of content over the last few years on the wave of an unprecedented global growth in video consumption.[12]

As smartphones reach more and more people, and people increasingly use smartphones to access internet services, the demand for online news services is expected to increase accordingly. This creates greater opportunity for MOJO, especially in India which has the second-highest number of smartphone users in the world, after China.

In many ways, MOJO has increased the dependency of media institutions on mobile and telecom Companies. The ease with which reporters can work on smartphones and transmit story feed to newsrooms depends largely on the new research in mobile and communication technologies. At the same time, the significant increase in video sharing and the growing importance of video-sharing platforms like YouTube have made it imperative for media institutions to create their footprints on them and cater to the growing demands of the new consumers of news. As the video traffic continues to grow at breathtaking speed, it will create more and more space for MOJO in the coming years.

Tips and Tools

Tips

- Mobile Journalism is not just video recording using smartphones. It is about using mobile phones for the creating content in a wide variety of forms, interacting and engaging with the audience in a more meaningful way.

- Deliver content to the audience where they are searching – they usually search on mobile phones.
- Journalists need to develop skills on how to create content for small screens.

Tools

Camera Apps: FimicPro, Camera+

Editing Apps: Kinemaster (iOS and Android), Luma Fission (iOS), I Movie (iPhone) Inshot (Android), FimoraGo (Android).

Questions

1. What is Mobile Journalism or MOJO?
2. What are the implications for newsrooms of shifting to MOJO?
3. Discuss the challenges and limitations of Mobile Journalism.
4. Discuss the advantages of Mobile Journalism.

Explore More

Mobile Journalism Guide: https://gijn.org/mobile-journalism-guide-how-to-get-your-mojo-workin/.

Stories of MOJO Challenge Winners: https://www.thomsonfoundation.org/latest/mojo-challenge-when-a-smartphone-wins-in-covid-19-coverage/.

Mobile and Social Media Journalism: http://mobileandsocialmediajournalism.com/resources/.

Top Tips to Help You Master Mobile Journalism: https://presspad.co.uk/top-tips-to-help-you-master-mobile-journalism/.

References

1. Rasmus Kleis Nielsen, Alessio Cornia and Antonis Kalogeropoulos, 'Challenges and Opportunities for News Media and Journalism in an Increasingly Digital, Mobile, and Social Media Environment', *Reuters Institute for the Study of Journalism, October 2016.*
2. Rima Marrouch, 'How Mobile Phones Are Changing Journalism Practice in the 21st Century', *Reuters Institute for the Study of Journalism,* 4 March 2014.
3. David Cameron, 'Mobile Journalism: A Snapshot of Current Research and Practice', *Charles Sturt University,* January 2008.
4. Gregory Perreault and Kellie Stanfield, 'Mobile Journalism as Lifestyle Journalism?' 16 January 2018.
5. Marc Settle, 'How to Get Started in Mobile Journalism, 12 Things You Need for Going Mojo'.

6. Anja Kroll and Nic Newman, 'How Journalism Faces a Second Wave of Disruption from Technology and Changing Audience Behaviour', 23 October 2015.
7. 'Mobile Journalism', Aljazeera Media Training and Development Centre.
8. Sajid Umair, 'Mobile Reporting and Journalism for Media Trends, News Transmission and Its Authenticity', *Journal of Mass Communication and Journalism,* 21 December 2016.
9. A. David A. and L. Levy 'A Case Study in Updating PSB in Politically Polarised and Cash-Strapped Times', June 2017.
10. Caroline Scott, '|Mobile Journalism Helps Reporters Get Closer to the Story, New Reuters Institute Research Finds', 17 July 2017.

Notes

1. 'The Mobile Journalism Manual', https://www.mojo-manual.org/.
2. '3 Stories for Better Understanding Mobile Journalism', *Shoulderpod*, https://www.shoulderpod.com/mobile-journalism.
3. Stephen Quinn, *Mobile Journalism in the Asian Region* (Singapore: Konrad-Adenauer-Stiftung, 2009), p. 7, https://www.readkong.com/page/mojo-mobile-journalism-in-the-asian-region-8308217.
4. Stephen Quinn, 'MOJO – Mobile Journalism in the Asian Region', p. 7.
5. Panu Karhunen, 'Closer to the Story: Accessibility and Mobile Journalism', *Reuters Institute for the Study of Journalism*, July 2017, p. 14, https://reutersinstitute.politics.ox.ac.uk/sites/default/files/2017-09/Karhunen%2C%20Accessibility%20and%20Mobile%20Journalism.pdf.
6. Marina Kamimura, 'Japan Launches World's First 3G Services', *CNN*, 30 May 2001, http://edition.cnn.com/2001/BUSINESS/asia/05/30/hk.japan.3g/index.html.
7. Panu Karhunen, 'Closer to the Story', p. 15.
8. 'Learn from the BBC: The Newsroom in Their Pocket', *shoulderpod*, p. 9, http://www.shoulderpod.com/mobile-journalism/.
9. Anthony Adornato, *Mobile and Social Media Journalism: A Practical Guide*, (California: CQ/Sage, 2017), p. 100, https://in.sagepub.com/sites/default/files/upm-binaries/83042_Chapter_5.pdf.
10. Manasi Sakpal, 'Gartner Says Global Smartphone Sales Grew 6% in 2021' *Gartner*, 2 March 2022, https://www.gartner.com/en/newsroom/press-releases/2022-03-01-4q21-smartphone-market-share.
11. 'The State of Mobile 2021', *data.ai*, https://www.data.ai/en/go/state-of-mobile-2021/.
12. Inmobi Press Center, https://www.inmobi.com/company/press/programmatic-mobile-video-ads-see-.194-percent-growth-in-india.

Chapter 8

Strengthening Journalism Using Artificial Intelligence

Rohit Gandhi

Artificial Intelligence (AI) can create a human-centered society that balances technological advancement, economic advancement, and spiritual advancement.

–Amit Ray

Introduction

Similar to most professions in the information space, the life of journalists has been changing at a phenomenal pace, often making it difficult to keep track of new developments. For a long time, our predecessors tried to hold on to the age-old practices, fighting tooth and nail to stay relevant – after all, journalists are, if nothing else, passionate and stubborn in their craft. However, after that decade of the disastrous intra-newsroom wars, today there's a consensus about keeping abreast of changes, rather than trying to resist them.

The picture from the past, of a journalist with a typewriter, will always stay embedded in our heads. In those days, hard-hitting legendary editors and reporters, whose one piece could bring down governments, were revered. They were the lords of their beats, yet answerable to the desk that could rip their story to pieces. With time and the advancement of technology, these roles changed, affecting the office dynamics. The newsroom culture became vastly different, with greater exposure to global media. As a person, the journalist needs to be multi-skilled and aware of the latest developments within the industry. The more up-to-date the journalist, the more impact his or her news has and, therefore, the more relevant their work. It is necessary to embrace these changes as frequently as they occur because, like the world around us, news and information is transforming at an extremely frenetic pace.

What Is Artificial Intelligence?

The crux of AI is to develop computer systems that can perform tasks usually performed by human beings. The program mimics human cognitive functions like learning and problem-solving. Whether it be answering direct questions or smarter systems that map users' habits, AI, though constantly evolving, has far-reaching effects.

AI is being integrated not only into our professions but also into our everyday lives as well. Take, for instance, our commonplace interactions with Siri or Alexa, scheduling our calendar, or even Google maps. Like them, there are far more complex systems that were originally coded by humans, their algorithms change as the system learns about new situations and updates itself.

When integrated into a newsroom, apart from the pros-and-cons debate of AI, there is an added dimension of ethical journalism. AI can be used to maps a user's online behaviour – links clicked, time spent and so on – and customise the newsfeed accordingly so that the user returns spends a longer time on the website. This means that the focus will shift from editorial to engagement in order to generate income. Another crucial point is about AI generating news by collating data. In such cases does a journalist disclose the source of the news as a certain company or app, or is it not necessary?

How Is AI Integrated in Newsrooms Across the World?

AI is used in newsrooms across the world in diverse ways – whether it is in natural language processing or collating data – to gather, generate, process and distribute content.

The *New York Times* used machine learning to make its archive of recipes and create the NYT Cooking app and used automation to digitally archive its photo collection.

In China, the app Toutiao makes use of computer algorithms to recommend interesting and important articles to readers. Newsfeeds are updated based on the reader's preferences, time spent on an article and location.

In the UK, a service called JAMES (Journey Automated Messaging for Higher Engagement through Self-Learning) is used by the Times and Sunday Times which will help learn about individual preferences and automatically personalise each edition in terms of format, time and frequency.

The Swiss newspaper *Neue Zürcher Zeitung* (NZZ) developed AI algorithms that are not optimized for clicks but to uphold journalistic standards.

Reuters in 2020 announced that it had used AI to enhance its entire video archive consisting of nearly one million clips dating back to 1896. This initiative was funded by the Google Digital News Innovation Fund. Reuters Connect helps publishers access all Reuters content on a single platform (Reuters Connect). According to Michael Friedenberg, president of Reuters, AI powers the news ecosystem.[1]

Full-Fact has developed AI tools to support fact-checking. It can detect and classify different types of claims. For example it produces a list of every claim found in each manifesto with labels showing what type of claim it is, for example, a quantitative claim, a prediction about the future etc. Fact-checkers then uses this list to organise their analysis of each manifesto.[2]

The journalism AI project of Polis, the journalism think-tank of the London School of Economics (LSE) has collated several case studies on how AI has been integrated in the newsrooms across the world.[3] All the case studies can be accessed here:

https://www.lse.ac.uk/media-andcommunications/polis/JournalismAI/Case-studies

In 2021, the Knight Foundation announced 3 million dollars to help local news organisations harness the power of AI. They analysed 130 projects to understand how newsrooms were using AI. According to the survey, almost half of the projects used AI for augmenting reporting capacity, which includes combing through large databases, social media analysis and scraping websites for some specific information. Other use-cases of AI in newsrooms were:

- *Reducing variable costs:* Tools that automate the process of transcription, tagging of images and video, and story generation
- *Optimising revenues:* This includes dynamic paywalls, recommendation engines, digitisation of the news organisation's archives and so on.
- *Engagement:* Sorting audience's questions and comments into manageable buckets.
- *Self Critique:* This includes work like fostering gender and racial balance in stories.
- *News reporting:* This refers to the situation where the result is the story for example election results.
- *Video editing:* We have all done video editing for years and we have numerous ways of cutting each story. Each time we decide how we will innovatively tell a story, it may change the story somewhat, and that is where our editorial judgment lies. We don't do innovation for its own sake. We do it because the story demands a unique way of storytelling. But many of the tasks are repetitive, such as understanding background sound, laying the video and so on. These are things a machine can do and it does not require human intervention each time they are done. The AI platform can learn from our review process as we make changes when we review the editing that the AI platform has done. At Democracy News Live we have been working on building videos using an AI platform and working on how to make them intelligent over a period of time. You have to start its journey by teaching the AI platform a few tasks and then it keeps getting better at what it does.

Journalism From the Ground: How Can AI Add Value to News Generation?

The cornerstone of journalism is great storytelling and ground reportage. Only with original on-ground stories can a journalist make a difference in his or her profession and society.

I remember that we were in Afghanistan in 2001 on the frontline, between the Northern Alliance and the Taliban. Northern Alliance was the force headed by Commander Ahmad Shah Massoud who fought the Russians first and then the Taliban later, for decades, successfully blocking the Taliban ingress into the North where the majority of the population was of Tajiks. The Taliban primarily consisted of Pashtuns. After months of stand-off and both sides eyeballing each other, the battle was finally unfolding. We were standing right outside Kunduz, the last remaining stronghold of the Taliban in Northern Afghanistan. At that time, at the place where we were stationed, two big mountains protected us from the direct line of fire of the Taliban. This mountain on both sides opened into a large valley controlled on each side by the Taliban and the Northern Alliance.

A few days before this, the US B-52 bombers started making sorties and aided by CIA's laser guidance on the ground, started targeted bombardment. Many of the Taliban positions were in the heart of the city, right inside the civilian population areas. This offered Taliban protection from the US bombers and gave sleepless nights to people who had to bomb these positions.

Now, the battle started enfolding. The troops began to march towards Kunduz. We were in a dangerous place. My trusted colleague and then my manager Satinder Bindra was with me. We discussed whether to stay on the frontline overnight or not. We decided to move back to safety at night to Taloqan. We moved away from the area of action on a promise from our source in the Northern Alliance that in the morning we would be given access to Kunduz if all looked safe.

The next morning at 11 a.m. we went live from Kunduz. That day, we were live on air continuously for almost four hours as history was unfolding in front of our eyes. This was the last stronghold of the Taliban in the North.

Amid such high adrenaline, dangerous and intense reporting, how can artificial intelligence help a reporter? It can't take over this story from the ground. But what it can do is something very different. While being reporters on the field we recognise the story that is unfolding in front of us, but at the same time we are far removed from the whole world. We don't know what answers people are seeking. The anchors from the studios are sometimes that voice.

In good journalistic networks, the anchor is usually a seasoned reporter who has travelled in these places for decades and is now back at the base, managing the coverage. He or she will know what to ask. But that may not always be possible. And here artificial intelligence can play the role in keeping the reporter ahead. It can be a tool informing the reporter about the narratives of the reportage circulating globally, what aspect of the story people have shown interest in, what is happening in the other areas of the war and so on. This perspective can be a boon to the reporter on the ground, cut off from the rest.

AI Helps Journalists Pre-empt the Answers to Questions

You may be the biggest icon in the industry but you will still have to continue to turn your attention to the story that is being told from places that may be difficult to access.

So when I hear things like machines will take over the writing, I know for a fact that it is not possible. I am personally aware of this because I have been working on an AI tool with a team of engineers as a part of my company's foray into making sure that journalists don't waste time when they are on the field to research and put context to their stories.

One of the biggest challenges of journalists on the field is contextualizing the stories, so teams sitting in a newsroom, even though may have more access to resources, will sometimes miss the big story because they weren't seeing what the reporter was seeing on the ground.

But AI helps fill that gap. It helps both the newsroom managers and reporters on the ground. AI takes a story and its context and takes references of other articles on the subject, and analyses what is missing in the story. Millions who search for the story or anything related to it leave a trace on the web, indicating what people are seeking. This information, on who is searching what, or rather the demographics of a search topic, changes every few minutes. There will be angles and elements, points-of-view and updates on facts that will continue to get added, and that helps us tell a far more wholesome and enriched story.

Data and Competition Mapping

With news coming in every second, it is very difficult to track and report on everything. However, having that data is crucial in bolstering our reportage, and a good reporter can spot the elemental story from the thousands of alerts coming in. Often what we miss will be reported by our competitors, hence it is important to keep a track of their output as well. Healthy competition leads to varied coverage and unearthing of information that we would have otherwise overlooked. Each story has different aspects and everyone digs up an angle to represent it the best, adding perspective and information to the pool.

There will always be stories that we may be looking for but can't get to fast enough. For example, let us consider reporting on riots in a city – we may be covering the story in one part of the city, while in another part there is something else enfolding with the potential to become the main news. We must always stay alert about these stories.

From the Ground

An instance of this was when I was in Sri Lanka in 2004 covering the tsunami. The devastation was so brutal that we had stories of tens of thousands who lost their loved ones, children being the worst hit. One morning, we saw a newswire cross that described the story of a child who was being claimed by seven parents. The child was named Baby 81, named as per the serial number of babies being brought to the hospital. The child had survived miraculously and was found floating in the sea on an old, discarded tyre.

I remember the day like it was yesterday. We were at President Chandrika Kumaratunga's house that evening for an interview. On realising that she was flying in a helicopter close to where this child was, we requested her for a ride. She dropped two members of her team as the helicopter could carry only so many people.

This solitary incident aligned with the stories of parents looking for their children that I was working on. To have personally encountered the loss and destruction after the tsunami, the heart-breaking incident about Baby 81 brings tears to my eyes even today as I write about it.

We told this story and it brought widespread global attention to the issue of lost children in the tsunami. It highlighted the need to provide psychological help to parents in the aftermath of such a huge disaster. It also resulted in DNA testing of parents to match the rescued children's. This is an example of how data and competition mapping can help align stories of interest with the welfare of the people.

AI is capable of helping competition mapping on the fly. It can help focus your attention on the stories that need to be looked at in your dashboard. The most precious thing for you as a reporter on the field is time because you have to react almost immediately, without prepping, to any information that comes in. As newsrooms become global, with easier access to information over the internet, and as the world shrinks, a journalist has to be tapped into this information flow to be able to do his or her job effectively.

AI fulfils that requirement. It is your assistant on the go who helps you focus your time on storytelling. As the area of coverage expands, AI will help you focus on geo-tagged content around you so that you can spot the stories from your neighbourhood and physically interact with them.

Tackling SEO as an Editorial Skill

There was a time in digital news storytelling when the writer would write a story and put an image. Post this, the digital team would take over the story and optimise its tags so that the story was found easily when searched on the web. There may be tens and thousands of stories written on the subject of your interest and in the middle of all this, your story can get lost in the internet universe.

If you want your story and your website to reflect as the topmost result on the internet, then you need to have the right keywords in the text of your story. In the world of AI, we call them 'entities'.

It is important to understand that the keywords are not just words splattered on your tags but a comprehensive part of your story, whether in text or video. Technology is running ahead faster than we think; the search engines can hear the spoken word in your video stories and written text on your screen. They can decipher the information to match the search criteria of people looking for content on the internet.

So get past the old way of doing search engine optimisation SEO. Each editor and writer must have access to tools that can do SEO on the story while it is being written rather than when it is finished. The editor and writer can then use the tools and fill these gaps and thus produces more comprehensive content. AI tools and software can provide you with this capability, making your work faster and easier. Keyword planner and Google trends can help you spot the important words or phrases that are being used by users in their search or in the stories they are reading, but an AI-based content generating system should have these keywords already integrated into the copy.

Opinion on Social Media

The most contentious topic is the relevance of social media in gathering and spreading of information. Tonnes of information is constantly shared on social media. Some relevant information is also shared around the story that you intend to write. Access to this content can uplift your story and add a layer to it. We cannot be at the epicentre of all, watching all the tweets that are flying around. Here, technology can come to our rescue. AI tools are capable of finding posts around your area of interest. It can further find those posts where audiences are constantly engaging, for example, Trendsmap.[4]

Let's be clear that I'm not saying at all that social media should drive your content. But it can add to your story to make it more engaging. Your story is what you have dug up from ground reporting, but social media reactions can, in many ways, add another point-of-view for layered storytelling. Social media may not always be reliable, but with journalistic rigour, we can identify authentic social media posts that help to shed greater light on your story. The ability to use them integrally in your stories helps generate better engagement with your audience. So much so that it has become an essential part of storytelling. This can help integrate the viewpoints of your audience in your story, their hopes and beliefs, and at times can it also pan out to become valuable leads to it.

Hence, it is extremely crucial to verify the source of social media-driven news and information flow. Quoting without cross-checking is irresponsible and faulty, often having a negative impact on the news itself. The world over, media agencies are facing the challenge of fake news over the internet and to counter it, you must go back to the basics of journalism – check your facts and cover your sources.

Video and Artificial Intelligence

Storytelling through video has become an integral part of our discipline. Although textual stories still manage to hold their own, giving us a perspective that a one-minute video can't, in this fast-paced world where everyone is short of time, videos are the need of the hour. They are informative and attractive, presenting facts that would have otherwise been dubbed boring. Videos have a greater impact on the human mind than a mere text piece. Almost all news media houses have realised and accepted the shift of audiences towards video for news consumption. But there's a whole lot of process behind making videos, including skill-based expertise.

The nuances of the language and the twists and turns of the story that a human being can provide, a machine will not be able to do that ever. Similarly, handling video is even more complex than handling text. The subtle juxtaposition of images, sound mixing and the structure of the video will always be a complex process determined by the aesthetics of the human mind. At the same time, multiple repetitive tasks need to be outsourced to machines. Machines can do repetitive tasks faster and better and deliver them back for review quickly. The review helps the machine learn what it needed to fix and over some time, the machine learns not to make the same mistakes again.

Let us say that a text story has been written and a video around that story has already arrived in your system. The AI platform is capable of delivering a script based on your text story, along with images that will go with the script of your story. It is also able to identify interview clips aligned with the text quotes you may have included in your story. The task of getting them all in line is done and after this the human comes in to review the work of the algorithm.

The review process of the AI now is resting on a learn mode, learning how the human makes changes to the system. After every review cycle, the machine gets better at its task. It also learns how to handle audio levels, like when the natural sound needs to be higher and when it needs to be lower. It also puts on name supers, location bugs and information crawlers on the story. If each of these tasks had to be done manually it would take the video editor much longer.

The repetitive tasks are handled on a cloud platform with commands from you and you don't need to download these files to your in-house computers. The cloud platform does not crash or hang. When one server goes down, it moves the task to another server. If the workload is more, it will increase the number of servers and at other times, it will optimise the usage of servers. Thus, the whole process of video creation becomes time and cost-effective.

The purpose of AI is to understand your routine or repetitive actions over a period of time and become better at implementing those actions. What technology brings to journalists is empowerment, with less dependence on sound recordists, editors, assistants, producers and others. AI empowers you to stitch your story together faster with the least technical knowledge. It is important to understand that technical people aim to build advanced technologies to empower non-technical people. For using hi-tech or AI, you don't need to have a technical degree. You just need to think logically and work systematically.

On a regular workday, you will go and capture your video story. To script, you will use the AI-based research assistant which will enable you to build a comprehensive storyline. And then you will upload your script into the AI-based video editing platform with your footage. Based on your text, the AI will suggest more images and videos from open sources. You will review the suggestions of the machine and make appropriate changes to the suggestions and the machine-edits of your video story. And then you are done for the day.

Summary

Artificial Intelligence and Machine Learning together can make the job of journalists easier. At the moment, to compete in the multiple mediums, one is getting burnt out, struggling to stay relevant within a small space and span of time. But Artificial Intelligence will bring cohesiveness and ease of doing a comprehensive story without going crazy on a manual treadmill.

The purpose of AI is to understand your mechanical and repetitive actions over a period of time and become better at implementing them. What technology brings to journalists is empowerment with less dependence on sound recordists, editors, assistants, producers and others. AI enables you to stitch your story together faster without needing to have any technical knowledge. It is important to understand that technical people aim to build advanced technologies to empower non-technical people. For using hi-tech or AI, you don't need to have a technical degree.

As we all restructure our lives to integrate AI, questions when and how to use it ethically are bound to arise, and it may take a while to solve them. But we must realise that AI is here for good and we must look forward, use safeguards and embrace the tides of change.

Tips and Tools

- Invideo: Video editing tool that can convert script into a video.
- Dataminr: Real Time alert for newsrooms.
- Chartbeat Software: It grows your audience through sight and action.

Questions

1. AI has the potential to automate several functions in journalism. How do you think this can help journalists?
2. Discuss a few use cases of Artificial Intelligence in journalism.
3. How are Indian newsrooms integrating AI in the news production and distribution process? Discuss with the examples.

Explore More

Exploring the Intersection of AI and Journalism: https://www.lse.ac.uk/media-and-communications/polis/JournalismAI/Case-studies.

A Global Collaboration to Experiment with AI: https://www.lse.ac.uk/media-and-communications/polis/JournalismAI/2020-Collab.

Journalism AI Case Studies: https://airtable.com/shrKhe7Js48HvBhmG/tblBcSZESOAuy5Q9A.

Journalism's Superfood – AI: https://knightfoundation.org/articles/journalisms-superfood-ai/.

References

https://www.techemergence.com/automated-journalism-applications/.

'Can you tell if this was written by a robot? 7 challenges for AI in journalism', *World Economic Forum*, 15 January 2018, https://www.weforum.org/agenda/2018/01/can-you-tell-if-this-article-was-written-by-a-robot-7-challenges-for-ai-in-journalism/.

'Artificial Intelligence Is Not the Future: It Is Happening Right Now' *Media News*, 11 November 2019, https://www.journalism.co.uk/news/artificial-intelligence-is-not-the-future-it-is-happening-right-now/s2/a747107/.

'Journalism's Superfood: AI?' *Knight Foundation*, https://knightfoundation.org/articles/journalisms-superfood-ai/.

'Reuters Applies AI Technology to 100 Years of Archive Video to Enable Faster Discovery, Supported by Google DNI', *Reuters Media Center*, 13 August 2020, https://www.reuters.com/article/rpb-lavita-video-archive-idUSKCN2591VO.

'Reuters Connect', *Reuters News Agency*, https://www.reutersagency.com/en/platforms/reuters-connect/.

'Survey of News AI & Automation Projects', *Google Docs*, https://docs.google.com/spreadsheets/d/1ze7CtNL6N-ha80kF81G9mQLKWLjXH4NgG3gRdINO7pM/edit?usp=sharing&usp=embed_facebook.

Notes

1. 'Reuters Applies AI Technology to 100 Years of Archive Video to Enable Faster Discovery, Supported by Google DNI', *Reuters*, 13 August 2020, https://www.reuters.com/article/rpb-lavita-video-archive-idUSKCN2591VO.
2. David Corney, 'How We Use AI to Help Fact Check Party Manifestos', *Full Fact*, 6 December 2019, https://fullfact.org/blog/2019/dec/how-we-use-ai-help-fact-check-party-manifestos/.
3. 'Case Studies', *London School of Economics and Political Science*, https://www.lse.ac.uk/media-and-communications/polis/JournalismAI/Case-studies.aspx.
4. Trendsmap, https://www.trendsmap.com/.

Chapter 9

Fake News, Misinformation and Disinformation: Tackling the Menace

Akhil Ranjan

Humans are a Post Truth species.

–Yuval Noval Harari

Everyone is entitled to his own opinion, but not his own facts.

–Daniel Patrick Moynihan

Introduction

It is increasingly rare nowadays to switch on a news channel, open a newspaper or scroll through a news website or social media feed and avoid an encounter with the phrase 'fake news'. The term is widely used to describe a complex phenomenon of information pollution in this era of digital media. There are many shades and components of this information pollution and hence, over time, it has been defined in many different ways. However, to those paying attention to when and how the term is invoked, it quickly becomes apparent that few who use or discuss 'fake news' seem to agree on what exactly it is or what to do about it. Hence there are many experts who have stopped using the term for reasons that seems to be justified. In this chapter we will cover the different terms that are being used in the misinformation ecosystem, their meaning and the context in which they are used, case studies from India and other parts of the world, researches in this area that helps us to understand the problem better and some online verification tools that a person can try to tackle this menace.

The Spread of Fake News

The term 'fake news' first gained global prominence in the run-up to the American presidential polls in 2016 when unverified, unsolicited and made-up stories concerning the two main candidates – Donald Trump and Hillary Clinton started pouring onto social media platforms, particularly Facebook. These completely made-up stories became viral and played a key role in forming people's opinions. In mid-2016, New York-based news website BuzzFeed traced the origin of these false or exaggerated stories to at least 140 independent websites run from Veles, a small city in the south-eastern European country of Macedonia. The authors of these sites were creating completely fabricated stories and posting them on Facebook. The language of the stories was designed to elicit an emotional response from people who read them. According to the BuzzFeed report, the best way to generate traffic to these websites was to get their political stories to spread on Facebook – and the best way to generate shares on Facebook is to publish sensationalist and often false content that caters to their supporters. These sites open a window into the economic incentives behind producing misinformation, specifically for the wealthiest advertising markets and specifically for Facebook, the world's largest social network, as well as within online advertising networks such as Google AdSense.[1]

The phrase again swept the media discourse when, in January 2017, US President-elect Donald J. Trump publicly labelled a number of respected national and international media houses as 'fake news' due to what he considered their false (and hence unfavourable) coverage of his campaign and the incoming administration. This was neither the first nor last time that a leader or a politician had used the term in an attempt to quell criticism. Syrian President Bashar al-Assad used the term in February 2017 to dismiss an Amnesty International report over the alleged extrajudicial killings of prisoners by government forces in Damascus between 2011 and 2015.[2]

The dissemination of the so-called 'fake news' by established media organisations has been used as a pretext by authorities in many countries to suppress media freedom. In mid-2018, Egypt criminalised the spread of false information while Vietnam cracked down on a local news website for allegedly spreading false news.

While the term 'fake news' often been used as justification to censor media, but politicians themselves have been guilty of engaging in the business of 'fake news'. Social media platforms and messaging apps have been assigned a new role as weapons for the political elite all over the world to spread fabricated content in a systematic way in an attempt to garner electoral benefits. A study by Oxford Internet Institute released in 2020 found organised social media manipulation campaigns were found in each of the 81 surveyed countries, up 15 per cent in one year, from 70 countries in 2019. Governments, public relations firms and political parties are producing misinformation on an industrial scale, according to the report. It shows disinformation has become a common strategy, with more than 93 per cent of the countries (76 out of 81) seeing disinformation deployed as part of political communication.[3]

The key insights from the study are:

- Private 'strategic communications' firms are playing an increasing role in spreading computational propaganda, with researchers identifying state actors working with such firms in 48 countries.

- Almost $60 million has been spent on firms who use bots and other amplification strategies to create the impression of trending political messaging.
- Social media has become a major battleground, with firms such as Facebook and Twitter taking steps to combat 'cyber troops', with some $10 million has been spent on social media political advertisements. The platforms removed more than 317,000 accounts and pages from 'cyber troops' actors between January 2019 and November 2020.

In India during elections, political parties hire professionals to spread propaganda on social media. WhatsApp has emerged as a key platform for such campaigns, particularly through the use of hyper-local messaging groups where tailored content can be targeted. WhatsApp engaged with the Election Commission of India to tackle the problem of fake news and misinformation during 2019 general elections. To verify the authenticity of the news or messages, it used the Verificado Model.

This model was first used during the Mexico elections in 2018. This initiative was led by ninety organisations including universities, media groups, NGOs and social media giants such as Facebook and Google to help tackle the problem of fake news. According to a *BBC* report,[4] this election was flooded by bots, trolls and fake accounts to sway the electoral vote. In this model, Krzna, an AI-powered search tool, was used to scan such posts.[5]

Fake News: What It Is Not

Prior to the modern mix of definitions, 'fake news' was a term used to refer to a particular form of satire and parody. Many people are familiar with American TV programmes that blur the line between news and satire such as *The Colbert Report*, *The Daily Show* and *Last Week Tonight with John Oliver*. A similar parody TV show in India called *The Week That Wasn't* started in 2006 and quickly gained popularity. There are a number of such news parody websites all over the world – *The Onion*, *The Daily Mash*, *Private Eye* and *Satire Wire* are some of them. Similarly, Indian meme websites like *fakingnews.com* and *unrealtimes.com* publish satirical content related to politico-social developments. Forms of parody and satire are popular and beloved arts, but they always run the risk of misinterpretation.

What Is Fake News and What It Is Not: Some Definitions

The examples mentioned reveal that 'fake news' has been used in different contexts and at different times to describe a variety of situations – everything from news satire or parody to news fabrication to advertising and propaganda. Broadly speaking, the phrase describes rumour, falsehood and distortion of information. To capture this breadth, but to narrow its scope somewhat, the Ethical Journalism Network (EJN) defines 'fake news' as 'information deliberately fabricated and published with the intention to deceive and mislead others into believing falsehoods or doubting verifiable facts'.

Claire Wardle, strategy and research director of First Draft News, says that 'fake news' is 'woefully inadequate' to describe the complexity of the current misinformation crisis. She prefers the term 'information pollution'. Emphasising the trend of world politicians terming media coverage critical of them as 'fake news', Wardle says that the phrase has been 'weaponized' and declares that media institutions have a responsibility not to use it.[6] Ethan Zuckerman, director of the MIT Centre for Civic Media, has also expressed his reservations, calling the term 'vague and ambiguous' because it has been used to describe a range of forms of information manipulation.[7] Even the social networking giant Facebook, which has often been at the heart of controversies concerning fake news, has shied away from the term, using 'false news' in informal communications.

Another section of media experts claims that avoiding the term distorts the issue. They argue that 'fake news' refers to a distinct phenomenon the world is facing. 'We can't shy away from phrases because they've been somehow weaponized. We have to stick to our guns and say there is a real phenomenon here, says David Lazer, a professor of political science and computer science at Northeastern University in Boston. Lazer cites an article published in 1925 to support his argument that fake news has been used to describe this problem for a long time. The article, published by Harper magazine, talks about the role of fake news and how information technology is rapidly spreading fake news around the world. He also criticizes the use of 'false news', saying that a media organisation might get something wrong and publish a false report, but such reporting should not be called fake news. 'We define it in a very particular way. It's content that is being put out there that has all the dressings of something that looks legitimate. It's not just something that is false – it's something that is manufactured to hide the fact that it is false,' concludes Lazer.[8]

The arguments presented here suggest that not only the nature of the content but also the intention behind its publication and circulation is important when deciding whether to describe a piece of information as 'fake news'. Given the complexity of the subject, Wardle aptly classifies 'fake news' into the following three categories:[9]

- *Mis-information:* Information that is false but not created with the intention of causing harm to anyone and shared unknowingly. For example, sharing an old picture or video with a claim to be of an incorrect event or place.
- *Dis-information:* Information that is false and deliberately created to harm a person, social group, organisation or country. For example, publication and circulation of morphed or doctored audio or visual material that has the power to harm or malign.
- *Mal-information:* Information that is based on reality and used to inflict harm on a person, organisation or country. For example, leaking someone's personal communications or any private content into the public space with the intention to cause harm.

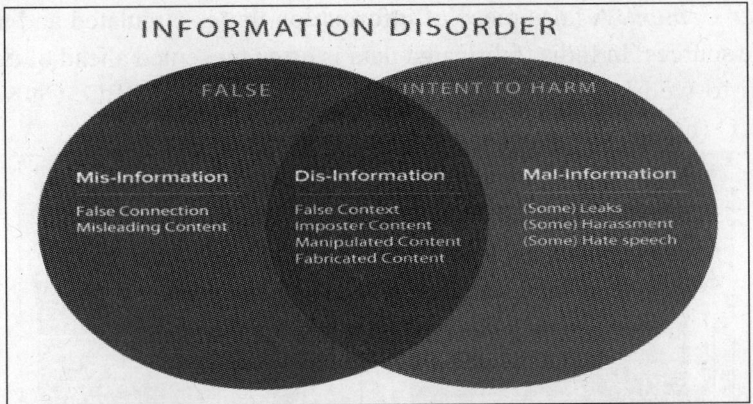

Figure 9.1: Information Disorder Diagram

Soure: https://miro.medium.com/max/1400/0*6h5O6NdCCm4DoFww.png

To understand examples of misinformation, Wardle and her co-researcher Hossein Derakhshan identified three key elements in their research paper published by the Council of Europe in October 2017.

1. *Agent:* Who created, produced and distributed the example? What was their motivation?
2. *Message:* What type of message was it? What format did it take? What were the characteristics?
3. *Interpreter:* How did the person who received the message interpret its content? What action, if any, did they take?

Given the complex scenario of information disorder and the wide spectrum of problematic content online, Wardle and Derakhshan's paper further classifies 'fake news' into seven categories:

1. *Satire or Parody:* A text piece or audio-visual content produced and circulated to exaggerate, ridicule, expose or criticise socio-political issues. Such content is aimed to be humorous, with no intention of inflicting harm, but it has the potential to fool. For example, the satire website *Duffel Blog* reported that an angry mob in Saudi Arabia beheaded 'Sophia', a female robot recently awarded citizenship, for 'strutting around the city without a male escort and without a hijab'. Tweets and posts from parody social media accounts of media organisations, politicians, or celebrities are also examples of such misinformation.
2. *Misleading Content:* Genuine content that is circulated with false association in an attempt to divert public opinion. For example, Pakistan's United Nations envoy Maleeha Lodhi tried to pass off a photograph of a Palestinian girl wounded in an Israeli airstrike as that of a Kashmiri girl wounded by a pellet gun fired by the Indian army.

3. *Imposter Content:* A false piece of information that is circulated and attributed to credible sources. In India, fabricated data is often presented ahead of elections and sourced to well-known international organisations like BBC, CNN, NASA or UNESCO (Figure 9.2).

Figure 9.2: Imposter Content

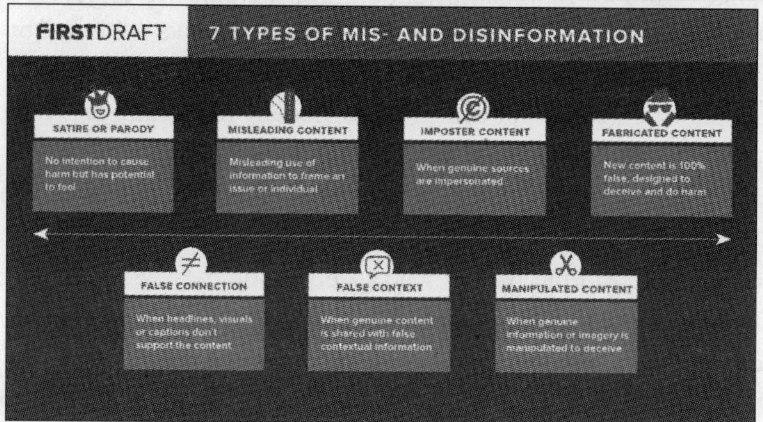

Figure 9.3: The Seven Categories of Fake News

Soure: https://miro.medium.com/max/1400/0*HsiKePQgAwYN1yKA.png

4. *Fabricated Content:* Completely false story of made-up content. For example, at the launch of the new ₹2,000 note in 2016, several Indian media organisations reported that the new currency would be equipped with a nanochip that could be tracked via GPS satellites.
5. *False Connection:* Popularly known as 'clickbait', this is another popular form of misinformation in Indian media. Tantalising headlines, captions or pictures lure people to click the link, but the promise of the headline usually goes unfulfilled.
6. *False Context:* An image or video is circulated with wholly incorrect context.
7. *Manipulated Content:* Genuine content is partially manipulated to deceive people and make them believe something that is not true. For example, screen grabs or video clips of a movie are distorted and circulated as real-life events.

The Technology Era

Of course, the dissemination of fabricated information is nothing new. A research paper published by the International Centre for Journalists (ICFJ) found the earliest traces of disinformation and propaganda in Roman times during the reign of Mark Antony (83 bc–30 bc). According to the paper, Octavian waged a malicious propaganda campaign against Antony in the form of 'short, sharp slogans written upon coins in the style of archaic tweets, painting Antony as a womanizer and a drunk'. Consequently, Octavian emerged as Augustus, the first Roman Emperor. ' "[F]ake news" had allowed Octavian to hack the republican system once and for all,' noted the paper. [10]

Technological advances have gradually increased the ease of disseminating misinformation. The printing press, for many centuries, held the honour of being the most influential invention for spreading information. The first large-scale news hoax through the press came to the fore in 1935 when the *New York Sun* published a series of articles about the 'discovery of life on the moon'. The ICFJ paper has further illustrated a number of examples, showing how territorial and ideological conflicts became 'markers for the dissemination of disinformation' throughout the twentieth century. From World War I and II to the Cold War, massive propaganda campaigns were used to suppress opposition. It continued in a much more lethal way with the start of the twenty-first century. The *New York Times* published several articles about the presence and production of 'biological weapons' in Iraq in the run-up to the US-led invasion. The paper later issued an apology over its unverified reporting on 'weapons of mass destruction' in Iraq.

The newest technologies in the media landscape – social media platforms and internet bots – have accelerated the spread of any kind of information to a pace never seen before. The result is a kind of 'information chaos' and the examples are many. At the start of the Syrian conflict, rivals took to social media and other digital channels in order to discredit one another. An Egyptian blogger in 2010 revealed how a local newspaper had published a doctored image to show President Hosni Mubarak at the front of a group of world leaders. In 2014, Buzz Feed reported that 'troll armies' were hired to flood social media platforms with anti-Western and pro-Kremlin posts during the Russia–Ukraine tussle over the territory of Crimea. According to media reports, these foot-soldiers were hired to open multiple accounts on Facebook and Twitter to post favourable news articles at least fifty times each. By the time of the US elections in 2016, Macedonian youths had turned this practice from political strategy into a money-making business.

Wardle notes that the emergence of these new technologies brought fundamental changes to the way information was produced, communicated and distributed. She identified the following characteristics and trends polluting the information ecology at present:

1. Widely accessible cheap, and sophisticated editing and publishing technology has made it easier than ever for anyone to create and distribute content.

2. Information consumption, which was once private, has become public because of social media.
3. The speed at which information is disseminated has been supercharged by an accelerated news cycle and mobile handsets.
4. Information is passed in real-time between trusted peers, and any piece of information is far less likely to be challenged.

Brian MacNair, professor of journalism, media and communication at Queensland University, writes in his book *Fake News: Falsehood, Fabrication and Fantasy in Journalism*[11] that the emergence of 'fake news' is a 'visible manifestation' of chaos arising from a 'combination of political, technological and cultural trends'. 'The phenomenon of fake news is one expression of a wider crisis of trust in elites, including political and mainstream media elites, whose members are struggling to maintain their traditional roles in our liberal democracies,' McNair observes.

According to a survey conducted by the BBC World Service in September 2017 in eighteen countries, 79 per cent of respondents expressed their worries over this information disorder[12]. But the situation seems comparatively severe in India, where 'fake news' circulated online has had real-life consequences. In addition to hatemongering and accentuating a divide in society, 'fake news' has led to many violent incidents. Nearly every case was spurred by false information spread through social media.

In May 2018, the ministry of home affairs demanded that social media firms take concrete steps to curb the spread of 'fake news' on their platforms. Subsequently, Google, Twitter and Facebook and its subsidiary WhatsApp announced several measures aimed to check the menace. Google launched a Google News Initiative (GNI) India Training Programme in July 2018 with an aim to train at least 8,000 journalists across the country in online content verification. Similarly, Facebook partnered with multiple fact-checking organisations to support them in the fight against misinformation. WhatsApp implemented measures like the 'forwarded' tag to indicate when a message had been copied directly from another chat and placed a limit on the number of messages to be forwarded as well as the size of groups that could receive forwarded messages in order to restrict circulation.

However, these measures seem inadequate to address the scale of the problem. India is the second-largest online market with over 800 million internet users. Wider internet penetration, easy availability of low-cost smartphones and an acute lack of digital literacy have made it easier to disseminate false information with unprecedented speed and effectiveness through the Indian populace. With a smartphone and an internet connection, everyone has become a consumer, producer, publisher and distributor of online content. Therefore, it has become necessary for every internet user to know some basic tools to be able to differentiate between fact and fiction amongst the forwards doing the rounds on the internet.

Online Content Verification

In India, online misinformation and disinformation mostly consist of photoshopped images and altered videos. In some cases, pictures or videos happen to be authentic but they are circulated out of context or with claims to be from somewhere else. Therefore, let us look at some basic tools to identify whether a picture or video is original or altered or edited and whether it is actually from the place or the event it claims. But first, we should learn to think critically about the authenticity of the content as well as the sources that present the information.

Thinking Critically

Most fake content has a certain emotional appeal, provoking or dramatic language, or clickbait-style headlines and captions, or a combination of these. If shocking claims in the headline sound unbelievable, they probably are. You must ensure that the story is authored by a source who has a reputation for accuracy and is someone you trust. If the story comes from an unfamiliar organisation, check their website and read their 'About' section to learn more about them. Ambiguous sources, conspicuous bias or one-sided information, credit-less and low-quality images or videos, and grammatical and factual errors are common features of fake content. In such cases, it is better to use the time-tested journalism check of five W and one H.

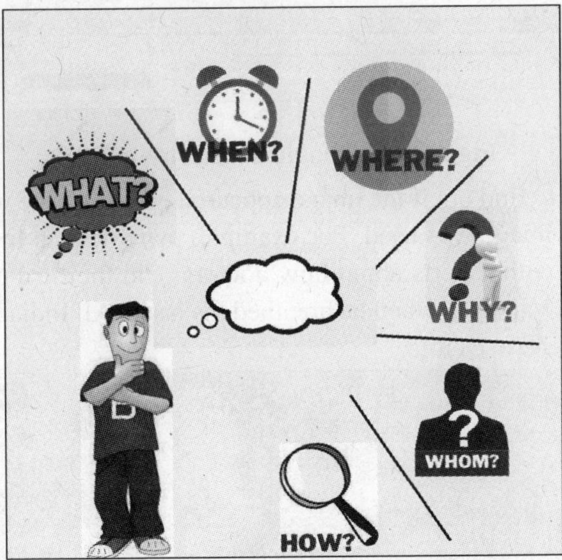

Figure 9.4: Five-W and One-H

Picture credit: Sarima Thakur

It takes only a few seconds to verify a news story with the help of a Google search if we dig a bit deeper to find answers for who, what, where, why, when and how. It is also useful to cross-check doubtful news articles with multiple sources to see whether any credible media platform has carried that particular story.

Technological advances have made it easier to alter audio-visual content in a sophisticated manner with huge potential to fool people. The same technology is adopted to help users verify the authenticity of any content.

Here are several useful online tools commonly used to verify pictures and videos. There are also tools to help ascertain the time and place of a particular incident based on features in the image or video. Finally, there are a few online tools to help analyse the credibility of the source of any information on social media platforms. With practice, you will learn which combination of tools to use in any situation when you try to authenticate a story that seems too good to be true.

Photo and Image Verification

Google Reverse Image Search: This is the easiest widely used tool to verify a photo. We use Google to search for images, but with the help of this feature, we can also use Google to search by an image. The Google search bar appears with a camera icon when we open the page image.google.com. Click the camera icon and the page will appear as shown Fig. 2. We can perform the reverse image search either by uploading the image or copy-pasting the image URL.

Figure 9.5: Google Search by Image

We will be able to find out if the image appeared earlier on the web, and if yes, then in what context the image was used. For example, many Indian media houses carried the image in Fig. 3 with reports about how doctors paid their tribute to former Prime Minister Atal Bihari Vajpayee when he breathed his last at All India Institute of Medical Science (AIIMS) in New Delhi.

Figure 9.6: Purported Farewell Image

However, a Google reverse image search found that the picture was actually from China's Guangdong Province and the medics were bowing to the body of a teenage organ donor. By using the Time Filter feature of Google Reverse Image Search, we also found that the picture in Fig. 3 was available before Vajpayee's death on 16 August 2018. The time filter is very useful in cases when the context added along an image claims that the event happened at a particular date or time. We can restrict our search results to a specific time period to find out if the image existed on the web before the time the uploader claims the said event took place. We can also pinpoint or specify our searches by using obvious keywords according to the images (Fig. 4).

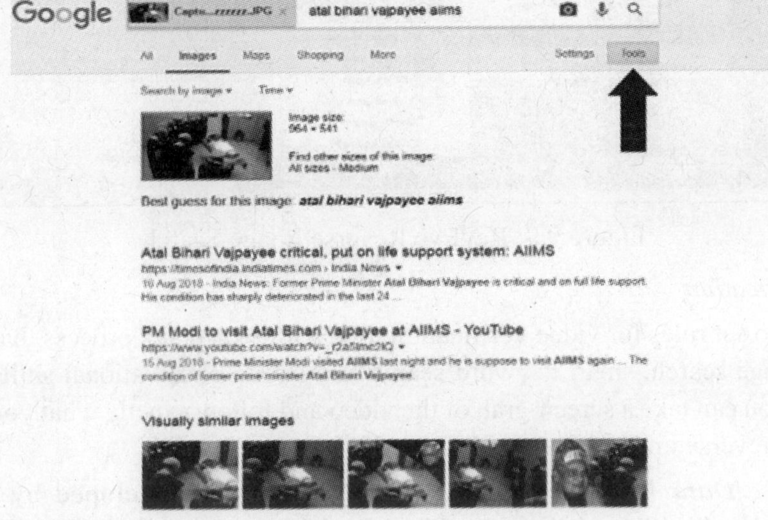

Figure Figure 9.7: Keyword Search

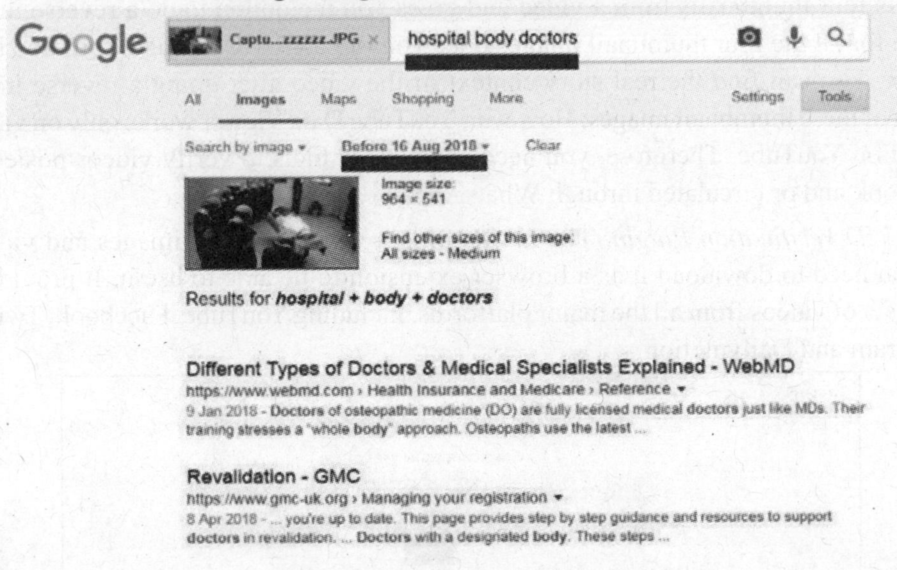

Figure 9.8: Keyword Search

RevEye Reverse Image Search: This is another good tool we can use to verify photos. The Chrome plugin of RevEye gives us the option to search an image across multiple search engines, including Google, Bing, Yandex, Baidu and TinEye. TinEye.com is also useful to verify an image and it replicates the functions of Google reverse image search.

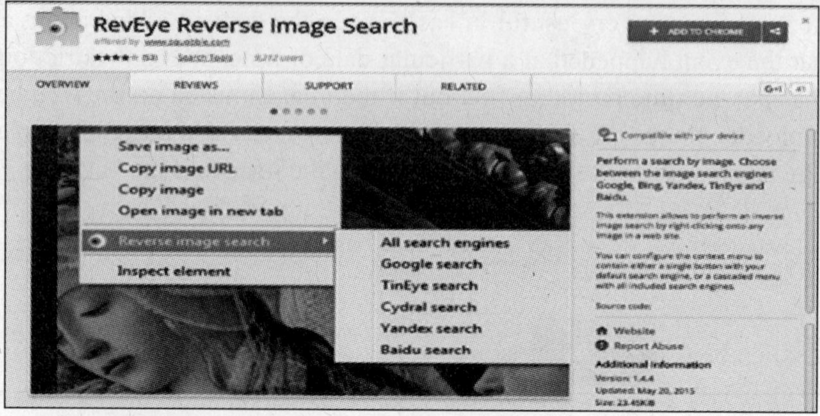

Figure 9.9: RevEye Reverse Image Search

Video Verification

There are no set rules for video verification. It is a little complex process that includes reverse image search, smart keyword search and strong observational skills. So as a first step, you can take a screen-grab of the video and follow exactly what you did with a picture – reverse image search with smart keywords.

YouTube Data Viewer: YouTube Data Viewer was developed by Amnesty International and it tells you the video ID, upload date and time of a YouTube video. It extracts four thumbnails from a video and gives you the option to do a reverse image search for all the four thumbnail images once you run the URL through YouTube Data Viewer. You can find the real story/context of the video after doing a reverse image search of these thumbnail images. However, YouTube Data Viewer works only on videos posted on YouTube. Therefore, you need some more tools to verify videos posted on Facebook and or circulated through WhatsApp.

InVID Verification Plugin: The InVID plugin works for both images and videos, but you need to download it as a browser extension to be able to use it. It provides a metadata of videos from all the major platforms, including YouTube, Facebook, Twitter, Instagram and Dailymotion.

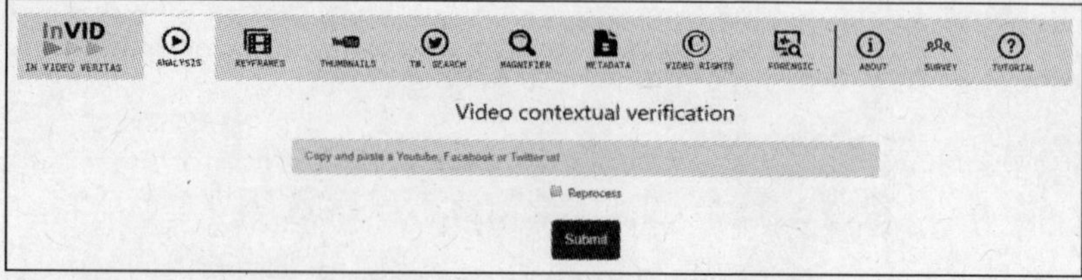

Figure 9.10: InVID Verification Plugin

The 'Analysis tab' provides enhanced metadata of a video posted on YouTube, Facebook, Twitter, Dailymotion and Instagram. It allows you to retrieve contextual information, location (if detected), interesting comments, apply reverse image search and check for tweets on the video (only on YouTube).

Key Frames: It segments a video in key frames that can be reverse searched with a right-click on Google, Yandex, Tineye and Baidu images. Similarly, the 'Thumbnails tab' allows you to quickly trigger a reverse image search on Google, Bing, Tineye or Yandex by images extracted from a YouTube video. The 'Twitter Search' tab allows you to do an advanced Twitter search by keywords or hashtag. The tab also gives you the option to search and verify videos using 'since' and 'until' operators, either separately or together to query within a time interval, up to the minute. The 'Magnifier' tab allows zooming in or magnifying an image/thumbnail image through a bicubic algorithm to help us discover implicit knowledge such as written words, signs, and banners (Fig. 8). The 'Metadata' tab provides Exif metadata of a picture in jpeg format or metadata of a video in mp4/m4v format, either through a link or through a local file. The 'Video Rights' tab gives information about video rights unless access is restricted by the content uploader or the social network and the 'Forensic' tab enables you to use eight different filters to detect digital image tampering.

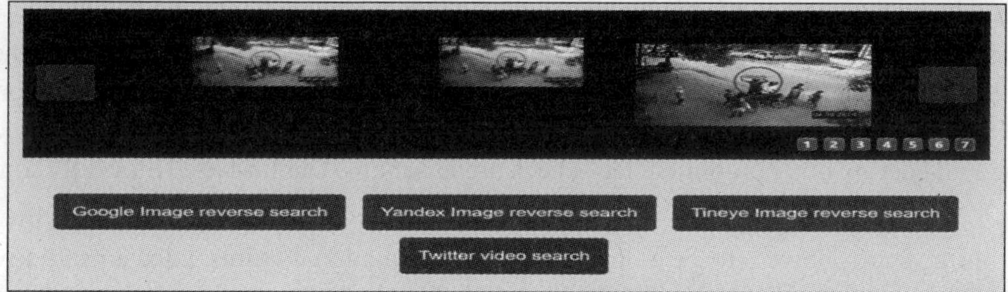

Figure 9.11: Metadata tab

Figure 9.12: Magnifier tab

Apart from these tools, it is extremely important to watch out for visual clues while analysing a photo or video – Buildings, Landmarks or Topography, Insignia, Number plates, Signages, Weather, Clothing, Language, Comments and so on. All these details reveal a lot about the image.

In addition to the photo and video verification tools discussed so far, there are many other tools which can be used to verify places, social media accounts and so on.[13]

Key Players

An endless discussion kicked off across the world over potential solutions as the problem of 'fake news' grew over the years. Tech giants like Google and Facebook announced steps to prevent fabricated websites from making money through their advertising platforms. Google came up with the Google News Lab initiative to bring together media professionals and techies to device new tools to help journalists to get their facts correct. Facebook also came up with a third-party fact-checking initiative and launched the 'Facebook Journalism Project' aimed at spreading digital literacy in January 2017. Apple also announced steps to systematically take down bot accounts and spread media literacy. Meanwhile, countries like Germany and Singapore came up with stringent laws to punish platforms for hosting fabricated content and not removing them within a certain time period.

These steps, however, proved insufficient to tackle the complex issue of misinformation. The need for fact-checking and online content verification has grown in relevance with the surge of 'fake news' worldwide. A number of fact-checking groups have come up to debunk misinformation and disinformation. US-based PolitiFact – a fact-checking website that rates the accuracy of claims by elected officials and other political influencers in the country – can be considered to be one of the oldest standalone fact-check organisations. It received the Pulitzer Prize in 2009. Fact Check.org, Snopes and Full Fact are other prominent fact-check organisations. Dublin-based Storyful claims to be the first social media newswire that contextualises and verifies social content.

First Draft News (to be relaunched as Information Futures Lab, an initiative from Brown's School of Public Health) is a global leader in terms of fieldwork, research and resources to address challenges related to the spread of misinformation. The organisation grew out of the collaboration between a number of organisations, including Google, Facebook, and Twitter. It started in June 2015 and partnered with newsrooms, universities, and rights bodies from across the world. First Draft joined the Shorenstein Centre for Media, Politics and Public Policy at Harvard's Kennedy School and operates as an independent entity headquartered in London. The non-profit organisation has also developed online courses and resource material to help media professionals and people, in general, to better distinguish good information from bad. It has organised pop-up newsrooms in collaboration with national and international media houses to debunk misleading claims ahead of elections in France, Brazil, and Nigeria.

The BBC spearheaded a similar pop-up newsroom in India in collaboration with First Draft, Google and a number of local media organisations ahead of state assembly polls in Rajasthan in December 2018. Indian fact-checking organisations like Alt News and Boom Live played a key role during the first such exercise in India. Besides, Alt News and Boom Live, FactChecker.in is one of the oldest fact-checking initiative in India. In the midst of election season, several Indian media organisations like TV Today Network and The Quint come up with dedicated fact-checking and online-content verification platforms. The Times Group, the largest media house in India, also started its own fact-checking imitative called Times Fact Check. Similarly, the highest-circulated Hindi daily, *Dainik Jagran*, launched a standalone website called Vishwas (trust) News to debunk 'fake news'.

The International Fact-Checking Network (IFCN), which certifies fact-checking organisations on the basis of non-partisanship as well as transparency of funding and methodology, has certified –a number of Fact Checking initiatives like Fact Checker and Boom Live TV Today Network Fact Check and Vishwas News. The IFCN seeks commitment from fact-checking organisations to tell their audience who they are, how they fund their organisation and how they do their work. The IFCN has chalked out the following Code of Principles for fact-checking organisations:

- A commitment to non-partisanship and fairness.
- A commitment to transparency of sources.
- A commitment to transparency of funding and organization.
- A commitment to transparency of methodology.
- A commitment to open and honest corrections.

Summary

It is clear that Wardle is correct in her assertion that we are living in an age of complex information disorder. The term 'fake news' is hardly adequate to encompass the wide variety of disinformation that we come across on a daily basis. It is also clear that journalists have a responsibility to approach new media with caution and to practise due diligence before adding to the chaos of rapid story-sharing. To maintain integrity as curators of respectable news production, we must train ourselves to make use of new media's gifts in order to fight its demons.

The issue of 'fake news' will likely have serious, long-term implications if not tackled effectively and soon. The current information disorder is not only spreading mistrust and confusion in the society, but it is also widening religious, racial, ethnic, nationalistic and cultural divides. The emergence of 'troll-armies' or 'cyber-troops' poses a serious threat to democracies across the world as they systematically misguide people and move them towards making ill-informed choices. Moreover, the weaponisation of social media to spread misinformation and gain electoral support as a tactic has gathered momentum worldwide.

WhatsApp and other social media companies claim to have taken steps toward addressing the issue of fake news, but inevitably technology firms, governments, media organisations, educational institutions, and society at large must all join hands to tackle this information disorder effectively.

All the following elements are essential parts of a strategy to counter fake news:

- *Awareness and digital literacy:* Technology firms and governments should invest in public education strategies to raise awareness of the dangers of misinformation. They should provide funding and data to research institutions to carry out empirical and solution-focused studies. Educational institutions should work with media organisations to create a standardised media literacy curriculum for journalism schools. Media organisations should moderate their platforms to halt the spread of fabricated content and produce news content to educate the general public about the threat of information disorder and ways to protect oneself from falling victim to misleading stories.
- *Fact-checking and content-verification:* Governments should ensure transparency of public-interest data, and tech companies should devise easy tools to help newsrooms in verifying content. Media organisations should ensure strong ethical standards while debunking false claims or fabricated content.
- *Diverse opinion exposure:* Tech firms and social media platforms should allow users to access diverse content and views by liberalising the customised feeds and search algorithms. These firms should ensure transparency over any algorithmic changes that down-rank content and curb computational amplification.
- *Laws and regulation*: Governments and concerned authorities should draft new legislation and regulatory frameworks in consultation with tech firms, media and research organisations to include measures that will help restrict the spread of misinformation. However, these law and regulations should not compromise or restrict media freedom or freedom of speech and expression.

Tips and Tools

Photo Verification

Reverse Image Search

Reveye

Tineye

Remove bg

Video Verification

YouTube DataViewer

InVID

Watch Frame by Frame

Verifying Places

Google Map

Bing Map

Mappilary

A detailed collection of verification tool is available at https://www.osintessentials.com/.

Questions

1. Why do a lot of experts have problem with the term 'fake news'. Discuss.
2. Identify one example each for the following types of misinformation and disinformation: satire, misleading content, imposter content, fabricated content, false connection, false context and manipulated content.
4. Visit the IFCN website and see how many websites from India are registered with them. Is there any from your area (state, city)? Visit their website to see the kind of misinformation and disinformation they are debunking and how.

Expert Speaks

Kristy Roschke is a media literacy educator and scholar. She is the managing director of the News Co/Lab, a Cronkite School initiative aimed at advancing media literacy via journalism, education and technology. In was conversation with Dr Anubhuti Yadav on 21 June 2021.

Why is there so much of misinformation and disinformation now?

Misinformation and disinformation have always been there. We see it more now primarily for three reasons. First, technological advancements. They have made creation and sharing of content very easy and fast.

Second, polarisation. We are at a time when countries are more polarised, political environment is more heated. People are at odds with one another more than ever before. They feed on one another. If we are polarised then we add disinformation to the mix and we become more polarised. So our reaction to it fuels the cycle.

Third, lack of media and digital literacy. We're using new technologies in a very complex media environment, but most of us have not received any formal training to know how best to deal with it.

Since the problem is so big that we cannot eradicate it completely, what steps can be taken to minimise it?

There is no one solution. There need to be multiple solutions to fight a problem like this. The first is fact checking and verification. We need people to continue to verify what's out there so that we have the best possible information. This not only includes journalists and fact checkers, but also the platform companies and other experts.

This has to be coupled with education about how these technology platforms work, and asking questions like why we're seeing what we're seeing. The platforms also have a responsibility and a major role to play in this. They are already moderating content and each platform has different ways of reducing the amount of misinformation and disinformation on their platform. I think they need to continue to do that but at the same time they should be more transparent about their efforts.

What is the role played by News Co/lab in promoting media literacy?

The News Co/Lab advances digital media literacy through journalism, education and technology. Since launching it in November 2017, we have partnered with news organisations and community stakeholders to help people comprehend the news and information environment.

This is done by conducting research and understanding the problem scientifically We also develop curriculum, helping journalists better understand the role that they can play in promoting media literacy. Good journalism and having good fact checkers is very important, but there's a limitation to its impact if you're not connecting those pieces to the public. So we position ourselves as a bridge between the news organisations and the community.

Notes

1. Craig Silverman and Lawrence Alexander, 'How Teens in the Balkans are Duping Trump Supporters with Fake News', *BuzzFeed News*, 4 November 2016, https://www.buzzfeednews.com/article/craigsilverman/how-macedonia-became-a-global-hub-for-pro-trump-misinfo.
2. Ben Mathis-Lilley, 'Bashar Al-Assad Uses Phrase *Fake News* in Dismissing Amnesty International Torture Report', *Slate*, 10 February 2017, https://slate.com/news-and-politics/2017/02/assad-amnesty-torture-report-part-of-fake-news-era.html.
3. 'Social Media Manipulation by Political Actors Now an Industrial Scale Problem Prevalent in Over 80 Countries – Annual Oxford Report,' *Oxford Internet Institute*, 13 January 2021, from https://www.oii.ox.ac.uk/news-events/news/social-media-manipulation-by-political-actors-now-an-industrial-scale-problem-prevalent-in-over-80-countries-annual-oxford-report.
4. 'AI to Help Tackle Fake News in Mexican Election', *BBC News*, 30 June 2018, https://www.bbc.com/news/technology-44655770.
5. '*WhatsApp to Bring Fake News Verification Model Ahead of 2019 Elections in India: Technology News', Firstpost*, 20 July 2018, https://www.firstpost.com/tech/news-analysis/whatsapp-to-bring-fake-news-verification-model-ahead-of-2019-elections-in-india-4780351.html.
6. DataJournalism, https://datajournalism.com/pdf/book.
7. Ethan Zuckerman, 'Stop Saying "Fake News". It's Not Helping', *Ethan Zuckerman Blog*, 31 January 2017. https://ethanzuckerman.com/2017/01/30/stop-saying-fake-news-its-not-helping/.
8. Robinson Meyer, 'Why It's Okay to Call It "Fake News" ', *The Atlantic*, 9 March 2019, https://www.theatlantic.com/technology/archive/2018/03/why-its-okay-to-say-fake-news/555215/.
9. Claire Wardle, 'The Age of Information Disorder', *DataJournalism.Com*, https://datajournalism.com/read/handbook/verification-3/investigating-disinformation-and-media-manipulation/the-age-of-information-disorder.
10. Julie Posetti and Alice Matthews, 'A Short Guide to the History of "Fake News" and Disinformation', *International Center for Journalists*, July 2018,

11. Brian MacNair, Fake News: Falsehood, Fabrication and Fantasy in Journalism (Disruptions), (Abington, UK: Routledge, 2017).
12. 'Fake Internet Content a High Concern, but Appetite for Regulation Weakens', *GlobeScan*, 21 September 2017, https://globescan.com/2017/09/21/fake-internet-content-a-high-concern-but-appetite-for-regulation-weakens-global-survey/.
13. Some more fact-checking tools: https://www.journaliststoolbox.org/2022/06/21/urban_legendsfact-checking/; https://www.osintessentials.com/; https://datajournalism.com/read/handbook/verification-3; https://firstdraftnews.org/long-form-article/newsgathering-and-monitoring-on-the-social-web/.

Chapter 10

Open Resources: Copyright to Copyleft; Understanding the Shift

Pawan Koundal

One of the most important social issues confronting humanity today is the sharing of information.

Introduction

Information is power only when all have access to it. The availability of information opens up a lot of opportunities.

The Information for All Programme (IFAP) was established in 2001 to provide a platform for international policy discussions, cooperation, and the development of guidelines for action in the area of access to information and knowledge.[1] The Covid-19 pandemic has also shown the importance of access to information during such a crisis. Lack of information can lead to several problems. As was witnessed during the pandemic, people fell for misinformation and rumours around Covid-19 due to lack of information from reliable and authentic sources. Journalists too faced the problem of getting reliable data related to the pandemic for their stories.

In today's digital world, there are several products built around information. People create their YouTube channels, blogs, websites, pages and reels on a variety of subjects for both information as well as entertainment purposes. Such initiatives require a lot of content. It is not always easy for them to create all the content themselves. In such cases, they rely on open resources.

Open Resources

What is an 'open resource'? Is this a resource that is available for all – free, easily accessible, and available for use? The answer is 'yes', but only partially. The resources are free and accessible but what you can do (edit, remix, distribute) with that resource is decided by the original author.

Before discussing open resources for journalism, we need to understand a little about the occurrence of 'openness' of the 'source' or the 'reason' behind it. According to UNESCO:

> Open educational resources (OER) are teaching, learning and research materials in any medium – digital or otherwise – that reside in the public domain or have been released under an open license that permits no-cost access, use, adaptation and redistribution by others with no or limited restrictions.[2]

In other words, these are resources that are openly available for journalists to use without an accompanying need to pay royalties or licence fees. They are resources that are released under a licence that facilitates reuse, and potentially adaptation, without first requesting permission from the copyright holder.

Lewis and Usher[3] identified four values of the open-source culture that connect with and depart from journalism – transparency, tinkering, iteration, and participation – and assess their opportunities for rethinking journalism innovation. Journalism and technology collaboration, with the open source ethos at work, has become an international phenomenon spanning traditional newsrooms to start-ups on the edges of the journalism field. Notably, journalists have new ways of achieving the best of traditional journalism; what open source has yet to do is push journalists beyond the newsroom, figuratively and literally. While open-source code implies that these tools may be applied by anyone online, many of these tools are designed primarily for newsrooms.

Journalism and Digital Technology

The 'traditional' form of print media is no more traditional now. Print newspapers have been around for more than a hundred years. In the 1930s they had their heydays as the most widely used news media in the world. It took fewer than fifteen years for the internet to claim this mantle, and by the end of 2010, according to the Pew Research Project, for the first time, the internet surpassed newspapers as the primary source of news.

The term 'online journalism' is mostly understood as publishing journalistic content on the internet. It may contain all sorts of content and is usually supported by audio-visual elements. Newspapers have been online for many years, where the news is produced and distributed through the internet. Thus online journalism has changed the way news is reported, written, designed, and delivered using different media elements, in isolation or combination.

Harcup's *Oxford Dictionary of Journalism* says that 'online journalism' covers different kinds of news disseminated via websites, social media, emails, newsletters, and other forms of online communication.[4] Russell says that:[5]

> It is about more than journalists using a digitally equipped public as a kind of new hyper-source. It is also about a shift in the balance of power between news providers and news consumers. Digital publishing tools and powerful mobile devices are matched by cultural developments such as increased skepticism towards traditional sources of journalistic authority.

These two definitions enable us to clearly distinguish traditional journalism from online journalism. Online journalism activities began in the 1990s and were strongly linked to the internet's vibrant business development.

The newspaper *Chicago Online, launched* by the *Chicago Tribune* in the United States, was the first American online newspaper, according to Carlson. The Slovak Republic's strategic geographic location in Central Europe helped spread the internet in the region of Central Europe. The Slovak elite daily newspaper *SME* started to publish on the internet journalistic material introduced by the Slovak Academy of Sciences in 1994 through their project 'Logos'. It had its own domain www.sme.sk (1996) and this newspaper became the first to enter the online world in Central Europe[6]. In China, the first online magazine *Shenzhou Xueren* was launched in 1995. The first online newspaper *China Trade News* was also published in 1995.[7] Online journalism in China has undergone the following four major phases: (a) the exploratory phase (1995–2000), (b) the booming phase (2001–2005), (c) the positioning phase (2006–2007) and (d) the new start (2008).[8]

Creative Commons: A Key to OER

Open resources allow innovative business models to emerge that rely on free and legal sharing and reuse. In the digital age, journalism students must do more than report, write and publish stories. The internet also offers students the ability to collaborate virtually, spread virally and create feedback loops that inform and deepen original stories. It is essential to have knowledge and to be proactive in applying open content licensing such as Creative Commons, to these web-based opportunities.

There are five key points (5R) to consider when using Open Educational Resource (OER) within the limits of Creative Commons licensing formulated by RMIT University:[9]

1. Reuse: Original content can be reused without alteration
2. Retain: For personal or reference use, copies of content can be retained
3. Revise: Content can be modified or altered to meet specific requirements
4. Remix: Adapting content to create something new using similar content
5. Redistribute: Whether the content is original or altered, it can be shared with anyone

Creative Commons is an incredibly powerful legal tool that many media outlets take for granted. Back in 2002, Creative Commons first published a set of licences that were meant to ease the way for creative work to be shared and reused. The licences allowed the owners of copyrighted works to release some privileges to anyone who agreed to follow a simple set of rules for using the work.

Attribution: CC BY

The license allows others to distribute, remix, tweak, and build upon your work, even commercially, provided they credit you. This is the most accommodating of licences offered. Recommended for maximum dissemination and use of licenced material.

Attribution: ShareAlike (CC BY-SA)

Under this licence, others may remix, tweak, and build upon your work even for commercial purposes, provided that they credit you and licence their new creations identically. All new work based on your work will carry the same licence, so any derivatives will also allow commercial use. This is the licence used by Wikipedia, and is recommended for material that would benefit from incorporating content from Wikipedia and similarly licenced projects.

Attribution: NoDerivatives (CC BY-ND)

This licence allows for redistribution – commercial and non-commercial – as long as it is passed along unchanged and in whole, with credit to you.

Attribution: NonCommercial (CC BY-NC)

This licence lets others remix, tweak and build upon your work non-commercially, and although their new work must also acknowledge you and be non-commercial, they don't have to licence their derivative work on the same terms.

Attribution: NonCommercial – ShareAlike (CC BY-NC-ŠA)

The license permits others to remix, tweak and build upon your work non-commercially, provided they credit you and license their creations identically.

Attribution: NonCommercial – NoDerivs (CC BY-NC-ND)

This licence is the most restrictive of the six main licences, only allowing others to download your work and share it with others as long as they credit you, but not to change it or use it commercially.

About CC0: 'No Rights Reserved'

CC0 enables scientists, educators, artists and other creators and owners of copyright – or database – protected content to place it as completely as possible in the public domain, so that others may freely build upon, enhance and reuse the work for any purpose without restriction under copyright or database law. This is in contrast to CC's licences which allow copyright holders to choose from a range of permissions while retaining their copyright.

Media Organisations that Embraced the Open Culture

ProPublica

Investigative journalism in the public interest is produced by ProPublica, an independent, non-profit newsroom. The mission is to expose abuse of power and betrayal of public trust by government, business and other institutions, using the moral force of investigative journalism to spur reform through the sustained spotlighting of wrongdoing. Each story that is published is distributed in a manner designed to maximise its impact. Many of their 'deep dive' stories are offered exclusively to a traditional news organisation, free of charge, for publication or broadcast. In addition to encouraging others to steal ProPublica's stories, ProPublica allows other sites to reproduce its stories as long as they are credited and linked under the Creative Commons Attribution-Noncommercial-No Derivative Works licence (CC BY-NC-ND).

The Huffington Post

The Huffington Post Investigative Fund is a professional newsroom that produces watchdog journalism and is staffed by reporters and editors from a variety of news organisations, such as the *Washington Post*, *Business Week*, *NPR*, the *Wall Street Journal* and more. It's a destination site with all news published under a Creative Commons Attribution-No Derivative Works licence (CC BY-ND).

Groundreport

It covers global news. An editorial staff of editors vets articles, photos, and videos that are submitted by over 5,000 contributors – citizen journalists from around the world. The Groundreport publishes stories on its site and through syndication partners such as Google News, the Huffington Post, and YouTube. It shares 50 per cent of its advertising revenue with its contributors, based on unique traffic to posts. Reporters retain rights to their work and can choose which Creative Commons licence to publish under.

Community-Funded Reporting

Al Jazeera

Al Jazeera was the first major news source to use Creative Commons. During the Gaza war, Al Jazeera built a Creative Commons video repository that is available to the public under a Creative Commons Attribution license (CC BY). Because Al Jazeera had access to the region amidst a scarcity of news footage available, the CC BY licence enabled other news organizations to report on the footage while crediting Al Jazeera—increasing both coverage of the war and Al Jazeera as the original news source.

Copyright and Plagiarism in the Digital era

In the Coronavirus era, the world has become truly digital. This has greatly impacted every sector. At time of crisis, digital technology provided many opportunities for dialogue, education, and cooperation. Besides causing a shift to digital, the Covid-19 pandemic has reignited numerous debates on copyright.

In 2020, the Registrar of Copyrights invited comments from industry stakeholders on amending the Copyright Act 1957, recognising that creative 'industries are performing and evolving in the light of changes brought about by use of internet, digitalisation and an increasingly globalised market for digital content'. India was given an opportunity to realign its priorities for creating and distributing creative content online, under a durable legal framework.[10]

Intellectual property has become more important as a result of new technology. The idea of copyright protection comes to mind when we think of original literary, musical, dramatic or artistic works. With the development of new technology, new concepts have been developed, such as computer programs, computer databases, computer layouts and various works on the web. As a result, it is very important to understand copyright when it comes to computer programs, databases and various cyber-based works. In the digital age, copyright is a key issue in intellectual property rights.[11]

The Rise of Plagiarism in a Digital World

The internet provides users with instant access to a wealth of information and knowledge in today's digital age. Although students benefit from information availability, it can also cause harm. The easy access to information and the synthesis of research may negatively impact digital natives' ability to cite original sources accurately in their writing, according to recent evidence and research.

Copying and publishing someone else's work as your own constitutes plagiarism. This category also includes text and ideas. Today, everything can be found online or in a digital format. As there is an (incorrect) impression that everything on the internet is free to use, you may end up copying someone else's idea or text into your own. This can get you into trouble. Even if you paraphrase from a source and give credit to the original source for the ideas, it may not be enough to protect you from being liable for plagiarism.

Copyright is protected by laws. In international copyright law, each individual's published work is automatically protected. It is illegal for others to copy the work without the author's permission and can result in legal action. In 1996, the US Senate passed the Digital Millennium Copyright Act (DMCA), which increased penalties for copyright infringements on the internet.[12]

Why Do We Cite?

- In order to acknowledge the contributions of other authors and researchers
- Giving credit to the authors whose words and thoughts you have borrowed.
- Respecting intellectual property rights of the contributors
- The best way to support your claims and assertions

It is possible to avoid plagiarism by following these steps. When writing papers, make sure you cite your sources.

There are different types of plagiarism, some of which are intentional, and others which are unintentional:

1. Contract cheating: Obtaining coursework from someone else (with or without exchanging money) and submitting it as your own;
2. Text manipulation: Deceiving plagiarism detection tools by swapping characters/ alphabets, replacing spaces with white text, insertion of images of text, Source code plagiarism – claiming to own another person's source code without attributing it to them;

3. Self-plagiarism: Reusing or recycling one's own words from previously published work;
4. Student collusion: Collusion between students to complete assignments that were intended for individual assessment.[13]

Plagiarism rules apply equally to news articles and scientific writings. Journalism often encounters three types of plagiarism:

1. Writing: Copying and pasting parts of another writer's article or words and passing them off as your own is plagiarism;
2. Information: When a writer uses information gathered by another reporter without crediting their sources, it's plagiarism;
3. Idea: Journalists who copy or plagiarise ideas or theories proposed by other journalists, theorists, or writers without giving them credit are considered plagiarists.[14]

Identifying Copyrighted Material: The Basics

In a world where everything on the internet belongs to someone, how can you find images, music, and other material for free to use in your projects? The solution lies in public domain and Creative Commons licenced content. For basic understanding, to know about the copyright material on the web, you can refer to the symbols mentioned below:

Traditional Copyright ©: Without the permission of the creator, the work cannot be published, adapted, or used.

Creative Commons (cc): The work can be used without permission, but there are certain rules which are set by the creators. These are:

Attribution		Using, copying, or sharing content requires crediting the creator.
Non-Commercial		Content cannot be monetised.
No Derivative Works		Content cannot be changed.
Share Alike		The content can be changed, but your new work must have the same license as the original.

Public Domain: Works published before 1923 by long-dead creators who have placed them in the public domain can be used, copied, adapted and published without restriction.[15]

Summary

Open Resources can help journalists in several ways. When uploading their work online, they should consider releasing it under a CC licence. The second way journalists – and everyone else for that matter – can use CC licences is to find work to build upon.

Questions

1. What makes any resource an open resource? Comment.
2. Discuss the six types of Creative Commons licences.
3. How can journalists make use of Creative Commons licences?
4. Make a list of news organisations in India which release content under Creative Commons.

Notes

1. Information for All Programme (IFAP), https://en.unesco.org/programme/ifap.
2. 'Open Educational Resources', *UNESCO*, https://en.unesco.org/themes/building-knowledge-societies/oer.
3. Seth C. Lewis and Nikki Usher, 'Open Source and Journalism: Towards New Frameworks for Imagining News Innovation', *Media Culture & Society*, 1 July 2013, https://doi.org/10.1177/0163443713485494.
4. T. Harcup, *Oxford Dictionary of Journalism*, 2014, p. 355 (i).
5. A. Russell, 'Networked: A Contemporary History of News in Transition', 1st ed. (Cambridge: Polity Press, 2013), p. 216, 9780745649528.
6. Jan Visnsnovskyy and Jana Radošsinskáa, 'Online Journalism: Current Trends and Challenges', in *The Evolution of Media Communication*, Edited by Beatriz Pena Acuna, https://www.intechopen.com/books/the-evolution-of-media-communication/online-journalism-current-trends-and-challenges
7. Z. Zhong, Wangluo Xinwen, *Internet Journalism* (Beijing: Peking University Press, 2002).
8. B. Yang, 'News Website Development in China', In Y. Yin, X. Wu, and R., Liu. eds., *Blue Book on New Media*, (in Chinese) pp. 45–55, (Beijing: Social Sciences Academic Press, 2010)., pp. 45–55.
9. 'Open Educational Resources (OERs)', in *Library Learning and Teaching Guides*, RMIT University, https://rmit.libguides.com/openeducationalresources.
10. Varun Ramdas and Shweta Venkatesan, 'Why India Needs to Modernise Its Copyright Laws for The Digital Era', *The Print*, 25 November 2020, https://theprint.in/opinion/why-india-needs-to-modernise-its-copyright-laws-for-the-digital-era/550243/.
11. Alok Kumar Yadav, 'Copyright in Digital Era', http://www.rmlnlu.ac.in/webj/alok_kumar_yadav.pdf.
12. Christensson, P. Plagiarism Definition, 5 September 2011, https://techterms.com/definition/plagiarism.
13. Chaitali Moitra, 'Rising Challenges of Plagiarism in the Era of Online Education', *Outlook*, 12 September 2021, https://www.outlookindia.com/website/story/opinion-rising-challenges-of-plagiarism-in-the-era-of-online-education/394368.
14. 'Plagiarism in Media', https://copyleaks.com/businesses/plagiarism-in-media.
15. 'Copyright and Fair Use', *GCF Global*, https://edu.gcfglobal.org/en/useinformationcorrectly/

Chapter 11

Digital Marketing

Dr Priya Sachdeva

Don't push people to where you want to be; meet them where they are.

–Meghan Keaney Anderson

Introduction

According to a recent article in the *Harvard Business Review*, 'content marketer' is another name given to journalists in the present times. Digitalisation in today's era has become the lifeline of the media landscape without which no news can exist or reach the target audience. Digital media has become a visionary asset for digging deeper into the realities and the essence of journalism. The numerous news sources through different outlets channelise and reach a persistent frequency, that has been amplified by the artificial intelligence interventions, detections and monitoring of different platforms presented by digital media. It has become compulsory for journalists to exist and survive in this continuous technological transformation with growth and updation to the new scenario of digital media, creating opportunities for them to upskill and enhance themselves and the content they create.

Digital platforms have a profound impact on the news supply, journalism and reporting pedagogy, which is an unequivocal success. Facebook and Google garner the lion's share of digital media revenues, for they have been designed for this and prove extremely productive at doing so. Digital news availability is rapidly opening to the participatory public. Digital media has initiated the age of profusion, attention-seeking and monetising that attention. With this, we have still not reached peak journalism, but it has offered a podium for multiple roles in journalism to create mechanisms in relationships and point to where deeper dialogue and consideration of new ideas may create equitable and sustainable outcomes. There may be a large amount of truth and an even bigger story about emotions in such thinking. But this is where journalism needs to adhere to the ties that bind them, which are set in the behaviours of their shared audiences. Getting a story out for news has never been this easy, and we should be grateful to digital media which makes this happen. Whether it's through social media platforms or news applications, the internet has given a dais to everyone to speak, to be heard and to disseminate news and information. It allows people to find a multiplicity of perspectives through postings and participation, which has opened up opportunities for citizen journalists. The only factor to be considered is that the news content itself should be alluring to the viewer's eye.

Journalists like Kate Roger (CNBC), Alexandra Bruell (CMO), Lauren Johnson (Business Insider) and so on are worth following on Twitter for their digital enhancement.

As rightly stated by McKeehan (Director-Asia, CNN Digital Worldwide) in 2020, 'Audience equals opportunity. With the right digital tools and by treating them as people with real interests, one can target readers effectively to the benefit of one's business.' Taking this perspective further, this chapter is written with the hopes to open a gateway to more insightful learning for passionate digital journalists to take their journey to the next level.

Why is digital marketing important in news?

'Newsrooms that don't embrace change are going to be left behind. We understood that if we analyzed data, combined it with the right sort of social media activity, our impact journalism could be extremely powerful and transformative,' stated Director digital Worldwide, CNN, Hong Kong in 2020.

Digital media has played a key role in the evolving media interface and has acted like a spine to businesses and journalism. It is a boon to news gathering and has helped progressive journalism immensely. News story production and its dissemination through different media channels has taken a totally new perspective in this transformational digital age as the news viewers have become very dependent and deeply engaged with the web for fresh and latest news, recommendations and real-time data for decision making. The drivers behind trends in technology innovation are the constant innovations by digital platforms like Apple, Facebook, Amazon, Microsoft, Google and technology vendors like Salesforce, Oracle, HubSpot, service providers like Mailchimp, independent standards bodies like Web Hypertext Application Technology Working Group (WHATWG), Internet Engineering Task Force (IETF) and so on.

Digital technology has enabled the target audiences to create, operate and produce user-generated content by using different digital platforms which provide them with a gamut of facilities and information. It was reported that globally, the audience of CNN on an average spends around ten hours every day on different media types with nearly 3-4 hours on their smartphones for viewing news and other information. It is quite evident that digitisation has brought a radical shift in the time people from developing countries devote to the internet, forcing news editors to make creative headlines and continuously update their homepages to retain attention and create captivating news, all the time keeping small screens in mind. Two out of three readers of news in India use their mobile phones to access it.

In 2019, twenty-seven out of the top thirty-nine stories in the most popular sections of CNN were videos. News channels have elevated digital video and newsroom resources during prime time by showcasing enticing stories, to gain higher rankings. These channels have created apps so their viewers can access content from anywhere.

Print and other media platforms are constrained by their distribution model, but digitalisation has provided flexibility. Digital marketing has taught news channels how to build, scale-up, and sustain their brand's reputation online on all digital platforms (what is called 'Online Reputation Management'). News channels thrive on their online presence, reviews and customer testimonials. The digital universe has offered the internet, apps, websites and live streaming TV services as platforms. The behaviour of audience and the functionalities of media platforms have evolved remarkably and constantly need alignment with the news rooms' broader spectrum of objectives. Digital marketing activities boost return on investment by running campaigns online. Digital practices like video advertising, email marketing, search engine optimisation (SEO), social media marketing and so on are an essential part of any customer engagement, for which news companies need to go digital.

Different Dimensions of Digital Marketing

Digital media is crucial for news and revenue generation. There are many aspects and dimensions according to which digital media operates. Let us look at them.

Engaging with the Audience

The customer is the soul of any business. Considering that, a digital engagement strategy is the most important factor to deliver a better customer experience and keep them elated. With digital linking in today's times, the spread of information is instant. So if consumers are dissatisfied, their entire social network becomes aware of it immediately. Being a journalist or news reporter, alertness is required to monitor the media platforms the reader chooses with the latest and fresh content consumption. Engaging the consumers with the recent news is quite challenging because all news channels are upgrading and enhancing their consumers' interest in the best possible way, giving them the edge to create their niches with the same interest, genre and desire and different levels of news consumption and participation. Product analytics is the key ingredient to framing any digital engagement strategy. Creativity and planned engagement strategy are crucial factors to utilise digital touchpoints that a consumer has with a brand, such as live chat messaging, webinars, email, paid search, social media, live streaming and the brands' website. Newsrooms must harness polling activities and consumer interactions on platforms into participatory insights. If the digital engagement is good, more consumer data and rich consumer involvement is achieved, which can lead to wonderful growth. Growth hacking is crucial in user engagement as it allows newsrooms to experiment and focus on the result, profits and growth, to scale the brand across all digital platforms, and to gain solutions with low-cost solutions and growth in revenues. User engagement computes the value a user derives from a product or service. Overall profitability is correlated high with user engagement.

To understand the response and scope of improvement, analysing customer engagement metrics is the best way to monitor and evaluate the digital standing of a news channel. These metrics include:

1. Conversion rates: Downloads, clicks and shares, signups, subscriptions
2. Pages per session: Internal links, site structures, quality of content
3. Net Promoter score: For measuring the loyalty of a consumer
4. Session Times

The tools for tracking user activity are Google analytics, Mixpanel and segment and adobe analytics. To measure sentiment value, you can use tools like Monkeylearn, Google Cloud NL UPI and so on.

It is necessary to keep abreast of the radical changes taking place. The uncertainty produced by advanced technology in the minds of customers can only be resolved by the best and creative planned engagement activities on all digital platforms so as to meet their expectations, wherever they are.

User engagement growth is likely to be very high in the coming decades with the advent of artificial intelligence and advanced digital technologies for the benefit of the consumer.

Understanding What People Want to Consume

Understanding what people want to consume is very vital as there are many interfaces on which data is crawling, indexed and searched. Tracking growth and formulating the best engagement strategies to ensure your brand landing pages should be leveraged by the best SEO practices to make great customer experiences. Impactful content writing and extensive and iterative A/B Testing are mandates to understand consumption on different platforms.

Table 11.1: Consumer Interest in News Content Categories

News content category	%
Region, town	63
International	51
Crime, security	48
Political	47
Health & education	44
Science & technology	36

Business, economy	**32**
Sports	**31**
Weird	**22**
Lifestyle	**22**
Entertainment & celebrity	**18**
Arts & culture	**17**

Source: Reuters Digital News Survey 2017

The feedback of consumers recommends a helpful 'high-altitude' perception of stimulating news. It is still reliant only on vague broad categories. According to a UK respondent, for example, 'international' news includes the whole lot from election news to trafficking in India, but for news start-ups in France, the news on corporate scam, terrorist intelligence operations, stalkers and so on is a part of 'crime/security' news. It is difficult to assess respondents' mindset and when to anchor a news preference picture in individuals' daily lives. The 'Most Shared' or 'Most Read' news stories lists are grounded on likes of news as measured by time spent, click-through rates and other forms of news story consumption.

Making Your Content Relevant for Search Engines

Some people find relevant stories which connect to their personal lives and have significant civic importance, while some avoid traditional political news. Creative and tailor-made digital news strategies help readers maintain a sensible outlook on issues and stories which provide them with information on recent happenings and allow them to absorb and conclude in their own way. Digital marketing extensively digs deeper into the core interests of the reader through its tools and techniques and provides them with interesting insights and experiences. Search engines have remarkable tools to get hold and crawl through data and provide the user with content they search in a fraction of a second. The Google AdWords, anchor texts, URLs, backlinking, Robot.txt, off and on-page optimisation, sitemaps and so on increase your website rank to the first page, if you follow suitable search engine optimisation practices. Newsrooms need to make their content relevant for search engines by regularly updating their landing pages with the most-searched keywords. This will make their landing pages appear on the first page of SERP (Search Engine Result Page) as Google crawls and indexes maximally fresh content and updated pages immediately and presents them to the reader in the first go.

Types of Digital Marketing

1. *SEO:* SEO stands for search engine optimisation. The goal is to make the brand rank higher on Google search results to boost web traffic to the website. It includes

context indexing, good link structure, content optimisation and keyword targeting on the SERP (Search Engine Result Page).

2. *Pay Per Click (PPC):* PPCs are paid advertisements (ads) and endorsed web results. The ad won't be published if you don't pay. It increases search traffic to an online business. The ads in YouTube videos on mobile apps, on the side and on top of the search result page, the ads while web browsing, are a part of PPC.
3. *SMM:* SMM stands for social media marketing, which connects the audience to the target segment via social media platforms like Twitter, Instagram, Facebook, LinkedIn, WeChat and so on. The aim to develop your brand, and increase sales as well as operating website traffic. It includes bookmarking sites like Flipkart, Pinterest, and so on, microblogging comments and forums, social review sites like Yelp, TripAdvisor and social news like Digg.
4. *Content Marketing:* This includes marketing practices like storytelling and sharing information to boost awareness of the brand. It entices the reader to take action, which converts a prospective customer into a real one, by providing data and information, enrolling in an email list or, finally, buying. 'Content' means blogs, white papers, digital videos, eBooks, podcasts and so on.
5. *Email Marketing:* This is a form of marketing that informs customers on their email about new products, services and discounts. It provides audience awareness, brand value and engagement offers. Email marketing campaigns can be used for special promotions of a new product or an eBook or a webinar. It is a fast, economic and flexible way of reaching prospective customers and retaining current customers by enticing them to visit the seller's website again and again. It enables the companies to create focused, personalised and direct messages. MailChimp, SendinBlue, MailerLite, SendPulse and Zoho Campaigns are a few examples of email marketing softwares.
6. *Mobile Marketing:* It aims at reaching the target segment through customers' mobile devices. It penetrates via direct live coverage and mobile apps, and has become a lifeline of today's generation of marketing.
7. *Marketing Analytics:* It consists of tools and technologies enabling marketers to assess the success of their digital initiatives. The dominant types are – Descriptive, Predictive and Prescriptive analytics. They are interrelated and offer different insights and solutions, helping businesses to make the most out of their big data.
8. *Affiliate and Influencer Marketing:* Affiliates or influencers enhance audience reach by creative engagement with their followers. They are well-known and respected within their industry and have several followers. They create content for news promotions and share links of brand websites. Every time a link is clicked or a sale is closed, the influencer/affiliate receives a payment.

SEARCH ENGINE OPTIMISATION (SEO)

During the last few decades, marketing and promotion practices have evolved swiftly. The popularity of internet and its billions of users has made businesses shift from old marketing to digital marketing, which has made everything massive, from exploring news on print media to PPC and social media. Everything plays an important role. SEO and its techniques help your webpage to rank higher than others. SEO provides many methods to get ahead of competitors in the virtual world. It basically helps in attracting traffic that is organic on SERP (search engine result page). For example, if you start a blog or a website for a bakery but your blog or the website is not among the first few search results, then the following reasons need to be checked:

1. Competitors have better online content than yours
2. Keywords are wrongly used
3. Your link building practices are not good
4. Your website's user experience is not good
5. You have used weak keywords
6. Your webpage's load time is slow
7. Your website is wrongly indexed

To say that without SEO newsrooms would not prevail, would not be wrong as news has to be necessarily on digital media and should reach the reader instantly. This is possible only through optimising search engines, as there are numerous other news channels putting fresh content and updating every minute. Hence keeping yourself updated in SEO is the only option.

Black Hat SEO: Violating rules, the SEO strategies for service in SERP that can get the website banned are Black Hat SEO. They are keyword stuffing and link manipulation techniques which create duplicate content articles inside landing pages. With this, attraction of the traffic to the site may be high, but Google charges a penalty which can crush their ranking quickly.

White Hat SEO: SEO tactics which are fair and in agreement with the search engine's terms of service are White Hat SEO. These techniques include creation of original content with quality and service area, mobile friendly websites, keywords in proper URL with meta tags and so on. These methods help in increasing search rankings and maintain the website's truthfulness.

Keyword Research: Before to all other actions, you need to do keyword research to build your content and metatag, and to choose primary and secondary keywords. Keywords are crucial in bringing traffic to your site when a user searches them on the search engine. Keyword research includes search volume, relevancy and competition. Tools like Ahrefs and Google keyword planner can be used to search for keywords. They optimise brand pages and increase website search.

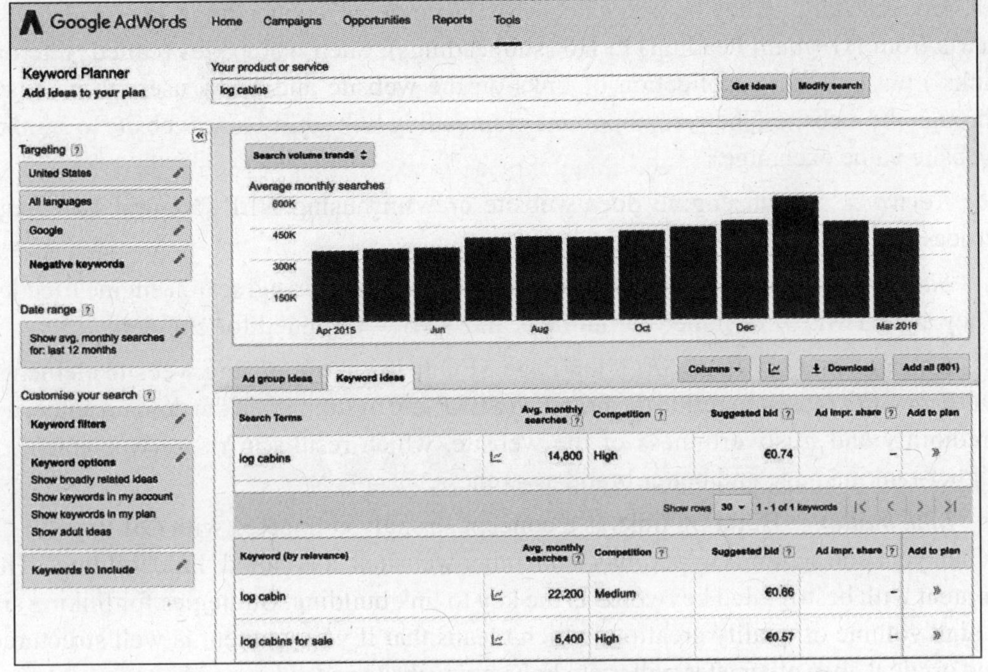

Figure 11.1: Google Keyword Planner

Source: https://www.woorank.com/en/blog/free-keyword-research-tools

The header element showing the website's content summary is called the 'Title Tag' on the search result page. Click through rate is influenced totally by Title Tag and it is important for On Page SEO search to display 50–60 first characters on it.

Figure 11.2: Title tag, URL, Meta description

Source: https://cvconnect.commercevision.com

Meta description: This is a short explanation that summarises the web page's content and gives more information about the site when it appears on the page of a search engine.

URL structure: It is a uniform resource locator and known as the best SEO-friendly practice. URLs are easily understandable and prevent the brand from getting lower ranks on SERP.

Header Tanks: They help to categorise the contents' subheadings and headings. It starts from H1 (main heading) to H6 (subheadings). Such web pages (called 'internal links') put together a collection of links on the website and allow users to navigate through the website. They are important in spreading link equity (one website to another website value exchange).

Keyword: Search engine does website crawling using NLP (Natural Language Processing) to find keywords and content.

Sitemap: They help in organising a website to make it user and search engine friendly. They are HTML5 – designed for humans and XML – designed for crawlers.

On Page and Off Page SEO: On Page SEO helps in optimising website elements. Off Page SEO is used to refine the brand on SERP and to strengthen the domain authority, credibility and trustworthiness of the website, which results in rising web traffic, a higher-ranking page and better brand awareness.

Link building: Building links is a concept strongly connected with Off Page SEO. When your site acquires hyperlinks from other websites, it is called 'link building'. The content with best-related keywords is the key to link building. Strategies for linking are a high volume of quality creation, which means that if your content is well structured and original, then other sites will try to link your website and enhance offsite engagement as well. It includes spending more time on different websites similar to yours which have appropriate content of relevance. It can be done vice versa as well. You can connect with them through social media also.

Metrics

The following tools helps in measuring the metrics are:

Rank Tank: Rank tank is a Google keyword rank searcher which allows you to paste into keywords lists, enter your domain, and fetch all the Google keyword rankings. It is free and built easily in a Google Sheet.

Google Analytics: It offers reporting and tracking of website traffic, giving insights of how users are finding your website, and tracking ROI (return on investment) for online marketing. This helps in measuring the individual campaign results in real-time and comparing data from previous periods.

Ahrefs: This is a search traffic growth checking tool, which checks why competitors are ranking high and helps monitor your niche. Ahrefs tools are Competitive Analysis, Keyword, Backlink and Content Research, Rank Tracking, and Web Monitoring.

Google AdWords

Google AdWords is a platform provided by Google to advertise business ads. Businesses pay Google to rank their ad on the first page of SERP. They are called PPC (pay per click). Signing up for a Google AdWords account is free. The brand will only pay you when your customers click the ad while they are visiting your website or call the brand.

For success, Google AdWords provides deep insights and reports which help to monitor, track and assess the ad costs and performance. It is the smartest tool if used intelligently. You need to choose very specific keywords which have the power to generate search leads, email sign ups help in enhancing brand recall and lead to sales generation.

When you are crystal clear about different objectives, you can run different advertising campaigns simultaneously on Google AdWords. The search for ads happens at a thunderbolt speed when you search anything on Google. Behind every click by the user, there is a big digital war happening amongst different brands to stay ahead on the result page because every click matters.

Hence, being a journalist, you need to use this tool very smartly. You need to stay ahead with fresh content and update it every day, to intrigue Google to crawl and index your brand page on the first SERP. It is not always good to be in the first position on the Google Result page, as Google AdWords gives a clear idea how you can reach your business targets and breakeven points.

AdRank is a formula to determine AdPosition. It represents your bid and quality, which is shown as a score based on your ad. It is believed that the higher your quality score, the better an ad position you can get. But sometimes this doesn't hold true. Structuring a successful GoogleAds account is like building a house for your brand. There are five parts to make a GoogleAds account:

- The Campaign is like the foundation of the house
- The AdGroup is like the building of the house
- Selection of Keywords is like interior decoration
- Making an AdCopy is like designing the exterior of the house

The different kinds of online ads are – Responsive, Text, Image, Video, Product Shopping, Call Only, Showcase shopping and App promotion ads. Designing a great ad to engage and attract traffic is an art, which should include your keywords relevant to your business, exceptional and compelling to make your brand stand apart.

Setting up Google AdWords Account:

1. Sign up with a Google Account
2. Budget setting
3. Target audience selection
4 Network selection
5 Keywords selection

Social Media Marketing

Social Media Marketing (SMM) means marketing the brand on social media sites like Facebook, Twitter, Instagram, LinkedIn and so on. In today's world of digital journalism, news as a brand, product and service should be present on these platforms in order to reach the reader instantly. When you choose social media marketing, make sure your content is always fresh, creative and engaging, as users constantly seek engagement and connectivity on these platforms. These platforms have their own tools and many strategies to reach the targets on the ads showcased on them. They have their different niche and campaign tools to operate, aimed at different target audiences.

Digital audiences are very vulnerable as they seek freshness and recent news updated regularly by the channels on these platforms. News journalists, reporters and digital marketers are blessed to have social media at their disposal as they can create, promote and generate leads in almost instantly. This technology connects users from different strata, and also gives them a platform for expression, innovation, opinions, reviews, comments and sharing. Social media websites provide tactics to segment, target, position and monitor brand performances, with deep insights.

Buffer says that Strategy, Engagement and Listening, Analytics and Reporting, and Advertising are the five major social media marketing pillars. Users always appreciate a human touch even in this digital age. Social media strategy encourages sticky content to entice, connect and engage the users for longer brand engagement. It is the only platform that allows user and organisation generated content to be available at all times, whenever the customer wants to refer or read. Hence, as a journalist, SMM is a great podium to exhibit your tailor-made creative stories with a stress on freshness to make your readers stay involved with your news.

Video Marketing

Videos act as the sweeteners for engagement. When you create videos to promote your news channels, drive sales in terms of news consumption, create awareness of your products or service, or engage with your customers, it is called video marketing. Videos serve as catalysts for building rapport, providing virtual experience, entertaining and engaging consumers through client testimonials, live-streaming events and delivering inspirational or viral (entertaining) content. Storytelling for your brand is the key to consumers' minds as it connects quickly and touches the emotions of the consumers, and helps in modifying buying decisions; videos help in storytelling. Videos also help in monitoring metrics to track customer engagement. Types of videos can be web series, short films, documentaries, client testimonials, a company culture video, a story, an explainer, a product demonstration, behind the scenes and so on.

A video marketing strategy requires:

1. Proper allocation of resources
2. Telling stories about your brand
3. Engaging consumers
4. Keeping the video short, sweet and simple
5. Publish the video in all social media channels like YouTube
6. Analysing the metrics

Tools to facilitate video marketing are available all over the internet. Through platforms like HubSpot, Forbes, and so on, videos can make connections instantly. They are considered a SEO gold mine, which builds backlinks to your website, increasing rankings, likes and shares, and drive immense traffic to your website. YouTube is owned by Google, so tagging with keywords/phrases will do wonders for your reach.

Videos increase brand retention. Research has revealed that video attracted 74 per cent of online traffic in 2017. Videos keep attracting more visitors onto the website and giving them opportunities to become brand leads. Emails that include the keyword 'video' get 65 per cent increase in brand click-throughs. It has been observed that 64–85% visitors are more likely to make a purchase after watching videos. The major challenges in video marketing are cost of equipment, monitoring and evaluation of the actual business through engagements.

As a journalist, you should be very conscious about which storytelling through video would bring the best engagement. After that, decide the metrics for assessment. Then test the video by publishing it on the chosen digital channels. Evaluate the feedback, improve and refresh every time to stay connected with the audience for a longer time. Videos can have a lot of emotion. Audiences love videos, so make them love you by providing them the best videos.

Email Marketing

Sending a viable brand communication specifically to the target audience through email is called email marketing. Emails are used to send ads, requesting business or signups or for sales. In spite of availability of diverse social platforms, email is still considered as the most important marketing method. An email provides personal attention to the user with creative content, provides value and, over time, it also helps in converting prospects into loyal consumers. Email marketing involves creation of persuasive email campaigns, understanding the most suitable audience outreach, analysing client data and interactions and making strategic moves for business growth. Email softwares provide multiple ways of sending emails and analytics of responses. The sender always has to monitor the 'open rates', meaning the percentage of recipients who opened the emails, and also the 'click through rate', which is the percentage of recipients who click the links in the email. The email marketeer needs to maintain a constant connect with the audience. To hasten decision making, they can generate a sense of urgency by mentioning limited time for product purchase. Emails should always be personalised by addressing the videos recipient with their names and providing them 'for you' offers ('Peter, unlock a special offer just for you'). It is necessary to always respect the recipients by giving them an open hand in setting their preferences – to subscribe or unsubscribe the emails.

Email marketing acts as a personalised tool which helps in reaching a large number of prospects in one shot, creating brand awareness, encouraging individual or one-on-one engagements with audiences, based on their own preferences, and building a bond between the brand and the consumer. Welcome emails, newsletters, dedicated and lead nurturing emails, sponsorship emails, transactional emails, brand story emails and engagement emails are different types of emails used in marketing.

Use of Digital Media by Newsrooms in India

ET Brand Equity: Digital Perspective

This is a brief interview with Prasad Sangameshwaran (editor-in-chief, *ET Brand Equity*).

ETBrandEquity.com is from the business newspaper *Economic Times* whose parent group is Times of India. It is the online incarnation of *Brand Equity*, which is a weekly print magazine that discusses, among other topics, start-ups and end consumer expectations from the contemporary market landscape, from pitches to movements, and challenges which brands may face in future. It is running a leading TV show for the Indian marketing and brand communications industry to report and relate to the latest developments and trends, discussing and taking perspectives of important personalities, hottest campaigns and leading agencies. It undertakes surveys and blogs like Most Trusted Brands, Ad Agency Reckoner and Most Exciting Brands. It monitors the most relevant stories on trends and happenings in the industry by tracking blog posts and tweets from leading publications worldwide.

An open-ended interview with Prasad Sangameshwaran gives an insight about newsrooms in today's digital world.

What is your take on digitalisation of media?

We have been witnessing the media for twenty-four years and seen a major breakthrough after the year 2000 when social media sites came into inception. From that time, the media industry has been globalised, personalised and mobilised with many digital interventions. Digitalisation has made us available with more options to explore, since we have been in print for thirty-one years and running a TV show from last decade, but now digital media is inevitable and many new newsrooms have come up with digital start-ups. So for keeping ahead, we need to focus more on consumers' digital expectations of readers. The internet is floating with content, but delivering reliable content is an art.

How do you think newsrooms have evolved and become digital hubs?

Digital start-ups have come into the picture now. Many new newsrooms are very well equipped with a team of journalists who are working in three shifts and sitting all the time catering to the higher demands of consumer preferences for news and making their relevant stories reach them with great ease via all social media platforms like Twitter, Instagram, Facebook, LinkedIn, etc. Traditionally, the news format was only to report 8-9 hours but it has completely shifted to 24x7. Though in *Brand Equity* we have a twelve-hour schedule, the team is not working in shifts but still we are leaders in dissemination of relevant and authentic content for news. News in the mainstream OTT segment has also increased which is giving a way to continuous improvement to us.

How do you think news in terms of reach and frequency is affected by digital media?

Frequency has been raised to the maximum by digital media platforms as now you need not wait for the news to be broadcast on TV or radio. Lot of content is there for discretion. You need to be on the ball. Digital journalism is playing its part so well that consumers won't miss any piece of information. You need to do a reality check for news before posting on websites and other platforms, but once you publish, the impact can be seen in seconds through Google Analytics and subscriptions. Our readership has improved by 70 per cent with digital access.

What are the best digital tactics you would suggest to newsrooms to stay ahead of competition?

The best digital tactic is to surprise the reader or consumer by information which is value added. Consumers are constantly looking and diving into content and if you provide recent, relevant and engaging stories, their quality will make you stay ahead. Keywords in all stories should be relevant and changed according to the content. Make the best use of live streaming news and always make sure that everything fresh is updated on websites for Google to crawl and index.

What new things have you started on the digital media front?

We were in print and TV initially, but now have entered mobile journalism and we have our own mobile application. On android phones, we have our social audio venture 'Clubhouse' and we are present on all social media platforms, but the stories always trend once we upload them on our website first. Then a synopsis is done which we link to these platforms. The texts on the sites have become hybrid including all types of news content, videos of the best stories to get the real flavour out. No doubt that video adds essence to the news story especially when to showcase retail revolution, like showing start-ups or showing some scams, interviews or breaking news. Consumers love live streaming and videos to get a feel of these things. In this process we make more loyal customers and they subscribe to our channel the most and bring in more visitors to the site. For feedback, we are doing personal calling as well as readership surveys and evaluating our growth on Google analytics. We are involved in email marketing, sending SMSs, WhatsApp and push notifications, through which we are doing Buzz and viral marketing for our trending stories. We are always focused on catching the eye and we have positioned ourselves as the most trusted news brand by getting the standing of 'most authentic content writers' in a report by TOI. We are conducting events like World

Brand Congress, Brand World Summit, and in the OTT segment also we are doing ice-stream for video and audio platforms.

What according to you would be the future of the digital world?

As you are aware that digital journalism has taken over. Newsbreak is happening within a few hours, analysis is happening in real time as monitoring updates in microseconds and milliseconds, you need to be on the ball always. There is no other way to keep pace with the growing digital interventions. We will partner Artificial Intelligence and other advancements and will become friends and make a collaborative shift in journalism in real time in coming times. The future of digital media would be more in paid form, as in, let's say 50 per cent would be free for readers and if they wish to know more, they have to pay 50 per cent more on the platforms and channels.

There is no other way than use digital media to the maximum in journalism. Digital media will become the base for future technological advancements. Being a journalist, taking real-time news with the best stories to the next level will be a challenge, accompanied by responsibility, and digital media would prove to be the biggest support.

Conclusion

Newsrooms have become digital in a major shift in the twenty-first century. The scenarios at newsrooms have changed and they are confined to internet web pages. The stories which were witnessed physically are now absorbed virtually. Brands have become storytellers and their own publishers and audience have their dashboards access in just a few instant clicks on smartphones or laptops.

The relevance of the news, audience connection and engagement are of extreme importance to all newsrooms and journalists. Digital technology is used everywhere in the form of digital content, digital platforms and digital storytelling. Demand for stories in this new media landscape requires devoted editors, journalists and digital marketers, who have to update the stories every minute, as no news channel wants to be left behind. Newsrooms have reincarnated into digital newsrooms which reach consumers 24x7. Newsrooms have become hubs of digital technology and the dissemination of information.

The best communication plans for any transformation begins with reliable connections by owned or earned media. Speed and quickness are the keys to unlocking news, reaching targets and communicating in real-time. This earns you consumer trust and provides clarity about consumer preferences so that you can make valid and informed choices for your digital strategies. So engineer your internet to make your story heard, touched and felt digitally.

Tips and Tools

Tips

1. Use the best SEO practices to make your message seen, heard and felt.
2. Be transparent and truthful in dissemination of digital news stories.
3. Be cautious and specific in choosing a digital platform for your brand.
4. Humanise your digital stories.
5. Invest in digital media and be alert and quick in communicating with your consumers.
6. Make sure your digital message is reliable and valid.
7. Use more engagement videos as a strategy for your news stories.
8. Never forget to update your content on websites and web pages if you want to rank on top of the search results.

Tools

1. Publish on social media platforms like Twitter, Facebook, YouTube, Instagram and so on to promote your news stories
2. Make use of softwares like Mailchimp, Zoho Campaigns, ClickFunnels, SendinBlue to reach your target audience
3. Do search engine optimization on Google with best practices like Google Ads, Google Keywords planner etc. to launch digital campaigns to stay ahead of competition.
4. Use Google Analytics to monitor your performance on search engines.
5. Be fresh and updated on Google AdRank index to make your AdPosition number one.

Questions

1. What is your opinion about the new digital media landscape in the coming decade?
2. How do you think news stories and newsrooms will evolve with new digital interventions?
3. What is your take on artificial intelligence peeping in the digital media landscape in newsrooms?

Explore More

Videos: How Is Digital Media Changing Journalism? https://www.youtube.com/watch?v=-7esKJDZqzQ.

Rickey Bevington, 'The Future of News Media in Our Hands, TEDExPeachTree', YouTube, https://www.youtube.com/watch?v=bVMna_zSGio.

The New Social Media Code – IN NEWS: https://www.youtube.com/watch?v=R0S5LYi1xJs.

References

https://digitalmarketinginstitute.com/blog/journalists-copywriters-pr-professionals-can-carve-content-marketing-career.

https://hbr.org/2014/07/the-content-marketing-revolution.

https://www.brainyquote.com/quotes/dan_rather_466507?src=t_journalism.

https://digitalmarketinginstitute.com/blog/journalists-copywriters-pr-professionals-can-carve-content-marketing-career.

file:///C:/Users/DR%20PRIYA%20SACHDEVA/Downloads/ACCCcommissionedreport-TheimpactofdigitalplatformsonnewsandjournalisticcontentCentreforMediaTransition.pdf.

https://digitalmarketinginstitute.com/blog/journalists-copywriters-pr-professionals-can-carve-content-marketing-career.

https://medium.datadriveninvestor.com/how-technology-is-shaping-journalism-in-a-positive-way-9bc6ed2adced.

https://www.forbes.com/sites/shamahyder/2020/04/09/how-content-hubs-are-redefining-digital-newsrooms-a-case-study/?sh=2c3616fb76ba.

https://directiveconsulting.com/blog/15-journalists-to-follow-b2b-digital-marketing-trends/.

https://wan-ifra.org/2020/02/how-cnn-uses-audience-insights-to-drive-newsroom-change/.

https://brandequity.economictimes.indiatimes.com/news/media/be-exclusive-cnn-eyes-big-indian-market-pie/68797996.

https://financesonline.com/video-marketing-trends/.

https://blog.thomasnet.com/types-of-email-marketing.

https://www.socialsamosa.com/2013/09/social-media-strategy-review-times-of-india/.

https://digital.hbs.edu/platform-rctom/submission/the-new-york-times-adapts-to-the-digital-age/.

https://digital.hbs.edu/platform-rctom/wp-content/uploads/sites/4/2016/11/Newspaper-Revenue.png.

https://www.webucator.com/how-to/how-create-google-adwords-account.cfm.

https://cvconnect.commercevision.com.au/display/KB/Page+Metadata+-+URL%2C+Title%2C+Description.

https://www.slideshare.net/TechedgeGroup/design-for-customer-engagement-digital-marketing-strategy.

https://www.woorank.com/en/blog/free-keyword-research-tools.

https://kinsta.com/blog/how-to-use-google-adwords/.

https://www.digitalnewsreport.org/publications/2019/news-readers-really-want-read-relevance-works-news-audiences/.

https://www.smartinsights.com/digital-marketing-strategy/digital-marketing-trends-innovation/.

https://www.zendesk.com/blog/4-customer-engagement-metrics-measure/.

https://www.edupristine.com/blog/importance-of-digital-marketing.

https://yourstory.com/mystory/importance-digital-marketing-2020-grow-business/amp.

https://www.bbntimes.com/technology/why-is-digital-marketing-the-future.

https://www.globecast.com/blogpost/key-2021-trends-media-technology/.

https://www.zendesk.com/blog/digital-customer-engagement/.

J. Jones, and L. Salter, *Digital Journalism* (Sage, 2011).

T. Aitamurto, and S.C. Lewis, 'Open Innovation in Digital Journalism: Examining the Impact of Open APIs at Four News Organizations', *New Media & Society*, 15(2), 314–31.

https://reutersinstitute.politics.ox.ac.uk/our-research/what-do-news-readers-really-want-read-about-how-relevance-works-news-audiences.

https://buffer.com/social-media-marketing.

https://www.ngdata.com/what-is-video-marketing/.

https://99designs.com/blog/video-animation/types-of-videos/.

https://www.nibusinessinfo.co.uk/content/advantages-and-disadvantages-email-marketing.

https://www.sas.com/en_us/insights/marketing/marketing-analytics.html.

https://www.investopedia.com/terms/s/social-media-marketing-smm.asp.

Contributors

Dr Abhay Chawla has worked with national and global media organisations on different media platforms in Hindi as well as in English. He can also read, write and speak Urdu and Persian. He is committed to providing authentic news, informative features and analytical articles to his audience. Dr Abhay Chawla did his BTech. in Electronics and Communications from IT-BHU, Varanasi (now IIT-BHU). After his graduation he started a career in the field of Information Technology having worked in various corporates. He did his PhD in the interdisciplinary field of New Media, Marginalisation and Communication from IGNOU and moved into academics. He has been teaching as a visiting professor in Guru Gobind Singh IP University, New Delhi, University of Delhi and Indian Institute of Mass Communication, Delhi.

He has written courseware for e-PG Pathshala, an initiative of the MHRD under its National Mission on Education through ICT (NME-ICT) being executed by the UGC, as well as IGNOU and University of Delhi. He has presented papers in national and international conferences as well as written on myriad topics for magazines and websites.

Clyde D'Souza is a VR filmmaker, speaker and published author. Living in different parts of the world, he loves interacting with people of diverse backgrounds and believing that a borderless, tech-driven world is the future. His book *Think in 3D* was peer-reviewed and recommended as essential reading by directors of blockbuster 3D films in Hollywood. His debut sci-fi novel, *Memories with Maya* was published by Penguin Randomhouse in 2015. Recent projects include setting up Media and VR Labs for government and educational institutions and VR masterclasses at Google MENA. He has trained journalists and crew while setting up an immersive journalism initiative at the TimesTV Network, India. His VR film *Dirrogate*, based on the book *Memories with Maya*, was licensed to Samsung's VR platform and became the first VR film distribution deal to be signed at Singapore's Asia TV Forum.

Sonia Bhaskar works with NDTV, India's first and most prominent private broadcaster, as Head of TV and Web Synergy for the group. She was involved in developing and executing digital and social media content and promotion strategies for television shows, events and brand solution concepts for sponsors across all channels of NDTV.

She has developed an online content strategy for numerous large-scale projects like 'Banega Swachh India', a campaign to raise funds to build toilets in rural India that has been praised by Prime Minister Narendra Modi as an important initiative to clean up India, and #MyFit100Days – 100 Days Fitness Challenge campaign that deployed gamification backed by an online content strategy which received over 2 million unique visitors on the site.

Dr Parry Aftab is one of the first cyber lawyers in the world and is known for her work in the emerging field of internet law. She helped establish best-practice standards for the internet industry. Dr Aftab works closely with law enforcement, the internet industry, educational institutions and government agencies worldwide. She is often called upon to create innovative programmes to address digital risks and is known for her practical approach. She is a legal and risk-management expert in all aspects of internet best practices, privacy, cybercrime prevention and abuse management. Her expertise extends to online gambling, cyber-terrorism/radicalisation, cyberbullying, violence against women, crimes against children and interactive gaming. She is an award-winning columnist for the magazine *Information Week* and has authored several books, including the first book in the world for parents on cybersafety in 1996. She helped design Singapore's PAGI programme, educating parents on cybersafety, in 1999. More than 21 years ago, she founded the first cybersafety help group, for which she still volunteers as Executive Director. She also founded Stop Cyberbullying Global and the new Cybersafety India Trust to address issues like cyberabuse, cybersafety, cybercrimes and digital literacy for all stakeholders in India. UNESCO appointed her to head its Innocence in Danger programme for North America in 1999, addressing online crimes against children. She also trains Interpol on cyberbullying, sextortion and online crimes against children. She was identified as 'the leading expert in cybercrime in the United States', by the *Boston Herald*. She has received numerous awards, including the Child Abuse Prevention Services Leadership Award and the 1998 President's Service Award from the White House.

Himanshu Shekhar Mishra works as Editor (Government Affairs) in NDTV India. As a TV news correspondent, he has extensively covered important developments in government, politics, foreign affairs and internal security for more than 18 years. He was a part of the Prime Minister's official entourage to the UN Annual Summit held in New York in September 2003 and later to the Indo-Turkish Summit held in Ankara and Istanbul in September 2003. Since then, he has had the opportunity to cover the Prime Minister's Office and the Indian Parliament and has extensively reported on all events and developments which have shaped Indian politics and government affairs. He has covered the Parliament since 2001 for national news channels and has reported extensively on important legislative and political developments in the country.

He has reported on internal security and strategic affairs from Jammu and Kashmir, Afghanistan and Pakistan. He has also actively reported and researched disaster management. He has presented papers at many national and international conferences.

Rohit Gandhi is an award-winning documentary filmmaker, journalist and news manager with 20 years of experience across forty countries and a proven ability to meet the pressing needs of global media companies in war zones and countries affected by crisis and natural disasters. He has strong leadership qualities, budgetary skills and over seven years of experience in managing multicultural teams. His technical expertise includes producing, shooting, editing and transmitting television stories. He has strong global networks spread across the media industry, non-governmental organisations and governments. He has received the Headliner Environment Award for Water World from PBS in 2010, Golden Cine Eagle Award for Afghan Warrior by National Geographic in 2010, Grace Award for Who Cares about the Girls in 2008 by American Women in Radio and Television, and Edward R. Murrow Award for Child Brides – Stolen Lives in 2008.

Akhil Ranjan is a Fact-Check Reporter at AFP and a Google-certified Fact-Check Trainer. He is a highly-motivated and enthusiastic journalist with expertise in South Asian geopolitics, He is a keen observer of contemporary media trends across the world. He has more than 10 years of experience working in national and international media organisations, and has led two projects aimed at spreading awareness against fake news.

Pawan Kaundal has more than 10 years of experience in teaching, training and publication of research journals and books. He has worked with Indraprastha College for Women, University of Delhi and was one of the founding members of the Centre for Media Studies at GGSIP University, Delhi, where he has taught print production and cyber production, and has handled a number of students' projects. He has been working as Assistant Editor in the Department of Publications at the Indian Institute of Mass Communication since 2011 and teaches print communication, layout and design.

Priya Sachdeva has a doctorate in Mass Communication from Amity University. She possesses 17 years of experience in teaching, industry, and research in advertising, mass communication, journalism, events and PR. She has authored three books on New Media: *Essence in Branding*, *Advertising Effectiveness: A Mantra to Brand Success* and *Connotation and Connection: Advertising Analysis with Semiotic Approach*. She has many research papers to her credit at national and international level. She is a curriculum developer for many graduate and PG courses. She is a Life Member of the Indian Society for Training and Development.

•••